Judy Upton Plays 2

Judy Upton was born in Shoreham-by-Sea, West Sussex. Her first stage play, *Everlasting Rose*, was produced at London New Play Festival in 1992. In 1994 she won the George Devine Award for *Ashes and Sand*, which was produced in that year at the Royal Court Theatre Upstairs, and the Verity Bargate award for *Bruises*, which was co-produced by the Royal Court and Soho Theatre Company at the Theatre Upstairs in 1995. Judy's other stage plays include: *Temple* (Richmond Orange Tree, 1995); *The Shorewatchers' House* (The Red Room, 1996); *Stealing Souls* (The Red Room, 1996); *Sunspots* (The Red Room, 1996, transferred to BAC); *People on the River* (The Red Room at the Finborough, 1997); *To Blusher with Love* (winner of the Open Stages Competition, 1997); *The Girlz* (Richmond Orange Tree, 1998); *Know Your Rights* (The Red Room at BAC, 1998); *Pig In The Middle* (Y Touring, 1998); *The Ballad Of A Thin Man* (Channel Theatre, 2000); *Sliding with Suzanne* (Royal Court/Out of Joint, 2001); *Team Spirit* (National Theatre Connections/Plymouth Theatre Royal, 2002); *Echoes And Shadows* (Ropetackle Arts Centre, 2008); *Gaby Goes Global* (New Wimbledon Theatre, 2009); *Flick To Kick* (co-written with Matt Merritt, Menagerie Theatre at Cambridge Hotbed Festival, 2009); *Noctropia* (Hampstead Theatre, 2009); *Lazarus* (Durham Mysteries 2010 for the Gala Theatre); *Come To Where I'm From* (Paines Plough, 2012); *82 To North Finchley* (Bread and Roses, 2012); *Undone* (Drayton Arms, 2013); *True Grit* (The Brockley Jack, 2015); *Milk* (Hen and Chickens, 2016); and *Lockdown Tales* (Youtube etc. 2020). Judy has also had seven original plays on BBC Radio 4.

T0347724

Other works by Judy Upton published by Methuen Drama

Plays

Bruises & The Shorewatchers' House

Confidence

Frontline Intelligence 3

Sliding with Suzanne

Collected works

JUDY UPTON PLAYS: 1

Ashes and Sand; Sunspots; People on the River; Stealing Souls; Know Your Rights

Judy Upton Plays 2

Bruises
The Girlz
Sliding with Suzanne
Gaby Goes Global
Lockdown Tales

With an introduction by the author

methuen | drama
LONDON • NEW YORK • OXFORD • NEW DELHI • SYDNEY

METHUEN DRAMA
Bloomsbury Publishing Plc
50 Bedford Square, London, WC1B 3DP, UK
1385 Broadway, New York, NY 10018, USA
29 Earlsfort Terrace, Dublin 2, Ireland

BLOOMSBURY, METHUEN DRAMA and the Methuen Drama logo are trademarks of Bloomsbury
Publishing Plc

This collection first published in Great Britain 2021

Cover design: Ben Anslow
Cover image © petoei / shutterstock

A catalogue record for this book is available from the British Library.

A catalog record for this book is available from the Library of Congress.

ISBN: PB: 978-1-3502-4916-5
       ePDF: 978-1-3502-4917-2
       eBook: 978-1-3502-4918-9

Series: Contemporary Dramatists

Typeset by RefineCatch Limited, Bungay, Suffolk

To find out more about our authors and books visit www.bloomsbury.com
and sign up for our newsletters.

Contents

Introduction

In the mid-1990s, when I started writing stage plays, I was surprised how few working-class dramatists there were, even at places like the Royal Court. I hoped this was something that would change in the future, but if anything there are even fewer of us now than then. With creative writing disappearing from the curriculum of non-fee-paying schools, reduced social immobility, and poverty on the increase, it seems it's becoming ever harder for a working-class writer to gain a toehold in the playwriting world.

My 1995 play *Bruises* was set in a down-at-heel bed and breakfast establishment in Worthing on the South Coast. It was a dark slice-of-life drama and, when it was produced, some people were dismayed that it depicted a young woman as the victim of violence. They compared it to the members of a female gang meting it out in my first play *Ashes and Sand* (published in Plays 1) and felt it somehow betrayed the feminist agenda. I had, however, not intended the earlier play to be a revenge drama. Hayley in *Ashes and Sand* is as damaged and damaging to those around her as Jay in *Bruises*. *Bruises* is undeniably a hard watch in places, and I've been asked why, when Kate has the opportunity of escape, she doesn't take it. My answer is that it felt in the closing scene that she hadn't yet reached the point where she was able to walk away. For me this uncomfortable ending felt truer than a neat resolution, even if that's what we would have all liked to see.

In *The Girlz*, I revisited teenage life for the first time since *Ashes and Sand.* Stacey has ambitions beyond those of her best friend Tara. Feeling threatened by the prospect of Stacey moving on without her, manipulative Tara plots to hold her back. It was originally written as a companion piece to a production of Shakespeare's *Macbeth*, whose lead character is also subject to the machinations of others. Stacey, however, remains true to herself, resists peer pressure and moves on.

Working-class women struggling to break out and make something of their lives continued to be a theme in *Sliding with Suzanne*. In the 1990s, I was still regularly seeing new plays where the women's roles were confined to one-dimensional girlfriends, who listened while the men had all the best lines, and occasionally still did the washing-up or ironing. It was enough to make anyone look back in anger. Had we really not moved on? It seemed to me that female characters, particularly working-class ones, were still too often passive and had things happening to them, rather than being the ones in control or moving the action on. They also often didn't have much to say. Suzanne, brought to life at the Royal Court by the wonderful Monica Dolan, had plenty to say and the action of the play revolves around her character. Suzanne is deeply morally flawed, but she's also a force of nature, needy, determined and outspoken. She has dreams of a better life, but she can't find her way towards it. Suzanne can be selfish and self-destructive, but a lot of the barriers she faces in life aren't of her making. For too many people the only jobs available are horrendously paid, depressing and temporary, with the benefits system still unfit for much beyond the crushing of dreams.

I returned to both the benefits system and a woman who drives the action in *Gaby Goes Global*. Gaby works at a job centre, where she herself is stagnating; bullied by her boss and treated with contempt by her 'clients' as from her own unfulfilling role, she tries to find something similar for them. Like 1989's *Confidence* the play is a comedy, as I'd always liked crafty, scheming heroines like Moll Flanders or Becky Sharp in *Vanity Fair*. When Gaby finds herself trending on social media due to a cruel trick, it proves to be the catalyst that allows her to change her life. Gaby seizes this flimsy opportunity with both hands and runs with it. She is soon, with few scruples, using those who have previously used her. If others have treated her badly, she doesn't see why she should behave any more generously when she is the one with the power. Even as her empire starts to crumble she remains indomitable and seeking the next opportunity.

The *Lockdown Tales* were all written during the first six months of the 2020 Covid crisis. At the start of the first lockdown, like many others, I felt compelled to start chronicling the unfolding situation. Since childhood I've written to try to make sense of the world and this was a new, intensely worrying set of circumstances which was changing daily.

Writing a full-length work about a fast-developing situation didn't feel immediately feasible. Instead I began a series of short plays, each around ten minutes in length, almost like diary entries or an artist's quick sketches. The only rule I set myself was that these plays and monologues should be able to be safely self-filmed or recorded by actors working from home and feature facets of everyday life during the pandemic.

I decided to offer my lockdown plays, as soon as each was written, to anyone wanting to collaborate to produce an immediate response to the pandemic. I quickly found myself working remotely with many incredibly talented actors, directors and producers, nationally and internationally. Writing 'stage plays' for actor-recorded YouTube films and audio podcasts was a unique situation, which by its fast turnaround and restrictive nature actually proved creatively liberating.

In the first of these dramas, *Signed, Sealed, Delivered*, I took the universities closing and students being sent home as the starting point for a drama that drew upon my interest in W. Reginald Bray, a man who became famous for posting himself.

In a second monologue, *Urban Foxes*, having noticed the increase of wildlife outside, I wrote a piece in which the lockdown and observing a wild fox give a young woman the courage she needs to escape a sex-for-rent arrangement

The White Hart came about as I could hear lorries thundering past my home at night, carrying goods to restock the supermarket shelves. As I imagined what it might be like to be a driver out on the otherwise quiet roads at night, I fed in the uncertainty that friends and myself were feeling early on in the pandemic, as to where we might be heading. I was thrilled when it won an OnComm Award for work broadcast or streamed during the coronavirus pandemic. In *Urban Foxes*, having noticed the increase of wildlife outside, I wrote a piece in which the lockdown and observing a wild fox give a young woman the courage she needs to escape a sex-for-rent arrangement.

People working largely unseen during the Covid crisis were also the theme of *Bees* in which a sewing machinist in a British sweatshop is labouring for a pittance in unsafe conditions to make cheap fashions for online retailers.

A Cat Problem was a two-hander, responding to the Covid situation in prisons and the struggles people on the outside were having to make ends meet. It also gave me the opportunity to write a conversation between two characters, where the fact that the actors were in two different places, communicating via their computers, could be incorporated creatively into the storytelling.

To begin with, referencing animals in the titles of all the *Lockdown Tales* was accidental but eventually became a linking motif for them as a collection, even though sometimes, as in *A Cat Problem,* which isn't about felines, and *Signed, Sealed, Delivered*, where 'Seal' is hidden away, it isn't always obvious.

Perhaps some of the characters from these shorts will re-appear in future work, but regardless they remain, both in script form and as internet productions, my small contribution to documenting a time like no other, and hopefully one we'll never experience again.

Bruises

A stage play

Judy Upton

Original Production Details

Date: November 1995

Venue: Theatre Upstairs, Royal Court

Director: Jane Howell

Designer: Hayden Griffin

Cast

Myrtle	Patricia Brake
Kate	Stephanie Buttle
Jay	Billy Carter
Phoebe	Anna Keaveney
Dave	Ian Redford

Act One

Scene One

A bed, back left. A kitchen, front right, with a long bar, dining table and chairs. Right back, the lights and beach hut backs of Worthing Prom. Beside the bed, a radio on the floor, lying on its side, knocked off its station.

Phoebe (*a smartly dressed woman of about forty*) *is lying on the floor, behind the bed.* **Jay** (*a young man, twenties*) *picks up the radio.*

Jay   Did you find the cricket?

Phoebe (*mutters*)   No.

Jay   What's that?

Phoebe (*close to tears*)   No, I said no.

Jay   It's probably on long wave. And you need an aerial.

Phoebe   Do I?

Jay   Or Persil, or something.

He tunes the radio.

There you go, Phebe.

Phoebe   Don't expect gratitude.

Jay   I said sorry.

Phoebe   Where's Dave?

Jay   Are you going to tell him?

Phoebe   If I did . . .

Jay   You know what he'd do?

Phoebe   Yes.

Jay   Is that what you want?

He offers her his hand, helps **Phoebe** *stand up. She sits down on the bed.*

Phoebe   No. But I –

Jay   Would you like a cup of tea or anything?

Phoebe   No.

Jay *sits down beside* **Phoebe**, *gently tilts her chin up so she is looking at him.*

Jay   It's funny, I feel really calm.

He pushes **Phoebe**'s *hair back out of her face.*

Jay   Are we friends?

He holds out his hand. She does not respond. He lifts her hand and kisses it.

Friends again. I can't really even remember why –

The entry phone buzzes. **Jay** *gets up, picks it up. Front of stage.* **Kate** *(in her twenties) talking into the other end of entry phone. She has a suitcase and bulging bags.*

Kate   Hello it's . . . Kate Milner . . .

Jay   Right? (*Mouths 'who?'*)

Kate   I phoned earlier, about a room.

Jay (*on entry phone*)   Right. It's open. Push it. Push hard.

He puts the phone down, it buzzes again. He picks it up again. **Phoebe** *carries her radio to the table, sits down listening to the cricket.*

Kate   I think it's jammed . . .

Jay   Push, push, PUSH! (*On the phone.*) Are you in?

Kate *downstage, carrying bags.* **Jay** *joins her.* **Dave** (*forties, built like a brick shithouse*) *is lying on the floor, not really noticeable until now.* **Kate** *looks at him with disgusted fascination.*

Jay   Just step on him.

Kate   Can you help me with these?

Jay *takes the bags, dumps them on the bed.*

Kate   Careful! Please.

Jay   A cheque will be okay today if it's all you've got, but after this week it's strictly cash okay? My dad's regs, no use moaning to me.

Kate   Can I settle up later, when I've had time to unpack?

Jay   Yeah, yeah.

Dave *gets up, tries to wander in.* **Jay** *pushes him out.*

Jay   Go and lie down, Dad.

Dave (*mutters*)   Fuck you.

Jay   My pleasure.

Kate   God, I'm famished. Could you bring me a tea and some toast or something please.

Jay   You have to make your own arrangements for lunch, I just do breakfasts.

Kate   It's only ten o'clock. Can't you get me a late breakfast?

Jay   There's a snack bar, not on this corner but the next. Food's pretty greasy and disgusting . . . yeah you might like it. Or you can get something from Marks – pack of sarnies.

Kate   Could I make myself a tea?

Jay   Not in my kitchen, no.

Kate   You're bloody helpful.

Jay   I officially knocked off ten minutes ago.

Kate   Suppose I paid you to make me a cuppa and a piece of toast?

She takes out her purse.

Jay   What do you take me for?

Kate   Two quid?

Jay   You're wasting your breath and my time.

Kate   Four quid.

Jay   I'm going home.

Kate   Five.

Jay   I'm walking out the door.

Kate   Six.

Jay   Kiss me.

Kate *looks at him in disbelief.*

Kate   Get out of here.

Jay *goes.*

Kate (*calls after him*)   Two slices of toast.

He comes back in, leans on the doorframe. She moves closer, looks into his eyes.

Jay   Marmalade or jam? Decision.

She kisses him on the lips. He makes no attempt to prolong the contact. She follows him to the kitchen area. **Phoebe** *gives her a small, tight smile, as she passes.* **Jay** *pops a couple of slices of bread in the toaster and puts the kettle on.* **Kate** *looks about the kitchen.*

Kate   Have you heard of Ajax? Vim? Jif? Flash?

Jay   You don't like grease and cockroaches? I cleaned this place from top to bottom before the weekend. Chrome you could see your face in. Then Dad decided to party. Major devastation. Ants, cockroaches, blowflies from miles around heard there was a good buzz around this place . . . No don't crinkle your nose up like that. This'll be good. As good as your mum makes. I promise. The best toast on the South Coast!

He takes out a jar of tea bags.

Kate   So –

Jay   So what's a nice guy like me doing in a place like this? So do you come here often? So have you got any plans for this evening? Well, no as it happens. I was going to stay in and wash my hair . . .

He pops up the toast, butters and jams it with flourish, plonks it on a plate, slides it along to **Kate***. He watches her while she begins to eat it.*

Jay   Good?

Kate   Okay. Mmmm, lovely!

Jay *makes the tea.*

Jay   Milk? Sugar?

Kate   Milk, not too much.

Jay   You're down from London. Just got fed up with your folks, all the rows, all the hassles . . .

Kate   I've come to see my mum.

Jay   She lives in Worthing?

Kate   The last address I have for her. She's stopped writing, stopped phoning . . . six weeks ago . . .

Jay   Is this a lovely cup of tea?

Kate   Good, yeah.

Jay   The odd compliment goes a long way, gets you anything around here. And I do mean anything.

Kate   Look –

Jay   I am. So are you.

Kate   Look, I don't know you . . .

Enter **Dave***.*

Jay   I've just made some tea.

Dave   Yeah.

Jay *pours* **Dave** *a tea.*

Dave   Harris called back?

Jay   Not yet.

Dave   You'll let me know as soon as –

Jay   Er, Dad this is . . . er . . .

Kate   Kate

Jay   Katie.

Kate   Kate.

Jay   Why don't you take a cup to Phoebe?

Dave   Fat old cow. Yeah, okay.

He pours another tea. He takes it to **Phoebe**, *sits down beside her.*

Phoebe   Thank you, love.

Dave   Have you been crying? You have been crying.

Phoebe   The cricket . . . when we're doing badly I always cry.

Jay   I'll introduce you to Phoebe sometime. She's lived here a dog's age. Always reliable with the rent. A good old girl. Lonely though, you know?

Dave *looks at* **Phoebe**, *she looks away. He gets up, walks out.*

Phoebe   Dave . . .

She follows him.

Jay   Then about a month back she and Dad teamed up, got it together, you know. Probably the drink has something to do with it.

Kate   Oh . . . he looks like a nice bloke.

Jay (*sharply*)   You think so?

Kate   Enough water for another cup?

Jay *checks the kettle.*

Jay   No, and I gotta be getting home. Just about have time to change and get to my other job. I work in a bar on the seafront afternoons, some late evenings, but not tonight, so if you want, maybe we could do something . . .

Kate *looks at* **Jay**, *trying to decide about him.*

Jay   Look at me properly. Come closer.

Kate *moves closer.*

Jay   Closer. You can't make an informed decision from there. Do you like blue eyes, or brown? Brown hair or blond? Younger or older? Pale or tanned? Innocent or . . .

Kate (*softly*)   And what do you like?

Jay   What I'm seeing.

She puts her hand on his shoulder, touches his hair.

Kate   Honestly?

Jay   Cross my heart.

She moves to kiss him. He shrugs her off.

Jay   I'll tell you when I want to kiss you.

He throws the cups in the sink, walks off. **Kate** *is startled.*

Kate   Hey! Hey, you . . . shit, I didn't mean to . . . you haven't even told me . . .

Jay   Yeah, well, I gotta go now.

He goes to exit.

Kate   Wait . . . Please. Do you know where Shelley Road is?

Jay   Ready to go now?

He puts on his jacket. He and **Kate** *walk to the back of the stage.*

Kitchen bench.

Myrtle *comes in with a Black Forest gâteau on a tray. She starts to cut it into slices.*

Jay   Will you be coming back to the B and B tonight or are you going to be staying with your mum?

Kate   I . . . I don't know. Depends if she's still with . . . Duncan.

Jay   I'll give you my number.

He writes a phone number on a piece of paper.

Kate   You don't live there?

Jay   Under the same roof as my dad? It would cramp my style. So . . . I might see you later then?

Kate   If not tonight, perhaps tomorrow or something?

Jay   Yeah sure, sometime, anytime.

He exits.

Kate *joins* **Myrtle***. They move to the chairs and tables.*

Myrtle   I hope it's defrosted properly. I've only just come back from Tesco's. I wasn't going to start on it till this evening. I'd have bought a bigger one if you'd written to let me know you were coming . . . (ex)cuse fingers.

She dollops a huge lump of gâteau onto a plate, hands it to **Kate***.*

Myrtle   Have some extra cherries.

She takes out a little plastic pot of glacé cherries, tips some on **Kate***'s plate.*

Myrtle   They never put enough in, do they? So how's college?

Kate   Why didn't you call me?

Myrtle   They cut off the phone.

Kate   Is . . . I mean are you still living with . . .

Myrtle   He's good for me. He makes me smile. I painted him, do you want to see? He said to never show anyone but . . .

Kate Then don't show me. I can't eat this. I'm sorry.

Myrtle Shall I make you something else? Salad? Something healthy? Have you gone vegetarian?

Kate Mum . . . I don't think I'll go back after the holidays. I don't fit in, I don't understand half the stuff they're trying to teach me, or why I should need to know those things. I thought I might try to get a job down here or something, so we could see each other sometimes . . .

Myrtle How's Mel?

Kate Dad's fine.

Myrtle I miss him.

Kate So why . . .

Myrtle I wish we were still friends.

Kate You can't be friends and love someone.

Myrtle Is this from experience, love?

Kate It's something I've been thinking about.

Myrtle Andy?

Kate He's my best friend, always will be . . . and no, no I do love him, but it's not like when you meet someone and you feel . . .

Myrtle That's exactly it. How it was with Duncan. I met him and I felt –

Kate I don't want to hear about Duncan!

Myrtle I was talking about me, my feelings.

Kate I hate Duncan.

Myrtle Kate, love, don't –

Kate I hate the way he treats you – it's all phoney, he's completely phoney – that's why I'm not going back to college.

Myrtle I don't see how Duncan –

Kate Don't you see! Everyone there, they're all like him!

Myrtle That sounds like his car.

Kate What! Shit.

Myrtle *stands, nervous.*

Kate I don't want to see him. We can't talk with him here.

Myrtle Don't go, Kate.

Kate I'm sorry, Mum.

Myrtle   Please. Please don't walk out.

Exit **Kate**.

The bar area.

Jay *is cleaning up.*

Enter **Phoebe**.

Jay   We're closed. Oh hi.

Phoebe   Your dad wants to know –

Jay   If Harris has called yet? No. My back is killing me.

Phoebe   Do you think he'll call tomorrow?

Jay   Phoebe . . .

He beckons **Phoebe** *over, holding out his hands.*

Jay   Feel them. My hands. Do they feel rough?

Phoebe *takes* **Jay**'*s hands.*

Phoebe   They're soft. Chapped and blistered.

Jay   Blistered where?

Phoebe   Between your fingers here.

Jay *sits on the bar studying his hand intently.*

Phoebe   What about a drink, love? Jay?

Jay   No.

Phoebe   Just a little one . . .

She moves to pull a pint. **Jay** *slams his hand down on the bar. She jumps.*

Jay   No!

Phoebe   Alright, alright . . .

Jay *moves away, looking at his hand. He piles washing-up into a bowl of soapy water.*

Phoebe   I'm going to move out.

Jay   Because of earlier –

Phoebe   I want a room with a sea view.

Jay   It'll cost more – do you think the DSS will stump up the difference?

Phoebe   I'll share with someone if I have to.

Jay   I thought you and Dad –

Phoebe   I still pay my rent.

Jay   You needn't though.

Phoebe   It wouldn't be right. It would be like I'm . . .

Jay   Screwing him to get free lodgings?

Phoebe   I'm going to move out.

Jay   And stop seeing my dad?

Phoebe   I didn't say that.

Jay   So it isn't Dad you want to get away from?

Phoebe   No.

Jay   Do you hate me?

Phoebe   I've told you I don't.

Jay   That's good, I'm glad about that.

Enter **Kate***.*

Kate   Hello.

Jay *looks up, smiles.*

Jay   See your mum?

Kate   Yeah.

Phoebe *gives* **Kate** *a small smile, turns to leave.*

Phoebe   . . . Jay. . .your dad said could you call in on your way home.

Jay   Say you didn't catch me. Say you got here and I'd already gone home.

Phoebe   I can't lie to him.

Jay   Everyone can lie.

Phoebe   I'll try, but he'll see it in my eyes.

Jay *takes some money from his pocket.*

Jay   Buy him some beers, Phoebe. Buy some for Dad, don't drink them all yourself, okay?

Phoebe   He's had enough today.

Jay   Not enough to stop him standing under my window screaming his head off. I can't take that tonight.

He takes out some more money.

Here, go have a few yourself first, okay?

Phoebe   Okay . . .

She exits.

Jay   She's a nice old girl, isn't she? Had a bad life, lots of husbands.

Kate *picks up a cloth, begins drying up.*

Jay   You don't have to do that.

Kate   It's okay.

Jay   I don't want you to do it.

He snatches the tea towel from **Kate**.

Kate   Oh fine. What do you want me to do? Talk? Keep quiet? Stay? Go away?

Jay *winds the washing-up cloth around the inside of a glass.*

Kate   Well?

Jay   Put your hand on my shoulder.

Kate   Which?

Jay   Left shoulder, left hand.

Kate *stands behind* **Jay**, *puts her hand on his shoulder. He continues washing up.*

Jay   And the right one.

She does so.

Jay   Got a boyfriend?

Kate   No. Have you got a girlfriend?

Jay   No.

Kate   Do you want me to stay like this, or do anything else?

Jay   You can stroke my neck, mess my hair, I don't know.

She does.

That's nice, feels good.

Kate   I don't know if I should've come down here. I don't know if I wanted to see Mum, or if she wanted to see me –

Jay   You gonna think about her or me?

Kate *kisses his neck.*

Kate   You're shivery.

Jay   Gotta be a good sign. Do I taste like stale beer?

Kate   Salty beer. Soapy beer.

Jay   God I'm not washing this! Look at this!

He holds up a dirty glass.

You get disgusting pigs in here, fat, smelly disgusting pigs.

Kate *strokes his sides.*

Kate   Hey, relax. I had a stupid fucked-up day too.

She lifts his shirt.

Scratches. On your back here, low down.

Jay   They're not scratches. That's where my dad used to hit me. There and lower down.

Kate   Can I see?

Jay   My arse? Turn around.

She does so.

Kate   My God, everyone can see in. We're all lit up and everybody out there, walking by, can see us.

Jay   Best thing about working here.

He sits on the bar.

I get my regulars most nights. When the bar's closed, there's just me clearing up, they come by, they walk past or stand looking in at me. There's a pale funny-faced one with corkscrew hair, there's a Spanish-looking one and her tomboyish friend. There're couple of freaky chicks from the art college, a couple of older ones, not that old you know . . .

Kate   And you what?

Jay   I watch them watching me.

Kate   Through the glass? You don't let them in?

Jay   The place is closed. They don't want to come in. They've got their own lives. That's not part of it. Sometimes I give them . . . a show, not always. I mean I dance, put the jukebox on and just find my way into the groove. Sometimes we play 'mirrors'. You know, shadowing each other's movements through the window. Getting in close, just the thin, cold glass preventing our fingers, our tongues, other parts touching. It's just a show. Best show they're going to find in Worthing. Sad or what?

Kate   We were . . . we were giving them a show?

Jay   I've finished here. Let's go home.

Kate   You're not coming back with me.

Jay   No not to that shit pit. You're coming back with me.

Kate   No.

Jay   What's the problem? So why did you come in here then?

They walk onto the beach.

Kate   Just thought we could talk . . .

Jay   About your problems? About your mum? I don't know what you should do. I don't particularly care.

Kate   You don't care, and you expect to fuck me.

She swings round to face him.

Dig yourself out of that one.

Jay   I meant I don't care for hearing about other people's problems, because there's nothing I can do about them. But I do care about you. When you first walked in the door this morning, I realised you were someone really special –

Kate   Oh shit. Don't give me that old 'you're really special' stuff. Don't start talking to me like that just because you're trying to get me in bed. Don't give me any lines like I'm just some girl and I don't mean shit! I can find my own way back from here.

Jay   Sure. Okay.

He hesitates, gives her a hug.

God, feel that. I'm as hard as a stick of rock . . . and it's got suck me written all the way through it.

He releases her and exits.

Breakfast is at nine. Fry-up, toast or cornflakes.

Blackout

Scene Two

Kate *is sitting at the table with* **Dave** *and* **Phoebe**. **Jay** *puts a plate of toast in front of* **Kate**. **Phoebe** *is feeding* **Dave** *with spoonfuls of cornflakes.*

Jay   Do you usually look this bad in the morning?

Kate   Wouldn't you like to know?

Jay   Sleepless night?

Kate   Yes.

Jay   Thinking about what you were missing?

Kate   You don't half fancy yourself.

Jay   Someone has to.

Dave   Jay, any word from Harris?

Jay *pours* **Kate** *a tea.*

Jay   No.

Dave   Do you think you should maybe give him another ring?

Jay   Later.

Phoebe   Maybe he didn't get your tape.

Dave   What if he hasn't got my tape? If it's got lost in the post or something.

Jay   I'll ring him later, ok.

Kate   Tape?

Jay   Dad's demo.

Kate   You're a musician?

Dave   Of sorts.

Phoebe   He's very good.

Kate   What sort of music, I mean what kind of things do you play?

Dave   Dylan covers, bit of Straits . . . You've heard of . . .

Jay   Course she has, Dad.

Dave   Well, a lot of these youngsters don't know what real music is, it's all rap and ragga and sampling these days . . .

Kate   I like a real song, you know with lyrics which mean something, words you can understand, that tell a story.

Jay (*grinning*)   'Words that touch your pain'. That's what Dad calls them.

Dave   Jay used to write songs. He's got them all in little jotters. Ask him to bring them in to show you.

Jay   I've ripped them up.

Dave   His band used to get played on the radio – Radio 1.

Kate   You made records?

Jay   We pressed a single, we once had a session on the John Peel show.

Dave   Just when they looked like they were going somewhere, were going to be the biggest thing ever to come out of Worthing, they broke up. Artistic differences! Artistic differences at seventeen!

Jay   I broke the drummer's nose.

Kate   What did you do in the band?

Jay   I was the singer, and no I won't let you listen to the tapes sometime. I was very young, all that stuff makes me cringe now.

Dave   But he's still got all the contacts in the industry, haven't you?

Jay   I don't know . . . there was a time . . . I don't know if Harris will call back . . .

Dave   Well, you're going to give him another bell later.

Jay   I don't know why you don't call him yourself.

Dave   Because he knows you, he's heard of you. He doesn't know me from shit.

Jay   God, I'm burning Kate's seconds!

He exits.

Phoebe (*to* **Kate**)   Dave and I are going down the ten pin this afternoon. It's a lot of fun. Well, it passes the time, you know.

Enter **Jay** *with burnt toast.*

Kate   Did you say you'd got the afternoon off?

Jay   Got to go to the dentist, have a tooth out.

Kate   Oh poor you.

Jay   Anything's preferable to ten-pin bowling. Don't get talked into it.

Dave *gets up.*

Dave   Well, I've got to go up the cash 'n' carry. Nobody want anything? Good.

He exits.

Jay   More tea, Phebe?

Phoebe   Ta, love.

Exit **Jay** *into the kitchen area.*

Phoebe   Don't break his heart, Kate.

Kate   What . . .?

Phoebe   I don't know what your plans are, how long you plan staying . . . Most people only stop here a few weeks. If they're young like you they drift along the coast to the bright lights of Brighton. Or if they're old like me /

Kate   You're not old, Phoebe!

Phoebe   / they just wither away.

Kate   How long have you been here?

Phoebe   Too long. Left my husband, just stuffed a few clothes and my nightie in a bag. The old story. My third husband. He was a bastard. Dave's not like that, he's gentle you know, a real gentleman.

Kate   Are there usually other guests here?

Phoebe   Only DSS, no one sticks around. Well, it's Dave's drinking and the brawls.

Kate   Brawls here?

Phoebe   In Worthing? I know it sounds unbelievable. I mean Dave and Jay. It's awful sometimes.

Kate   What do they fight about?

Phoebe   I . . . I don't know. I don't want to know. I lock my door and wait for it to end. Jay usually comes out of it worse, well, Dave's a big bloke, built like a brick shonny and when he's drunk . . .

I've noticed that you and Jay seem to be getting on –

Kate   Doesn't he 'get on' with all the girls who stay here?

Phoebe   Keeps himself to himself, keeps out of the way mostly.

Kate   Yeah?

Phoebe   Jay needs someone to . . . I don't know, do you mind me talking frankly? He needs someone to give him a bit of stability, a bit of affection. It might be all it takes to change him –

Kate   Change him?

Front of stage converts to a ten-pin bowling lane. Juke-box music plays.

Phoebe *and* **Kate** *walk to the far end.* **Phoebe** *picks up a bowling ball.*

Enter **Dave** *eating some chips.*

Dave   Swing it, Phoebe.

Phoebe *bowls, hits only a few skittles.*

Dave   That was rubbish, love. Make way for the pro.

He gives his chips to **Kate**.

Dave   The boy's on form tonight.

Dave *polishes the ball on his shirt.*

Kate   No ball tampering.

Phoebe   Or I'll tamper with yours in a minute.

Dave   Is that a threat or a promise?

Kate   Get on with it.

Dave *bowls; it's a powerful shot, demolishing the skittles.*

Dave   Nice one.

He takes his chips back.

Dave   Think you can finish it off, Kate?

Kate   I'll try.

She is about to bowl.

Enter **Jay**.

Jay *comes up behind* **Kate**, *puts his arms around her as she bowls. She misses the skittles.*

Dave   Foul. No sexual harassment allowed.

He picks up another ball, demolishes the skittles. **Jay** *and* **Kate** *move away.*

Kate   Was I sad or what?

Jay   Are you going to join them at the bingo tomorrow night?

Kate   Bingo?

Jay   In London you have nightlife, in Worthing you have bingo.

Kate   It's nice here though.

Jay   Did you see your mum again?

Kate   Yeah.

Dave   Jay, you haven't had a chance to call / Harris yet –

Jay (*snaps*)   Not yet.

He rubs his jaw.

Jay (*to* **Kate**)   Come for a walk?

Kate   Okay.

Kate *and* **Jay** *walk along the beach.*

Kate   I've never seen a beach with so much seaweed.

Jay   In summer it's always packed . . . with seaweed flies!

Kate   Everyone here seems to be old. It's like the whole country come here to retire.

Jay   To die. Friday night, you'll still be here?

Kate   Yeah . . . I don't know.

Jay   I'll take you into Brighton, there's bound to be a good all-nighter.

Kate *takes his hand.*

Jay   Or a gig.

Kate   I'd like to hear you sing.

Jay   No you wouldn't. It's colder than I thought. Don't really fancy a paddle after all. Tell you what, we could go back to my place, I'll cook us something.

Kate   No . . .

Jay   Christ, Kate, what is it with you? What do the guys you usually go with do? Do they have good jobs, a car, a nice place? Do they live somewhere exciting? Do they have lots of money?

He pulls her against him.

Bet they don't smell of stale beer and fags and chips.

Kate   You smell very nice today.

Jay   Not nice enough though obviously.

Kate   Let me go.

Jay   My pleasure.

He shoves **Kate** *away from him, turns.*

Kate   Hey, don't just walk away from me. Hey.

She catches hold of **Jay***, tries to turn him to look at her, catches his face. He lashes out, hits her across the face, sends her staggering. She looks at him in horror.* **Jay** *stands looking at her.*

Jay   Shit. Are you . . .? God, did I? Kate!

He hugs **Kate***. She is still stunned.*

Jay   Are you alright? I didn't mean to, I just caught you.

He leaves her, crouches down.

I'm sorry. You caught my jaw, I've had two teeth out and stitches.

He wipes his mouth with a bloodstained tissue.

Shit. I'm sorry.

Kate *sits down beside him.*

Jay   You're sure you're alright?

He wipes his mouth.

That dentist's a bloody butcher! Thank Christ it's at the back. Are you alright?

He gently examines **Kate***'s face.*

Jay   You're not crying?

Kate   Just my eye watering a bit. What're the grey birds?

Jay   Seagulls.

Kate   I thought gulls were white.

Jay   Even the gulls are grey in this place.

Kate   Have you always lived here?

Jay   Not always.

Kate   Where're you from?

Jay   Does it matter? London. Like you. That's why I could tell, see? Is my face swelling?

Kate   It looks okay.

She brushes her fingers across his cheek. He takes one in his mouth, releases it.

Jay   Kiss me, Kate.

Kate   No –

Jay   Oh Christ!

Kate   It'll hurt.

Jay   Any excuse not to.

He sighs. She kisses him gently; he holds her head to prolong the kiss.

Jay   Kiss me deep.

She starts to but stops.

Kate   You're still bleeding. I can taste it. It must hurt.

Jay   You're worth it. What's a bit of pain?

They get up. He takes her hand.

I'm only going to be able to manage soup for dinner, but I'll cook you something special . . . you are coming back to mine?

Kate *smiles.*

They walk off and exit.

Blackout.

Act Two

Scene One

Kate *is in bed. She rolls over, sits up.*

Enter **Jay** *with breakfast on a tray.* **Kate** *smiles.*

Jay *sits down beside her, feeds her.*

Kate   It's delicious.

Jay   Will madam be requiring seconds?

Kate   I know what I'd like for seconds.

Jay   Mmmm, but I've got to see to Phoebe.

Kate   Couldn't your dad?

Jay   He could, but if he does I won't get paid. The DSS left a message to say they were sending us three more punters. You never know if they're going to turn up or not, or whether Dad's going to scare them out of the place within the day, but whatever, I've gotta go, sweetheart.

Kate   When will you be back?

Jay   I haven't got to work late. You could drop by the Mermaid about seven'ish.

Kate   Okay, I'll do that.

She gets up, they kiss.

Jay   See you later then.

He exits.

Kate   Jay!

Jay *comes back in.*

Kate   Can I come back again tonight? I mean you do want –

Jay   What do you take me for?

Kate   I don't know if this is something serious to you . . . our relationship . . .

Jay   Or whether you've just been fucked over. If that's what you think, you can just fuck off.

Kate   What do you want –

Jay   My mouth's bloody killing me. My gum's turning black. The last thing I want to do is talk! There's a spare door key in the kitchen. If you want to shift your stuff over here, do it.

Kate   What'll your dad –

Jay   Kick my arse for losing him a punter . . . and kick my arse for not getting his old tart her breakfast, if I don't go.

He exits.

Beside the table, **Dave** *sits picking at a guitar.*

Jay *comes in, tries to exit before* **Dave** *sees him.*

Dave   Jay.

He beckons **Jay** *over.*

Dave   Harris left a message for you on the answer machine.

Jay   Yeah? What he say?

Dave *puts the guitar down, goes to answerphone, plays back message. 'Hi, Jay, it's Harris. I'm away for the next couple of weeks, give me a bell sometime after that, yeah?'*

Dave   What do you think? Why doesn't he mention my tape? He must've got it by now.

Jay   Probably hasn't had time to listen to it yet. Probably gets a lot of tapes . . .

Dave   But he knows you. If it was your tape he'd have listened to it by now, wouldn't he?

Jay   I don't know. I doubt it.

Dave   Course he would. Well, you played on it.

Jay   On one track.

Dave   Did you tell him that?

Jay   No I –

Dave *approaches him.*

Dave (*sharply*)   Why not? You're ashamed of me!

Jay   No.

Dave *slaps* **Jay**.

Dave   Why didn't you tell him?

He hits **Jay**, *knocks him back.* **Jay** *retaliates. They exchange a series of quick blows.*

Jay   He's not interested in you, or me!

They circle around each other like boxers.

Dave   You want me to fail, just because you have.

Jay   I'm not failing.

The fight starts to get nasty.

Enter **Phoebe**.

Phoebe   Oh God! Dave!

She tries unsuccessfully to part them. **Dave** *slams* **Jay** *hard against the wall. Freeze.*

Blackout.

Exit **Dave** *and* **Phoebe**.

Lights up, front of stage. **Kate** *comes into* **Myrtle**'*s flat.*

Kate   Mum, did you know you've left the front door . . .

She looks around. She sniffs.

God!

She rushes into the kitchen area, turns the gas off.

Kate   Mum. Mum!

She rushes out.

Back of the stage.

Kate *runs in.* **Jay** *is sitting alone on the bench, back to her.*

Kate   Jay! Help, something's happened to Mum . . .

He doesn't turn round.

Her front door was left open. There was no sign of her or Duncan. And the gas was on – the oven door was open . . .

Jay   Was her head stuck in it?

Kate   No!

Jay   That's okay then.

Kate   But why would she . . .

Jay *turns round. He has a bruise on his face.*

Jay   I don't bloody know! Shit, my mouth's bleeding again, I think I've busted my stitches.

He spits in the sink. **Kate** *gives him a glass of water.*

Kate   I'm so worried.

Jay   Perhaps she's trying to scare him.

Kate   What? Who?

Jay   Got a tissue?

He wipes his mouth.

Your mum's bloke. Perhaps she's trying to scare him, make him think . . . I don't know. Women are so cruel. Don't look like that, I don't mean you, not in particular, but I've known some girls and they always surprise you, with the things they're capable of. Shit. I'll have to go back and have it re-stitched.

Kate   Your face is really starting to bruise now.

Jay   I know some places she might be. Places I go when I want to think, when I'm feeling a bit down.

He takes **Kate**'s *hand.*

They exit.

Phoebe, *back of stage, is joined by* **Dave**, *clutching a bottle.*

Phoebe   Are you alright, love? You look awful.

Dave   He's a bastard. He's not a son, I don't want him for a son. Give me a son, Phoebe! Give me a proper one.

Phoebe   I've already got a couple of sons. Lovely sons.

Dave   Shaun and Richard.

Phoebe   Richard and Shaun. My lovely boys.

Dave   When am I going to meet them?

Phoebe   Soon.

Dave   When's soon, Phebe? You're ashamed of me, I'm never going to get to meet your kids.

Phoebe   You are.

She takes the bottle, swigs.

Dave   When?

Phoebe   At the wedding.

She chokes, spits out the beer.

A decent skirt and that'll stain.

Dave   Whose wedding, you crazy old cow?

Phoebe *stumbles against* **Dave**, *slides down him, fondles him.*

Phoebe   Dave, will you marry me!

Dave   People are looking, keep it down.

Phoebe   Dave, I am asking you to marry me.

Dave   Are you serious?

Phoebe   I love you!

Dave Me too love.

Phoebe Well?

Dave Christ! . . . Okay let's go get some bubbly to celebrate, shall we? Let's paint the town red tonight, Phoebe! Let's eat oysters. What do you say, huh?

Phoebe Are you going to say yes, Dave? You're supposed to say 'yes'.

Dave Yes, I do, whatever. Let's get rat-arsed darling.

He hauls **Phoebe** *to her feet.*

Dave The man's really supposed to do the proposing.

Phoebe It doesn't matter. Equality and all that.

Dave What about your other three husbands?

Phoebe They won't mind. I'm divorced, lover.

Dave I mean, did you propose to any of them?

Phoebe All of them. Each of those bastards.

They exit.

Jay *and* **Kate** *enter,* **Myrtle** *between them, on* **Kate***'s arm.*

Myrtle I put the oven on, meaning to warm up a pie for Duncan's dinner. I looked in the fridge for the pie. I'd forgotten to buy it. How utterly stupid! I went straight up the shop to get him one. I suppose I left in a hurry, without locking the door, I've been more lax about things like that since moving down here, it's so much quieter . . . I didn't have very long, or it wouldn't have had time to cook through properly and brown on top. Sometimes he's home by quarter past five. I must've left the door right open, and the oven door, and the wind blew the gas out.

Kate I thought all sorts of terrible things –

Jay Have you got the pie now?

Myrtle Eh?

Kate The pie for Duncan's dinner.

Myrtle That's the really funny thing. Halfway to the shop I realised – it's Thursday. Duncan works late on Thursday evenings. He won't be in until seven or so. The sun was shining down on me, I could smell the salt on the breeze, so I decided to take a little walk on the prom just to stretch my legs, I haven't left the flat all day . . . Then I saw you –

Kate And you tried not to look at me, Mum. You kept your head down and tried to walk on by.

Myrtle (*laughs nervously*) I thought to myself, 'There's my Katie. Oh, and it looks like she's found herself a young man. I won't call out and disturb them.' Then you both came running over. (*To* **Jay**.) It's very nice to meet you.

Jay   Kate's told me a lot about you.

Myrtle   I'm sure in due course she's going to tell me a lot about you. Or maybe you'd both like to come back for dinner this evening, unless you've other plans –

Kate   Well, actually, Mum –

Jay   We'd love to come over, Mrs Milner. Wouldn't we, Kate? When I finish work, about 7.30?

Myrtle   Duncan will be so pleased to see you, Kate. And to meet Jay too. I better get another couple of pies.

Front of stage.

Phoebe   You shouldn't have opened the champagne. It'll go flat before he gets here.

Dave   Shall I ring him again?

Phoebe   I expect he's gone out for the evening.

Dave   With Kate? Sod him, sod them both, let's finish the bubbly.

Phoebe   Let's take it to bed.

Kitchen area.

Myrtle *dollops some gâteau onto a plate for* **Kate***.*

Jay   Not for me thanks, Mrs Milner.

Myrtle   Myrtle.

Kate   Jay's only just had a couple of teeth out.

Myrtle *opens the pot of glacé cherries, shakes some onto* **Kate***'s slice of gâteau.*

Myrtle   I wondered about the bruise. Didn't like to ask, you don't do you. You should've seen me when I had my wisdom teeth out – face out here.

Jay   I've got that joy to come.

Myrtle   The body's a great healer though.

Jay   Yeah, it's a miracle how it can take so much.

Myrtle   Life itself is a miracle. As you get older and you have less of it left, you really start to appreciate just what a precious gift it is.

Jay   This is lovely coffee, Myrtle.

Myrtle   It's only instant I'm afraid, though they keep telling us on telly how good it is and that you can't tell the difference. Same with butter and all these new spreads, and half-fat butters – they all look like proper butter and don't taste bad –

Jay   But then you try to cook with them.

Myrtle   Disaster. Can't even grease a tin properly. Do you do much cooking, Jay? I suppose you have to – you're a single young man.

Kate   Jay works in the bed and breakfast hotel where I'm staying.

Jay (*edgy*)   Just to fill in while I'm deciding what I want to do.

He takes hold of **Kate**'*s hand, squeezes it hard.*

Jay   It's just to help my dad out actually. Now winter's coming and trade's tailing off, he'll be able to manage without me. I've got a few ideas about what I want to do. I'd like to start my own business, be my own boss –

Kate   That's something I've always thought about too.

Jay   I was thinking about doing something in the catering line –

Myrtle   Cakes – decorating them like Jane Asher –

Jay   Maybe a sandwich franchise . . . Kate could help me if she likes, we could be partners.

Kate   Hey, that's an idea –

Myrtle   Perhaps when she's finished college –

Kate   I'm not going back to college, Mum.

Myrtle   Oh, Kate, please think about it carefully –

Jay   More coffee, Myrtle?

Myrtle   Oh where is he?

Kate   Late at the office, eh?

Myrtle   He works long hours, but it's a good job, a career with prospects and there are too few of those around these days. That's why I think getting a good education is important –

Jay   Couple of my mates have got 'A' levels and they've both been on the dole for three years now . . .

Myrtle   But Kate's going to be a teacher. They always need teachers.

Kate   I don't want to be a teacher.

Myrtle   You do, you did –

Jay   You've got to let Kate make her own decisions. If she doesn't want to be a teacher, she doesn't have to.

Myrtle   Of course she doesn't, I'm just asking her to think things over.

Kate   I have been –

Jay   Of course she has.

Myrtle   I just don't want to see her stuck in some dead-end job . . .

Jay   In some dead-end town with a boyfriend with a dead-end job.

He gets up.

Thanks for the pie, Mrs Milner. I'm sorry you don't think I'm fit to grace your table.

Myrtle *gets up.*

Myrtle   I didn't mean . . . sit down.

*She catches hold of **Jay**'s sleeve. He pushes her away.*

Jay   Let me go. I need to throw up. Your pie's left a nasty taste in my mouth

He exits.

Myrtle   I'm sorry, Katie. I didn't mean to offend him.

Kate   You're a snob, Mum. Dad's only a fitter. But you still married him. Oh but I forget, you left him for Duncan. Duncan with his flash job in computers, his flash car, his whiny posh voice, his golf clubs . . .

Myrtle   I left your father because we'd grown apart. Duncan was only a friend then . . . Oh where is he? And where's your young man gone. Is he feeling sick, did he say?

Kate   Sick of you, Mum. And so am I.

She exits.

(*Shouts back offstage.*) You and Duncan deserve each other.

*Enter **Dave** and **Phoebe** back. They have finished the bottle and are very drunk. **Dave** props **Phoebe** up.*

Phoebe (*slurring*)   We should've waited for Jay.

Dave   He's useless. All that stuff with his friend Harris being able to give me a break was all a big wind-up, a big piss-take at my expense.

Phoebe   Jay never promised Harris could help get you bookings . . .

Dave   Jay, Jay, Jay, he's all you seem to want to talk about tonight.

Phoebe   Well, he is going to be my stepson.

Dave   I suppose there is that.

Phoebe   And I don't really feel quite right about it. I feel it's a bit –

Dave   I know when you came to stay here, you and Jay . . . you two kind of became quite close for a while . . . I mean he befriended you, showed you around town. But you never . . .

Phoebe   Dave –

Dave   You and Jay. . . .

He laughs.

You and him, I can't see it somehow. You know what he calls you, you know what he says about you and me? He thinks we're too old for sex, he thinks it's obscene, it's filthy. That's what he said. He calls you my old tart . . .

She looks at **Dave***, stricken.*

Phoebe   He begged to sleep with me. He begged for it.

Dave   No, Phoebe, no, no.

Phoebe   Dave I . . . it was a mistake. I didn't say 'yes', but he assumed . . . I don't mean he raped me . . . he was nice . . . and sweet . . . the first time . . . but after that . . . Oh, Dave, I wish I hadn't, I wish I'd been stronger. I was weak, I was stupid, I'm sorry.

She reaches out. He moves away from her.

Dave   Don't come near me.

Phoebe   But that's over, Dave.

Dave   It's over. Get your things and get out.

Phoebe   Dave . . .

Dave   Marry me so you could carry on seeing him, that it? I tried to ignore it, tried to intercept those little glances and smiles and keep them for myself. I tried to kid myself it was me that was keeping you here. I tried to ignore the fact that I'm old and fat and pissed and I can't play the bloody guitar. Tried to forget I have a son with the kind of looks I've never had –

Phoebe   It's over with Jay. I don't love him, I love you. You're lots of things he's not. You're kind, you're gentle –

Dave   And you're a whore. Get out!

Blackout.

Lights up on the bed.

Jay *and* **Kate** *lying together.*

Jay   Was that good, Kate?

Kate   Better than good . . .

Jay   Do you love me?

Kate   I do.

Jay *nuzzles her, smiles.*

Jay   Your mother doesn't think I'm good enough for you.

Kate   She's always like that with everyone. Lots of questions.

Jay   With your other boyfriends?

Kate   Yeah.

Jay   I thought you said you hadn't got any others.

Kate   Previous boyfriends I should've said.

Jay   Sure. Of course. Tell me about them.

Kate   What?

Jay   A list, first names only if you like, and what you did with them.

Kate   Don't be stupid.

Jay   Tell me. Names and what you did, everything you did.

Kate   That's private, personal. It's none of your . . . well, you tell me about your previous girlfriends then.

Jay   Okay. Fine. Let me see . . . You really want to hear this?

Kate   I do.

Jay   I fucked Phoebe.

Kate *hits him across the face. She tries to jump up.* **Jay** *pulls her back down by her hair.*

Kate   Shit . . . Oh my God.

Jay   And the others, starting in chronological order with my cousin Juno when I was eleven . . .

Kate   No! No!

She struggles, breaks free. She grabs a cup and hurls it at him, sitting on the bed. It misses narrowly. He looks startled, then angry. He gets up, she backs up.

Jay   I'm going to fuckin' kill you.

Kate   Keep away. Keep back. I'm going.

Jay *stalks* **Kate** *around the kitchen bench. She backs up, fearful.*

Kate   Jay, let me go.

Around the bench again, and again, **Jay** *with deadly intent.*

Kate   Please Jay.

Jay *wavers, looks about to back off, lunges over the bench, grabs hold of* **Kate**. *She cries out.*

Jay   You're an evil bitch. Someone's got to teach you a lesson.

He thumps her back hard against the cooker, and again, until she sinks to the floor. He kicks her as she curls into a foetal position to protect herself. He kicks her again.

Blackout.

Lights come up.

Kate *alone, curled up where* **Jay** *attacked her, shaking. She gets up slowly, painfully, looks about her. She begins to clear up, smoothes her hair, straightens her clothes.*

She goes to sit on the bed, picks up the pillow, hugs it. Suddenly she drops the pillow with a look of repulsion, starts punching it hard, repeatedly. She sobs, for the first time.

Jay *appears in the doorway, dishevelled, his face bewildered, frightened. Seeing* **Kate** *he starts to cry, quietly. She hears his breathing and looks up, her eyes wide like a cornered animal. Her face hardens, she sits up, defensive. He is shaking.*

Jay   Kate, I . . . I can't believe that I . . . I'm going to end it, I've got some pills in the kitchen. There's nothing I can say to you. I mean sorry's not enough, it's pathetic. I'm a shit. Death's too good for me, but . . . I don't know what else . . . . I'm sorry . . .

He runs into the kitchen. Pours a glass of mineral water, takes a little pot of pills back into the bedroom.

Jay   I'll take the whole pot.

Kate, *horrified, gets up, approaches him warily.* **Jay** *swallows a couple of pills, stops.*

Jay   I love you, Kate.

Kate *takes hold of* **Jay**, *meaning to snatch the pills, ends up hugging him. He hugs her tightly.*

Jay   I love you, baby. God, I love you. Forgive me, sweetheart, please, please . . . Kate.

Blackout.

Scene Two

Jay *is wiping the bench.* **Dave** *hunched over a bottle of beer.*

Jay   Phoebe not up yet then Dad?

Dave *grunts.* **Jay** *discovers the champagne bottle.*

Jay   Someone's birthday? Phoebe's?

Dave   She's forty.

Jay   She was forty back in May.

Dave   She told you that? What did you give her for a birthday present, eh?

Jay   Nothing . . .

Dave   Nothing!

He lurches over and leans over **Jay** *as he scrubs at a non-existent stain on the bench.*

Look at me when I'm talking to you, son.

Jay looks up, wary. **Dave** *tilts* **Jay***'s chin up, gently, caressingly, so he is looking into his eyes.*

Dave   Look at me, that's right, look at me.

He smashes his other fist into **Jay***'s face.* **Jay** *sinks down.* **Dave** *kicks him, walks off.*

Blackout.

Lights up.

Jay *sitting on the floor.* **Phoebe** *has come in. She takes a chipped, floral-patterned mug from the bench.*

Phoebe   I'm not leaving my mug. My Richard gave it to me, brought it back from Australia. Do you mind if I go upstairs and collect the rest of my things?

Jay (*dazed*)   Be my guest.

Phoebe   I flung some things into a bag last night, but I was a bit gone and forgot all my undies and my make-up. Actually I'm still a bit gone. I waited outside across the road until I saw him leave just now.

Jay *tries to get up. His legs won't let him.*

Phoebe   My God, are you alright?

Jay *drags himself up against the bench.*

Jay   Yeah. I . . . I only came back to tell him I'm quitting.

Phoebe   And he laid in to you for that?

Jay   I don't think . . . I don't think I got round to telling him. I think he just . . . hit me . . . I think . . . I don't know . . .

Phoebe   Look at me.

She tries to tilt **Jay***'s head.*

Jay (*horrified*)   No!

Phoebe *jumps back, fearing a blow.*

Phoebe   You might be concussed. You ought to go up casualty. Is Kate up yet? She'll help you get up there. Shall I go up and call her?

Jay   She's at my place. It's okay, I'll go home in a minute, she'll look after me. She's a good girl, she's an angel . . .

Phoebe   I told Dave about us. Maybe that's why –

Jay   I told Kate.

Phoebe   What?

Jay (*exasperated*)   About us!

Phoebe   What did she say? Or did she hit you too?

Jay   She forgave me.

He staggers and grabs hold of **Phoebe***, tries to kiss her.*

Jay   She'd forgive me anything.

Phoebe *pulls away.*

Phoebe   Poor girl. Well, I don't forgive you! It's your fault everything's in tatters. Dave was so good to me, so gentle. It was real with him. I'll never forgive you.

Jay   What? For what? It was real with me. It made you cry. What have I ever done to you –

Phoebe   Hit me!

For a moment in his concussed state **Jay** *thinks she is asking him to hit her.*

Phoebe   You hit me. The day Kate moved in, just a stupid row about the stupid cricket on the radio. You nearly killed me.

Jay   Liar. You're pissed and you're making up stories. Get your things and go. I might've slapped you once because you were calling me names. You couldn't decide if you wanted a son or a lover, and England were being thrashed by the Aussies, so you took all your confusion out on me.

Phoebe *cradles and strokes the floral mug.*

Phoebe   I just didn't want to be alone. Even you are . . . were better than an empty room, an empty bed.

She exits.

Jay *picks the up the phone, plays back the answerphone messages. The one from* **Harris** *is still on the tape.* **Jay** *listens, scowling.*

Jay   Bastard.

Another message: 'This is Sandra, at Worthing DSS /

Wankers!

/ we've a Mr McKenna needing a room immediately. Can you call me straight back please?'

Can you suck me off please . . . Sandra?

He switches off the machine.

Bollocks.

He dials a number, makes a hash of it, dials again, listens, waits.

Jay   Come on, answer it. Come on, Katie.

Lights up over the bed.

Enter **Kate** *and* **Myrtle**.

Kate *makes a dive for the phone. At that moment* **Jay** *slams his phone down. The phone stops ringing.* **Kate** *picks it up.*

Kate   Missed them. It's not the first time that's happened.

Myrtle   Here?

Kate   A couple of times I've answered Jay's phone and the person the other end's hung up on me. Probably an ex-girlfriend, do you think?

Myrtle   You could ask him –

Kate   I think it's best not to delve.

Myrtle   Are you cold?

Kate   No.

Myrtle   The way you're sitting. The damp down here plays havoc with my rheumatics, but at your age –

Kate   I'm fine, Mum.

Myrtle   Your face, is that a bruise?

Kate   I borrowed Jay's mountain bike, went for a ride out into the country yesterday morning – fell off. No damage done. The bruise didn't start to show until this morning.

Myrtle   Are you sure you're really alright? You're pale. Are you eating? Does he cook for you?

Kate   Yeah.

Myrtle   I brought you a cake, I hope it hasn't got too squashed. I've got all shapes and sizes of tupperware but I can't find any of the right lids.

She hands **Kate** *a box containing a gooey cake.*

Myrtle   Shop bought I'm afraid. Not as good as I used to make, but I can't get used to the kitchen in the flat, gas when we always had electric. I suppose your dad has to cook for himself now that you're –

Kate   I think Penny cooks.

Myrtle   Penny next door?

Kate   Didn't you know, Penny and Dad. . . .

Myrtle *turns away.*

Myrtle   We always used to laugh about her didn't we? Call her Miss Moneypenny, because she was the spinster of the parish. Never had a boyfriend in her life.

Kate   Well, now she's had Dad.

They both snigger, **Myrtle***'s laughter sounds strained.*

Kate   I came home from college without letting him know, just walked in and they were on the sofa . . . well . . . I mean I just burst out laughing, couldn't help myself. Dad and Penny, it was unearthly. Weird. Then I felt awkward, I was dying of embarrassment. I couldn't stop there, under the same roof. I decided to come down here, and come and see you.

Myrtle   And tell me.

Kate   No, not necessarily. I mean you've both got your own lives now. You've got Duncan.

Myrtle (*unsteadily*)   I'm glad your father's happy . . . if he is happy, do you think he is?

Enter **Jay**.

Jay   I've quit that piss-stinking bar too . . . ahhhhh, hello Myrtle.

Myrtle   My God, your face.

Kate   Jay, did your dad . . .

Jay   Take me up the hospital? No I told him I was okay, thought I'd better come home like I was planning or you'd worry.

Myrtle *examines* **Jay***'s face.*

Myrtle   What happened?

Jay   Fell off my mountain bike.

Myrtle   Are those things safe? At the very least you ought to get it checked over.

Jay   It wasn't the bike's fault, it was some guy in a Capri that decided to overtake me.

Myrtle   Was it the brakes? Did you say it was the brakes with you, love?

Kate   Jay, I was just telling Mum how I fell off your bike yesterday.

Jay   And bruised your face, yeah. Nothing compared with mine though is it? Think I've loosened another couple of teeth. Do you think they can do something to hold them in? I don't want to lose any more. I'll need a plate before I'm twenty-five at this rate.

Myrtle   It looks like you'll have to miss out on my cake again. I wanted to bring you something, Jay, that's why I called round – to make my peace, I wanted to bring you a peace offering.

Jay   Yeah, I'm sorry we had words. It'd been preying on my mind. I'd meant to ring you and apologise. We talked about it didn't we, Kate?

Kate   Yes . . .

Jay   Duncan arrived home safe and sound?

Myrtle (*startled*)   Duncan? Yes, yes he did.

Jay   I think that's partly why we ended up having words – you were worried that he was so late.

Myrtle   No harm done anyway. Well, I must be on my way. Duncan will wonder where I've got to.

Kate *goes to the door with* **Myrtle**.

Kate   Bye, Mum.

Exit **Myrtle**.

Jay   Great minds think alike, love.

Kate   What?

Jay *puts his arms around* **Kate**.

Jay   Both of us using falling off my bike as an excuse. It shows how in tune we are – two of a kind, eh?

Kate   Hadn't you better see a doctor, at least the dentist? Jay, promise me you'll keep away from your dad. He'll kill you otherwise. One day he'll kill you.

Jay   He's getting old, he won't be top dog for much longer. I'll crush him, I'll smash his stupid head to pulp.

Kate   I don't want to hear you talk like this. It's killing us, Jay. It makes me scared of you.

Jay   You ought to be a little bit scared, that's what makes a relationship. Mum was always terrified of Dad. That's what made her respect and love him. She never looked at another man once during their marriage.

Kate   But eventually she left him?

Jay   She died. Brain haemorrhage. I discovered her lying at the bottom of the stairs where she'd fallen. I was fourteen.

Kate   I'm sorry.

Jay   She must've got up in the night and tripped.

He holds his head suddenly, sits down.

Kate   You really did ought to see the doctor.

Jay   You think she'd buy that load of bollocks about the mountain bike?

Kate   If you're saying my mum's gullible –

Jay   I'm saying my doctor has my medical records, including X-rays sent down from casualty over the past twenty-odd years. She's started to ask awkward questions.

Kate   Why not answer them? Why protect your dad?

Jay   I don't want the world knowing my business. If he was charged, if it came to court, everyone would know. I don't want people knowing, I don't want their sympathy. I'm not a battered baby, I'm not a victim. He might get a fine or something but I'd be humiliated in public. I'd look like some weedy wimp. Anyway things are going to be different now. Where do you live at college?

Kate   On campus.

Jay   Big room?

Kate   Tiny, cramped.

Jay   It would only be for a short time.

Kate   I told you, I'm not going back.

Jay   Kate, love, you have to.

Kate   And what about you?

Jay   We'll both have to make do with your little cramped room until I can get on my feet.

Kate   We're not allowed boyfriends in the halls.

Jay   Hardly a hanging offence is it? You won't get, what do they call it – sent down?

Kate   They might ask you to leave.

Jay   Well I'm prepared to risk it. So what's the problem? There's someone else isn't there? Some smart-arsed college jerk . . .

Kate   There's no one else.

Jay   You're scared I won't fit in with your clever, clever friends? Think I'll embarrass you?

Kate   No. . . .

Jay   Well I've got GCSEs you know. I just decided to live in the real world . . . And my dad made me leave school.

Kate   You'll get on fine with my friends. You can cook, they'll love you.

Jay   I thought we could leave tomorrow, if that's alright with you.

Kate   I'm worried about leaving Mum.

Jay   I'm glad she came round and forgave me. We'll be able to come down at weekends and see her. And she's got what's-his-name hasn't she?

Kate   I don't like Duncan.

Jay   I'll have to reserve judgement until I meet him.

Kate   He's a complete prat. A waste of space.

Jay   You shouldn't talk like that – about anyone. You should respect other people if you want them to show you any respect.

Kate   I don't like him, that's all.

Jay   Then I probably won't either. How are they off? He's got a good job didn't she say?

Kate   Something in computers and merchandising.

Jay   He's not short of a bob or two.

Kate   I don't –

Jay   Because the the only way I can see us getting anywhere is if you borrow a bit off of your Mum.

Kate   I don't know –

Jay   And you can get a student loan right?

Kate   I already have.

Jay   Well, try your mum first then.

The phone rings. **Jay** *looks at* **Kate**.

Kate (*shrugs*)   It's probably for you.

Jay *picks the phone.*

Lights up back of stage.

Dave *on the phone*

Jay *mouths, 'It's Dad'.*

Dave (*on phone*)   Jay . . .

Jay (*on phone*)   Yeah, Dad.

Dave   Are you alright? I don't know what came . . . well, I do, it's the drink right? It makes me like another person, or brings out the worst in me, the evil inside /

Jay *passes the receiver to* **Kate**.

Jay   He's mumbling.

Dave   / I've got to make a decision. I have made a decision. I'm giving up the booze /

Kate   He says he's going to stop drinking.

Jay   Yeah, he always says that. Then he starts talking about old times.

Dave   Jay, I want to be some sort of father to you, like I used to be /

Jay   When I was ten – and had a fit.

Dave   Remember how I used to look after you then? Do you remember when you were about ten, your mother was visiting her sister. You were playing out in the sun and then suddenly you were rolling about on the ground like you were having some kind of fit /

Kate, *uncomfortable, passes the phone back to* **Jay**.

Dave /If I'd have panicked, if I hadn't known exactly what to do you'd have died. Do you remember when we went camping in Belgium? And . . . and the model glider we built in the back garden. Mr know-all nextdoor didn't reckon it would fly. You were six years old. You told him he was wrong, of course it would fly – your dad had built it, your dad could do anything. We took it down the beach . . . and you just looked so proud, you were so proud of me . . . even though it only flew a couple of yards and nose-dived straight into the sea.

Jay He's talking about how I used to be proud of him. I've never been proud of him.

He offers **Kate** *the phone. She moves away.* **Jay** *leaves the receiver lying carefully beside the phone.*

Dave Jay, I'm sorry, son. It'll never happen again, I promise you, on my life I promise you. I'll never get pissed again. I'll never lay another finger on you /

Jay This is where he starts losing it. Leave him to talk. Let's go out. How about a day in Brighton?

Kate You're just going to leave that . . .

Jay He keeps ringing back if I put the phone down. He'll ramble on for hours, now the mood's on him. He'll start crying in a minute, I can't listen to that. It's too depressing. We can go to the pictures, a cafe on the seafront, have a look at the shops, go to a club tonight.

Dave, *sobbing now, incoherent. See monologue below.*

Kate Do you really feel like it?

Jay Getting out and about is the best cure for the blues. Grab your coat.

Exit **Jay** *and* **Kate**, **Kate** *with a backward glance at the phone.* **Dave**'s *monologue continues.*

Dave . . . I will stop drinking. Things are going to be so different, believe me, Jay. I'm gonna change, I swear to God. What I'm trying to say is . . . I mean I know I haven't been much of a dad to you . . . but things haven't been easy. Things haven't been easy since your poor mother passed away. God I miss her, she was a good woman. A good woman, your mother, I miss that girl so much. You know, when I look at you sometimes I can see her standing there looking right back at me. I can hear her saying, 'Stop it, Dave, stop this madness now' . . . but I can't stop it, I can't help myself. I don't know what comes over me, Jay. But I'm going to get help . . . and things will be the way they used to be . . . when your mother . . . when there was the three of us . . . and we used to have some laughs, we used to have some good times, didn't we . . . God, I miss her, I still miss her so much. Sometimes I was very hard on her, I admit it. But she knew when she married me that I've a short fuse, and she had a temper too, it wasn't all on my side . . . but we had some laughs, some good times, didn't we?

Blackout.

Act Three

Scene One

Dave *and* **Phoebe** *sitting at the bar.*

Dave   When you weren't at the station I knew you'd be here.

Phoebe *sips her drink.*

Phoebe   Why can't you let me go?

Dave   I am. I will. I just want the answer for one question. Him or me?

Phoebe   I told you, Dave, I . . . I had a . . . relationship with Jay when I first moved in. I didn't know you then.

Dave   Tell me about it.

Phoebe   He carried my cases up to the room, then he just stood there. I didn't know whether I should tip him –

Dave   Tip him!

Phoebe   I'd been to hotels, proper hotels years ago with my second husband. I didn't know if this was a hotel, or a hostel or what. It says hotel painted on the flaking brickwork, but the metal sign hanging in your garden, says 'B + B, DSS welcome'. I didn't know if I should tip him. He's standing there, I'm wondering if he'll say something, or whether I should ask him . . . and how to ask him. I'm thinking how handsome he is –

Dave   Did you think I was handsome?

Phoebe   I could tell immediately you were father and son.

Dave   So Jay stood there, you stood looking at him –

Phoebe   Then he smiled.

Dave   And that clinched it? I should've knocked all his fuckin' teeth out. And?

Phoebe   Dave –

Dave   Was he good?

Phoebe   He was rough –

Dave   You like that?

Phoebe   After the first time he was rough and he didn't think of me, he didn't have any respect for me. If I made a sound, if I protested that he was gripping me too tight, hurting me . . . he'd tell me to shut up. Once when I didn't, he slapped my face.

Dave   I'll paste the floor with him.

Phoebe   Then he wouldn't sleep with me anymore, he just started behaving like it hadn't happened. On the day Kate arrived, he came into my room. The first time he'd come in for a month at least. I was embarrassed . . . I was seeing you, I was in love with you –

Dave   You weren't in love with Jay?

Phoebe   No. And I've always been faithful to who I'm with at any time. That's one of my rules. I put the radio on, pretended I wanted to listen to the cricket. He hadn't said anything, I didn't know what he wanted. I couldn't ask him, he'd think I was coming on to him, you know? I put the cricket on but it was all hisses and crackles. He said he'd tune it in properly for me. It annoyed him to hear it like that. I wouldn't give him the radio, I clutched it. We started having a tug of war. I tried to prise his hands of it. He was gripping so tight. I tried to uncurl his fingers, one of my nails must've scratched the back of his hand. He swore, put his hand up to his mouth. He punched me in the face. Knocked me on the floor.

Dave   Phoebe! Why on earth didn't you tell –

Phoebe   I'd seen you kicking the shit out of him once, I didn't want to see it again.

Dave   You were still in love with him.

Lights up back.

Both scenes continue simultaneously.

Enter **Jay** *and* **Kate** *arguing.*

Jay   The way that guy was looking at you, Kate!

Phoebe   I was never in love with him!

Jay   And you were lapping it up. Wetting your knickers over him.

Kate   You . . . I was not. I can't even remember this –

Jay   You don't? You don't want to remember making such a complete disgrace of yourself. God, how do you expect me to respect you –

Exit **Jay** *and* **Kate***.*

Dave   I just want you to come home?

Phoebe (*bitterly*)   Home? No, Dave.

Dave   What've I done? Have I ever hurt you? Have I ever raised a finger to you? Have I?

Phoebe   No, no you were kind, good . . . to me, but the way you treat your son –

Dave   He hit you. You said so. He deserves it.

Phoebe   No one deserves it. I couldn't let you near my sons –

Dave   I wouldn't hit them! . . . They're nice, well-behaved lads, you said so yourself.

Phoebe   I'm not coming back, Dave.

Dave   I . . . I don't know what to say. I really . . . shit.

He wipes his eyes with his fist. He stands up.

I've been too bloody nice, is that it? If I'd treated you like shit you wouldn't be walking all over me! You'd still want me, hell you would! You'd still love me!

He exits.

Exit **Phoebe** *in the opposite direction.*

Enter **Jay**, *dragging* **Kate**. *She struggles, screams, fights against him. He grips her with one hand, pounds her with the other fist.*

Jay   You bloody whore! You think you can treat me like shit!

Kate *breaks free, back up, stumbles around the bed.*

Kate   No . . . no . . .

Jay   I'll fuckin' kill you!

Kate   I'm leaving . . .

Jay   You think so?

Kate *makes a break for the kitchen. She grabs the carving knife from the drawer.* **Jay** *pursues her, snatching up another knife from the drawer. Heading for the door,* **Kate** *is caught in the open. She swings the knife to keep* **Jay** *away from her. He goes on the attack; the blades clash.* **Kate** *screams. The blades clash again. They circle each other.* **Jay** *lunges at* **Kate**. *She fends the knife away. They fight on. The phone rings.* **Jay** *is momentarily distracted.* **Kate** *tries to barge past him. He lunges at her again. She swings her knife up near his face. He flinches back. She knocks his knife from his hand.*

Kate   Get out.

She jerks the knife at him.

Out.

Jay *opens the door, exits.*

The phone starts to ring again. **Kate** *runs to answer it, panting for breath, looking fearfully towards the door.*

Kate   It's who . . .? Mum? What . . . what do you. . . .

Blackout.

Lights up.

Myrtle *lying in bed.* **Kate** *sits on the bed.*

Kate   Why?

Myrtle (*hoarsely*)   I don't know? I . . . I suppose I ought to have a reason but I don't. No reason at all. The pills were just there and that was that.

She starts coughing. She dribbles, wipes her mouth.

Myrtle   I'm sorry.

Kate *squeezes her hand.*

Kate   It's alright, Mum.

She looks around.

Where's Duncan? Have they let him know?

Myrtle   Duncan?

She laughs suddenly.

Duncan left me six months ago. Didn't I tell you?

Kate   No . . . No you didn't.

She hugs **Myrtle**

Kate   Oh, Mum.

Myrtle   I was thinking about your father. I could see his face in my head. If you love someone, Kate, if you love someone totally unthinkingly, you love every part of them, you could forgive them anything – if you ever love someone like that – don't leave him, promise me you won't leave him. Promise?

Kate   I've left Jay.

Myrtle   Do you love him?

Kate   No. I don't know.

Phoebe *comes into the kitchen area, puts the kettle on, sets out two cups.*

Enter **Jay**.

Jay   Is she here?

Phoebe   Kate?

Jay   I don't know what I'm going to do. Where do you think she's gone?

Phoebe *shrugs.*

Jay   I've got to find her and say sorry. She can't leave me without giving me a chance to explain. She can't.

Phoebe   I'm making some tea.

Jay   Yeah, thanks. Change your mind then?

Phoebe   About Dave? Yes. I'm staying.

Jay   Why?

Phoebe   Because I want to stay with him.

Jay *moves beside her, looks in her eyes.*

Jay (*gently*) Why?

Phoebe (*quietly*) Because he looks –

Jay Like me?

He hugs **Phoebe**.

Phoebe What about Kate?

Jay Do you mind about Kate?

Phoebe Yes. I don't know.

Jay I didn't mean what I said to you. I think you're beautiful.

Phoebe Oh no, no you don't . . . you don't know what you think or who or what you want. My love, my beautiful love.

Enter **Dave**.

Quietly he makes the tea. **Jay** *notices him, releases* **Phoebe**, *scared.*

Dave No, don't mind me. Carry on. I said carry on, or shall we move upstairs? Yes, take him up to your room. Shall we?

Dave *grabs* **Jay** *by his hair, drags him across the stage.* **Phoebe** *follows.*

Phoebe Dave! No, oh no . . .

Lights up on the bed.

Kate *is sitting there, talking on the phone. Her case and bags are on the bed.*

Kate (*on phone*) You're bound to feel a bit sick. Having your stomach pumped, yeah. I'll be in later, yeah. I'm moving my things over to your place right now. I don't know where he is. I don't care actually.

Jay *hammers on the door.* **Kate** *jumps, frightened. She stands up.*

Kate See you later, Mum. Bye.

She puts the phone down, looks warily at the door.

Jay (*outside, scared*) Kate! Kate, let me in!

Rattle of keys.

Kate Go away. Go away you bastard.

Jay I can't find the lock.

He rattles the door.

I can't see the door! Kate, help me! I can't see anything. I'm blind! I've gone fuckin' blind. Help me!

He sobs. **Kate** *goes to the door. She opens it a crack.* **Jay** *almost falls into the room. He stumbles around as if blind.*

Jay   I can't see you. I can't see anything. Where are you?

He blunders into the kitchen bench.

Help me, come here!

He stumbles into one of the chairs, falls down.

(*Quietly.*) Kate . . . Kate . . .

Kate *goes to him, wary, takes his hands.*

Kate   I'm here. Look at me.

Jay   I am. I can't see you.

Kate   Yes you can.

She moves her hand in front of his face.

Jay   I can't see you! Christ!

Kate   I don't believe you . . . I . . .

Jay *pulls away from* **Kate**, *stands, walks towards the bed, arms stretched out in front of him as if he is blind.*

Jay   Where's the bed? Where's the fuckin' bed? Help me! Help me, Kate. My God, help!

Kate *runs to him.*

Kate   Did Dave do this? Did he do something to your eyes?

She holds on to **Jay**.

Jay   It's my fault.

Kate   What happened?

Jay   It's happened before . . .

Kate   What has?

Jay   I've not been able to see. Sometimes I've not been able to move. I've been paralysed. It's not real, it's my head. If I can relax it goes away. The more scared I get, the worse it is. Hold me. Tight.

Kate *hugs him tight.*

Jay   Do you forgive me?

Kate   Forgive you? No . . .

Jay   Say it!

Jay *sobbing, clinging to* **Kate**.

Jay   Tell me you forgive me everything. Things I've done, when I've beat up on you, other things I've done . . . names I've called you . . . things that you don't even know about, that I couldn't tell you. Something my dad made me do . . .

Kate   What?

Jay *drops to his knees, clings to* **Kate**.

Jay   I'm never going to be able to see you again.

Kate   What happened? It might be where Dave's hit you. It might be the effects of that –

Jay   It's in my head. It's a kind of blackness I make around myself. I've got to fight it.

Kate   Fight it then. You fight everyone else. Fight yourself and drive it away.

Jay   I can't. I'm scared. It's never gone on this long . . .

Kate   When did it happen? Did everything just suddenly go black?

Jay   I was talking to Phoebe. Dad came in and saw us. He got angry. Jealous. He dragged me up the stairs. He . . . he made me and Phoebe . . . he made me . . . And I couldn't. I couldn't do it. He started screaming at us, saying he'd kill us both if I didn't fuck her, but I couldn't . . . and he started talking about Mum. He told Phoebe he'd throw her down the stairs and kill her – like he'd done with Mum. I threw up, I was sick over Phoebe, I couldn't stop myself, and then I must've passed out. Then I . . . I was awake again but I couldn't see anything. They'd both gone, or they were silent and I couldn't see them. I can't remember putting my clothes back on, or how I got back here. I just remember thinking over and over, 'I must get home, I must tell Kate I'm sorry'. Help me on to the bed.

Kate *helps* **Jay** *on to the bed.*

Jay   Lie me down.

Kate *helps* **Jay** *onto the bed. He lies on his back.*

Jay   And he beat me. When she had gone. Or maybe he had gone and she beat me.

Kate   I'll, I'll call an ambulance.

Jay *grabs her arm, grips it.*

Jay   No! Just say you forgive me. And kiss me.

Kate   I can't. I can't kiss you any more. You scare me . . .

Jay   Do it! My God do it!

Kate *leans over* **Jay** *and kisses him.*

Jay   And kiss my eyes. Kiss me on each eye.

She does so

It hasn't worked! I still can't see anything! Help!

She lies down beside him. He rolls over, knocking her case on the floor.

What was that!

Kate   My case. I was packing.

Jay   Everyone leaves me. Everyone hates me.

Jay *tries to get up.* **Kate** *stops him.*

Kate   I don't hate you. Lie still.

Jay   Don't leave me, if you leave –

Kate   Don't blackmail me, don't you!

Jay   I'm not. Go then. But you'll kill me. If you want to go, go, but I won't be here anymore to come back to if you change your mind. And you'll never find anyone who loves you as much as I do, or who you love more than you do me. Where are you going to run to, Kate? Can you get me out of your head? Can you leave me to die and be happy? Have you loved any of your previous boyfriends more than you love me? Can you honestly say you have?

Kate   How can you say you love me and treat me like a punchbag.

Jay   You'll never find anyone who loves you as much, you know that's the truth! Believe me, darling, you'll never find anyone who needs you more –

Kate   . . . Who treats me worse. I can't take it. And why should I? I'd be crazy to stay with you. I couldn't go home, I couldn't go back to college, so I let myself be taken in –

Jay   I can't live without you.

Kate   That's complete crap! You treat me like shit and then you try to make me feel guilty!

Jay   I don't want you to feel guilty. It's my fault.

Kate   Well, do something about it!

Jay   I've already given up drinking, but it doesn't seem to stop my rages. I just heat up as if I've got some kind of fire in my head. Then it's like it's not me. I go so far and then I lose control. I'm not making the decisions anymore. You know how it is when you're doing something stupid – usually you can rely on a little voice in your head saying 'this is crazy, stop this now'? Well, when I get angry I don't have that little voice there. There's nothing to check me, nothing to stop it. It's scary, scary for me too. I lose everyone I love. One day I'll lose everything, lose my grip on life.

Kate   Don't say that –

Jay   I'll keep away from Dad. I'll get some sort of help. I'll change, Kate. I promise.

Kate *gets up.*

Jay   Where are you? Where are you going? You're not going!

Kate *looks towards the door.*

Kate (*softly*)   I'm still here, love.

Pause.

But I don't know what we're going to do.

Jay *sits up.*

Jay   You won't leave me? I can see you. It's alright now. Thank you, Kate.

He goes to **Kate** *and kisses her.*

Jay   We're be alright, won't we, baby?

Kate *looks over his shoulder, her face exhausted, haunted.*

Blackout.

The Girlz

A play

Judy Upton

Original Production Details

Date: March 1998

Venue: The Room, Orange Tree Theatre

Director: George Ormond

Designer: Tim Meacock

Cast

Mr Kelsey	Kenneth Harvey
Tara	Heidi James
Stacey	Nicky Marks
Roxanne	Hilary Perkins
Shaun	Danny Spring

Act One

Scene One

Centre stage a low brick wall. To one side, chairs and desks. **Stacey** *and* **Tara** *come running in, laughing. They're carrying bulging sports bags. Both are aged sixteen.*

Tara   Wait for me! Wait up!

She clutches her stomach.

Ow! Ow!

Stacey *stops.*

Tara   I've burst my appendix or something.

Stacey   It's cramp that's all. You're so unfit.

Tara   I so am not.

They sit on the wall, bulging bags on their laps.

Stacey   That's smoking forty a day that is.

Tara   Well, how many do you smoke then?

Stacey   Not *that* many.

Tara   You do. Whenever I think of lighting up it's always cos you're already puffing away.

Stacey   I don't smoke as many as you. I've always got like three or four left at the end of the day.

Tara   So you smoke thirty-seven fags a day. What's the difference?

Stacey   Thirty-seven' not as many as forty.

Tara   Yeah, yeah.

They both look at each other then grab the zips of their sports bags.

Tara   Ready?

Stacey   Ready.

Tara   You first . . .

Stacey   After you.

Tara   Bet mine's worth more.

Stacey   Bollocks.

Tara *takes a bottle of Darling from her bag.*

Tara   Darlin' by Kylie . . . that's how much?

Stacey   £15.99?

Tara   You're joking. Twenty easy.

Stacey   In your dreams.

She takes a bottle of perfume from her bag.

Allure. £44.99

Tara (*impressed*)   Give it here.

Stacey   Shut up.

Tara   I want to smell it.

She takes the bottle.

S'alright that. By Chanel, innit? Loads better than that Victoria Beckham one you're wearing.

Stacey   I'm not wearing Intimate actually. This is Glow.

Tara   Don't make you look like J. Lo though does it? And that all you managed to jack today – one bottle of Chanel?

Stacey *delves in her bag, takes out more bottles, one by one.*

Stacey   Paris's Heiress, Jordan's Stunning . . .

Tara   What? I don't think she is . . .

Stacey *shows her the bottle.*

Tara   Oh yeah right.

Stacey *looks in her bag again.*

Stacey   And I got Britney's Fantasy and Lovely by SJP.

Tara   Shame the Kate Moss had sold out.

Stacey   Or all been jacked for other people's e-shops before we got there.

Tara   Joleigh was great. Wish my sister was like her.

Stacey   She's good for stuff like that . . . causing distractions in shops and things . . . but she can be such a pain. Always wanting me to babysit.

Tara   You should charge her.

Stacey   She's skint. And you can't really charge your sister, can you? I just hate babysitting.

Tara   Cos you don't have a man to drop by.

Stacey   No. I just hate where she lives. So depressing. There's never anything in the fridge and the only DVD she's got is *The Little Mermaid.*

Tara   Not good for a kiddie that.

Stacey   *The Little Mermaid*?

Tara   Living in a damp flat.

Stacey   She's written to the council, her MP and everything.

Tara   Is she still suing the council?

Stacey   Probably. And her old job for sacking her. Gotta be better odds than the lottery. So what did you get then?

Tara *takes a fancy pen from her bag.*

Tara   Real ink . . . £22.99.

Stacey   A pen? Shit, Tara . . . What do you want that for? You never use the one you've got.

Tara   Well, I know someone who does, don't I?

Stacey   Who? Me?

Tara   You? Shut up. You can jack your own. Anyway you use shite biros. It's for Jon.

Stacey   Oh Jon. You and Jon. Tara and Jon. But he doesn't let you call him that does he?

Tara   He will.

Stacey   Yeah right.

Tara   He will! The way he was looking at me in English.

Stacey   When he realised you hadn't done your homework. How many other lessons have you been to this week – apart from English?

Tara   Chemistry . . . had to get that money off Luanne.

Stacey   Cool.

She sniffs her own wrist.

The Glow's really nice when it's been on a little while.

Tara grabs and sniffs **Stacey**'s wrist.

Tara   Smells alright on you . . . but it might smell different on me.

Stacey   Cheaper.

Tara *shoves her.*

Tara   You cow. You know what, like, puzzles me? Would it smell the same on a guy?

Stacey   J. Lo's perfume on a bloke? Don't think he'd be our type.

Tara   What I'm saying is, does perfume smell the same to guys? I mean do they like the same scents we do?

Stacey   You want a perfume that says' Fuck me, Mr Jon Kelsey'. I read this survey . . . in *Marie Claire* or something . . . where they got all these blokes and women to smell a lot of scents. Course the blokes all liked the ones the women didn't. Typical, eh. But there was one all the guys thought was classy . . . Can't remember what it was . . .

Tara   Fat lot of good that is.

She sniffs the 'Allure'.

This one's quite classy, innit? Here.

Stacey *sniffs it.*

Stacey   If I knew what classy smelt like.

Tara   Like me. Even my farts.

An electronic bell rings. **Stacey** *gets off the wall.*

Stacey   Coming.

Tara (*without moving*)   Yeah. Just for English. I'm not stopping for double maths.

She gets up.

Stacey   Who is?

They go and sit down at a couple of tables, take out exercise books covered in scrawl and pictures from their bags.

Tara   You're gonna bunk off? Thought you'd forgotten how.

Stacey   Not where maths is concerned. Well, that was a pretty profitable lunch hour.

Tara   It will be, you mean, once we've shifted some of these bottles. Wish I'd had time to eat my sandwiches.

Stacey   Scoff 'em now.

Tara   Don't want Jon to see me with crumbs all over me lips. Ere give me that Allure.

Stacey   Fuck off. Think I might keep it.

Tara   Give it.

She tries to grab **Stacey***'s bag. It develops into a not-too-serious tug of war.*

Enter **Roxanne***, age sixteen, all swagger and sneer.*

Roxanne *goes up to where* **Tara** *is sitting.*

Roxanne   Out!

Tara   What?

Roxanne   Out of my seat now!

Stacey *gets up threateningly, stands close to* **Roxanne**.

Stacey   Got a problem, Roxy?

Enter the teacher **Jon Kelsey**.

Mr Kelsey   Everyone sit down. That includes you, Roxanne and Stacey.

Roxanne   Tara's in my seat.

Mr Kelsey   Well, sit somewhere else then.

For a moment **Roxanne** *stands her ground, then abruptly goes and sits down.*
Mr Kelsey *takes a pile of books from his bag, plonks them down on* **Stacey**'*s desk.*

Mr Kelsey   Stacey, I've remembered the books you wanted. These cover most of the syllabus . . .

Tara *looks amazed.* **Stacey** *looks at* **Tara**, *embarrassed.*

Tara   What? *Books?*

Roxanne *laughs.*

Roxanne   Becoming a swot are you, Stacey?

Mr Kelsey   It seems Stacey's finally woken up and realised that exams do matter.

Tara (*to* **Stacey**)   It's a wind-up, right? Is it, Stace?

Mr Kelsey *sniffs.*

Mr Kelsey   Funny smell around here.

Roxanne   It's Tara's knickers, sir.

Mr Kelsey   Alright, now let's have a bit of quiet . . .

Without warning loud dance music cuts in. Lights flash. **Mr Kelsey** *and* **Roxanne** *exit.*

Scene Two

Tara *and* **Stacey** *are dancing in a nightclub. It's Saturday night.*

Stacey   Which one?

Tara *nods in the direction of someone else in the club.*

Tara   Over there. See, *him.*

Stacey   Where? The blond guy?

Tara   Urgh.

Stacey   Not that blond guy, *that* one.

Tara   Not him!

Stacey   Which bloke do you mean then?

Tara   Can't point can I? He'll know.

Stacey   So? I mean I don't give a fuck.

Tara   You will when you see him.

Stacey   Yeah?

Tara   Well, you ought to. What is it with you?

Stacey   What?

Tara   Ain't there anyone is this town good enough for you?

Stacey *shrugs.*

Tara   When you do meet a guy you fancy you never do anything about it.

Stacey   So.

Tara   It's not . . . natural, Stacey.

Stacey   It's not natural that all the guys in this town are off the ming-ometer

Tara   Only most of 'em, Stace. Not all of them.

Stacey   Well, even with the good-looking ones . . . I can never really feel like . . . wow, I want some of that . . . I just can't make myself get interested . . . I mean I just don't think I've anything much in common with them.

Tara   You don't have to have anything 'in common' with them. That's not how it works. (*Beat.*) Oh no . . .

Stacey   What?

Tara   He's leaving. No, hang on, he's coming this way.

Enter **Shaun** *crossing behind them, drink in hand.* **Tara** *backs up as she dances, knocks against him.*

Tara   Watch it!

Stacey *smiles.*

Shaun   Only if it's worth watching. So, Tara . . . how's things?

Tara   Yeah, fine, y'know. Shaun, you know my best friend Stacey don't you?

Shaun *turns his attention to* **Stacey***.*

Shaun   Stacey . . . how ya doing. Know your sister . . . Joleigh, innit?

Stacey   Yeah.

Shaun   Used to know my brother. Got a little 'un now hasn't she?

Stacey (*Flatly*)   Yeah, stupid cow.

Tara *starts to move away.*

Shaun   I like kids, me. Last Christmas, right, I went round like every fuckin' shop trying to get a Transformer for Kyle . . . that's my nephew. Only eighteen months he is . . . So . . . Stacey, what do you like then?

Stacey   Like? What do I like doing you mean?

Shaun   Well, yeah. That's a start, innit.

Stacey   This . . . you know . . .

Shaun   Chatting up guys. Right.

Stacey   I meant dancing. I like dancing.

Shaun   Right . . . So Stacey, you still at school or –

Stacey   Yeah, still at school.

Shaun   It's a drag, innit?

Stacey *looks round for* **Tara**. *She's a little way off, in the gloom, watching.*

Stacey   So's a lot of things.

Shaun   Yeah? Yeah, you've got a point there.

Stacey   . . . but I've got plans to –

He can't really hear her over the music.

Shaun (*interrupting*)   What?

Stacey (*louder*)   Plans –

Shaun (*interrupting*)   Plans! Yeah, I like plans, yeah. I mean it's a good idea to make 'em isn't it? So what you planning then? Like, your future or . . . or something?

Stacey   Yeah. I want to go to college . . .

Shaun   Right. (*Beat.*) Do you like cars?

Stacey   Cars?

Shaun   Just got a new car, haven't I?

Enter **Roxanne**.

Shaun   Well, when I say a new car, I mean a car that's a bit newer than my last one . . . It's an Audi TT. Now I know some people think they suck . . . maybe it has a bit of an image problem, but that's not always what matters, if you know what I'm saying . . .

Roxanne *walks right up to* **Shaun**. *She is a confident mover.* **Shaun** *is immediately drawn to her.*

Shaun   Roxanne . . .

Roxanne   Hear you've got a new set of wheels, Shaun.

Shaun   Yeah . . .

Roxanne   So're you gonna take us for a spin sometime are you?

Shaun   Yeah, just say the word.

Roxanne *starts to manoeuvre* **Shaun** *away from* **Stacey**.

Roxanne   Quite fancy a drive tonight as it happens – nothing going on in here.

Shaun   Where d'you wanna go? Anywhere special?

Roxanne   Just feel like sitting back, music playing, the wind in my hair . . .

Shaun   Yeah, well I've got a sun roof.

Roxanne   Yeah? Sounds cool . . .

Shaun   Stacey! Stacey, I'll see you around, right?

Exit **Shaun** *and* **Roxanne**.

Tara *rejoins* **Stacey**.

Tara   Shit! I don't believe you!

Stacey   What?

Tara   Come here.

Tara *drags* **Stacey** *to one side.*

Tara   I don't believe this. You're a disgrace you are. And that slag Roxy. How could you let *her* do that? Everyone fancies him. But he likes *you*. For fuck's sake wake up, Stacey! You had your chance there. But you went and blew it big time. You let that slapper Roxanne walk all over you.

Stacey   It's no big deal.

Tara   The fuck it isn't! It'll be all around the school on Monday. She'll be flaunting it in our faces. 'Me and Shaun', 'he says you're a nothing', 'he thinks you're a dog', 'I just left you standing, Stace'.

Stacey   Look, if Shaun wants to go off with poxy Roxy or some other sad tart that's his problem . . .

Tara   No it's *your* problem, Stacey! It's your reputation on the line. Look, they haven't gone yet. Quick, grab your chance to smack her down!

Stacey   I told you to forget it. I don't care. He's a complete prat. The car probably isn't even his. It's probably nicked.

Tara   So? He's cool, Stace, he's fit. He's exactly the sort of guy you need to get yourself seen with.

Stacey   And what about you?

Tara   I can always go back to Ben. He'd drop that slapper he's shagging and come running, if I snapped my fingers. But I've got to chill on him for a bit . . . if I'm gonna stand a serious chance with Jon.

Stacey   You don't stand even a non-serious chance with 'Jon'. A fucking teacher, Tara.

Tara   And everyone knows he fancies me. Everyone's talking about it. (*Beat.*) And people are talking about you . . . cos you've never had a guy . . . Everyone thinks you're a bit . . . weird, Stacey.

Stacey   Yeah, yeah. And I've told you I've better things to listen to than that shit.

Tara   It's not shit, Stacey. People are trashing your image, girl. And this isn't just your problem, it's mine as well . . . people are taking the piss out of us both – just cos you can't get a bloke.

Stacey   Look, Tara . . .

Tara   You've got to deal with this thing okay? You've got to deal with it soon.

Stacey   Yeah, okay –

Tara (*interrupting*)   Right, who else in here do you fancy . . . well, nearly fancy at least?

The music fades away, lights stop flashing. Exit **Tara** *leaving a depressed* **Stacey** *alone.*

Scene Three

Mr Kelsey *is packing up his things at the end of the lesson.*

Mr Kelsey   Is everything alright, Tara? You're usually the first out of class when the bell goes.

Tara   Yeah, well I want to talk to you, sir. Er . . . in private . . . if that's okay, sir . . .

Mr Kelsey   I see. Is it about the homework you were supposed to hand in over a week ago? So what's today's excuse, Tara?

Tara   It's not about homework . . . well, it is and it isn't. I mean I'm getting worried . . . with my exams coming up and everything . . . and you see I was wondering, Jon . . . Er, can I call you Jon?

She sits on the edge of the desk.

Mr Kelsey   Mr Kelsey will do just fine.

Tara   I'm getting really worried about my exams, Mr Kelsey, and I was wondering if you could help me . . .

Mr Kelsey   If you want to borrow any books –

Tara (*interrupting*)   No . . .

Mr Kelsey   You could share the ones I've lent to Stacey.

Tara   I don't want more books to read. They take so long. I haven't had time to finish *Hamlet* yet.

Mr Kelsey   So you've made a start on it at last.

Tara   Well, nearly. (*Pause.*) Look, I am gonna read it . . . but it's so hard, all Shakespeare's language and that. It's alright in class when you tell us what it's about . . . but then when I have to read it at home . . . it's just really difficult to concentrate. (*Pause.*) Which is why I thought . . . I thought maybe you could give me some after-school lessons.

Mr Kelsey   What? First it's Stacey asking for a reading list and now you're asking for extra tuition.

Tara   Yeah, so what about it, sir? You know, just you and me, after school.

Mr Kelsey   If you came to my class more often, you'd have no need of extra tuition.

Tara   I have been coming to your class . . . whenever I can. When I've got time. I come to your class more than I do anyone else's. But it's not the same trying to learn stuff when Roxanne and her lot are pissing . . . er messing about. They're holding me back, sir. If I had you all to myself with no distractions I'd just learn so much faster . . .

Mr Kelsey   Well, maybe, but I'm still not sure there's really a lot of point, Tara, until you've actually read the play . . .

Tara   I'll read it tonight. (*Pause.*) I really will.

Mr Kelsey   All of it?

Tara   If I do, er manage to read the first few chapters . . .

Mr Kelsey   Scenes, Tara.

Tara   If I read the first few scenes tonight, we could discuss it after class tomorrow.

Mr Kelsey   I'm not free tomorrow night, Tara.

Tara   Well Monday night then. Nobody goes anywhere on a Monday do they, sir?

Mr Kelsey   If I did agree to give you half an hour extra tuition . . .

Tara   One to one.

Mr Kelsey   . . . on Monday night, how do I know you'll turn up?

Tara   Because I will. I'll give you my word. I'll swear on Stacey's life. I promise, sir. I really will.

Mr Kelsey   The trouble is, if I start giving one of my pupils extra teaching . . .

Tara   People will talk? So what? We don't have to listen to them do we, Jon . . . er, sir? Anyway, no one'll know. Nobody sticks around long after school do they? Well, unless they're in detention.

Mr Kelsey   What I meant is there're lots of other pupils who might benefit from some additional teaching . . .

Tara   What? In our class? Has anybody else asked you about it? But I'm willing to learn . . . anything you want to teach me.

Mr Kelsey   Oh?

Tara   Yeah. I only need a little encouragement, Jon.

Mr Kelsey *moves away a little.*

Mr Kelsey   Alright, Tara, if you really are serious about wanting to pass your exams . . .

Tara   I am. I've just like suddenly realised how near they're getting and everything . . .

Mr Kelsey   Well then, read *Hamlet* this week, and I'll see you after class on Monday evening.

Tara   Thanks, Jon. I knew I could rely on you.

Scene Four

Enter **Tara** *and* **Stacey**. *They sit on the wall.*

Tara   He was *so* gorgeous, Stacey . . . so handsome, so sexy. I ask him how old he is, right? Twenty-four!

Stacey   No way was he twenty-four. He had spots.

Tara   He did not! We got in his car right, and we're snogging . . .

Stacey   What kind of car was it?

Tara   I don't know! I wasn't too bothered about that was I? It was one with a comfy back seat, that I do know. We're in the back and he's burrowing under my clothes . . . got his hand down my Calvins . . . and I think he's gonna finger fuck me.

Stacey   Tara!

Tara   He had this ring and it was so cold when –

Stacey (*interrupting*)   I don't want to know all the gory details, alright?

Tara   And then he's like undoing his jeans and getting his dick out . . . and he's like this big . . . (*She indicates.*)

Stacey   Shit. No way. Really?

Tara   I swear to you, Stace. So then he grabs my hand and puts it on it.

Stacey   Shhh, don't tell the whole street.

Tara   And he's really hard, you know.

Enter **Roxanne***, unnoticed.*

Tara   So I jerk him off, right . . . and he comes all over my skirt.

Stacey   Urghh! Tara! That's so disgusting . . .

Roxanne   Getting an education, Stace?

Stacey   I wondered what the smell was.

Tara   Smell of dog.

Roxanne   Fuck off, Tara. I only dropped by to offer Stacey my sympathy . . .

Stacey   And why would I possibly want your sympathy, Roxanne?

Roxanne   Well, you never manage to get laid do you?

Tara   Course she does. She just doesn't need to brag about it like some do.

Roxanne   Like you do, you mean? Okay then name a guy you've shagged, Stace. Come on, I'm waiting.

Stacey   What's it to you? Why should anything I do be your business?

Roxanne   Well, I'm getting a bit concerned about you. I mean like on Saturday night, you went home empty handed again didn't you?

Tara   It was a crap night. Nothing there worth having, was there, Stace?

Roxanne   Not even Shaun? Oh, but then I forget. He left with me, cos he likes a girl with a little experience, if you know I'm saying, Stacey?

Tara   Stacey's got experience . . .

Roxanne   Yeah? (*Pause.*) Yeah, but it's not with guys though is it?

Tara   What?

Roxanne   I mean I think you ought to know the kind of things people are saying . . . about you two.

Stacey   Just fuck off, Roxanne.

Tara   We don't care what people are saying . . . so why don't you stop sticking your big nose in where it's not wanted.

Roxanne   That's right, you stick up for her, Tara. You know you're just so close you two, it's not really normal is it? No wonder people are talking. (*Pause.*) Saying you're lesbians and that . . .

Stacey (*laughs*)   Oh that's it, is it? That's just pathetic.

Roxanne   Yeah, well, you've never been seen with a man, Stace, you're so tough and you're always protecting Tara, aren't you?

Stacey   It's called friendship, Roxanne, something you wouldn't know anything about.

Roxanne   No, I get it – who needs blokes when you're girlfriends right?

Stacey   Why don't you just piss off you stupid slag . . . you're asking for a smack, aren't you?

Roxanne   She's so tough, isn't she, Tara? You must feel really safe and protected with a best friend like that. Hanging out with Stacey . . . it must be almost like having a bloke around all the time.

Stacey *gets off the wall.* **Roxanne** *backs up slightly.*

Roxanne   Oh I get it, three's a crowd sometimes, innit? . . . and you two clearly want to spend some time together alone . . .

She exits.

Stacey *sits back down, close to* **Tara**. **Tara** *moves away from her a little.*

Stacey   Little-Roxy-No-Friends, she's really sad.

Tara   Yeah . . . I mean you don't have to listen to anything she says . . .

Stacey   She's so full of shit.

Tara   . . . But, Stace, this whole thing with you and blokes . . . I mean you must feel a little bit embarrassed about it sometimes . . .

Stacey   What?

Tara   And sometimes . . . sometimes I feel embarrassed for you.

When people are whispering and that.

Stacey   People are talking about me? So what? I've not done anything for them to talk about.

Tara   Yeah, exactly . . .

Stacey   Not like my sister. Do you remember when everyone used to be gossiping about Joleigh? Calling her a slag and that . . .

Tara   This is different, Stacey.

Stacey   Yeah, people talked about Joleigh cos she was putting out like . . .

Tara   Putting out big time.

Stacey   And now what? They're talking about me cos I don't have a boyfriend? That's so pathetic. I don't see why what I do is anybody else's business.

Tara   Yeah, you're right it isn't. But things like that can still damage your reputation.

Stacey   I don't care about my reputation.

Tara   You do. You're always going on about how you're the hardest girl in our year.

Stacey   Only cos it's true.

Tara   But sometimes being the toughest isn't enough. Other things matter too.

Stacey   Like getting my exams, I know. That's why I asked Mr Kelsey for those books . . .

Tara   I'm not talking about fucking exams. I'm saying that if people think you're a dyke . . . (*Pause.*) And cos we're always together and that . . . I mean if they start thinking you're gay, then they're start thinking I am too.

Stacey *laughs.*

Tara   It's not funny. It's not at all funny if every time we go out people are talking behind our backs . . .

Stacey   Okay, so what do you want me to do? Walk around with a big placard saying 'I'm not gay'?

Tara   Don't be stupid. You just need to find yourself a boyfriend.

Stacey   'Find yourself a boyfriend' – that's all I hear from you.

Tara   What is the problem? Don't you like guys? Losing your cherry's no big deal. Honestly.

Stacey   Yeah, I know. I've told you before . . . When I meet the right guy –

Tara (*interrupting*)   You've met loads of 'right guys'.

Stacey   Like who?

Tara   Joel, and Ryan, and Luke. And what about Shaun the other night?

Stacey   Who? Look they're okay, alright. But I don't just want to meet a guy and do it . . . then they start talking about you, don't they? Like people talked about Joleigh.

Tara   That's completely different. Joleigh used to be, like, with a different guy, every night. I mean people say about her going with, like, two at once . . .

Stacey   That's a lie. She told me she never did that. But I don't want people saying shit like that about me.

Tara   They won't, Stacey. If you just like go with one guy. Somebody cool, somebody everyone wants . . . you'll get rid of your fucking virginity and stop all the gossip about us . . . you being gay . . .

Stacey   Yeah, well, I shouldn't have to do that, just cos of what people think. You should help me, Tara. You're supposed to be my friend, and stick up for me. You should start spreading the truth about me, instead of listening to lies.

Tara   And what is the truth? What is the truth, Stacey?

Stacey   That I'll have sex when I'm ready to.

Tara   And it'll be soon, won't it? Okay, great. As soon as you meet some gorgeous guy . . .

Stacey   But don't start pressurising me, alright?

Tara   Just don't leave it too long then.

Stacey   There's no hurry, Tara. Especially if I might be going to sixth-form college next year . . .

Tara   You can't wait that long . . . I mean you don't want to still be inexperienced when you get among all those college boys.

Stacey   Look, you're starting to piss me off, Tara. I don't want to hear any more about it. It's all sex, sex, sex with you, as if nothing else matters.

Tara   You're be hearing plenty more about it at school, even if you don't hear it from me.

Stacey *gets up.*

Stacey   Either you talk about something else, or I'm out of here.

Tara   Okay, let's go and get some chocolate or something.

Stacey   Yeah.

Tara *gets up.*

Tara   We can go to the garage shop. You know, the garage where Shaun works? When you were talking to him the other night there was definitely something between you two . . . some chemistry.

Stacey   That's it!

Tara   What?

Stacey   I'm going home.

Tara   Stacey . . .

Stacey   See you tomorrow, Tara.

She exits.

Tara   Stacey! Oy, don't walk off when I'm talking to you, girl! Stacey!

She exits.

Scene Five

Mr Kelsey *is talking to* **Tara**. *She is sitting on his desk and leaning towards him.*

Mr Kelsey   Who does Hamlet suspect of killing his father?

Tara   The soldiers.

Mr Kelsey   Soldiers?

Tara   Or the ghost. Yeah the ghost.

Mr Kelsey   I thought you were going to read it over the weekend . . .

Tara   I watched the DVD. Just missed the beginning didn't I? But I saw the rest. Mel Gibson kills his mum . . . Maybe he thinks she did it . . . and he kills this other young bloke in a sword fight . . .

Mr Kelsey   Tara . . .

Tara   Look, I stayed in and watched the whole DVD, and there was hours of it, not including all the extras . . . that shows you I want to learn doesn't it?

Mr Kelsey   It's not the same as reading the play . . . or completing your essay.

Tara   The bit I've done is alright though isn't it?

Mr Kelsey   Since you've only just got round to giving it to me I haven't had a chance to read it properly yet.

Tara   You're not a very fast reader are you, Jon?

Mr Kelsey   Not when you keep distracting me all the time.

Tara   So I distract you, do I, Jon? But you kind of like being distracted by me, don't you?

Mr Kelsey *moves away a little. He looks at his watch*

Mr Kelsey   Tara, er, listen, I can't really spend anymore time talking about this now . . .

Tara   Talking about what, Jon?

Mr Kelsey   *Hamlet*. I don't think there's much point in us talking about your essay until you've completed it.

He offers her the essay back.

Tara   If we talk about it now, I might feel . . . inspired to finish it. You're so good at explaining it all . . . like Hamlet's feelings and stuff . . .

Mr Kelsey   Well, maybe we can talk about it some more next Monday, but I'm having to cut tonight's session short, as I need to be home by half four.

Tara   Excuse me – I thought we had a class. A thirty-minute class.

She looks at her watch.

And you've only given me seven minutes' worth, Jon.

Mr Kelsey   I'm sorry, Tara.

Tara   Charming, innit. I go and tell Stace I can't see her 'til later, and then you go and stand me up.

Mr Kelsey   Look, alright, I'll try and find some other time to discuss your work . . .

Tara   Oh Jon . . .

Mr Kelsey *packs up his things.*

Mr Kelsey   . . . Maybe if you come in ten minutes early on Monday morning. I'm sorry I can't stop longer, but my wife's not well and –

Tara   Your wife! (*Beat.*) You never told me you were married. I've never heard anyone say anything about you having a wife. You don't wear a wedding ring, do you?

Mr Kelsey   It's not compulsory.

Tara   And I thought . . . by the way that you behave with us . . . with me . . .

Mr Kelsey   How do I behave with you, Tara?

Tara   Like you're free. Available. The way you look at me in class . . .

Mr Kelsey   What about the way I look at you?

Tara   You want me, Jon.

Mr Kelsey *laughs.*

Mr Kelsey   In your dreams maybe, Tara.

He picks up his case.

Tara   And in your dreams, Jon. Yeah alright, Mr Married Man, go running home to your cocoa and biscuits . . . and dream about what you're missing.

Scene Six

Music playing. **Tara** *and* **Stacey** *are in the toilets of the nightclub.* **Tara** *is smoking a joint, keeping a wary eye on the exit.* **Stacey** *is making up her face.* **Shaun** *is at the bar, drinking.*

Stacey   Is it just the light in here or does this lippy look disgusting?

Tara   It's fine, Stace.

Stacey   This was supposed to be non-clog mascara. I'm still getting little bits in my eyes. I'm gonna take it back.

Tara   Did you keep the receipt?

Stacey   When I nicked it?

Tara   How much longer you gonna be? If you're not careful someone else'll distract him again.

Stacey   There's plenty more guys around. Why's it have to be him?

Tara   Because he's cool. You ask anyone at school who they'd most like to go with. This'll stop all the gossip once and for all. After tonight it won't matter what people write on the wall.

Stacey   Who do you think it was, Tara?

Tara   I told you I've been trying to find out . . . but nobody's saying nothing.

Stacey   Yeah, they're scared of what I'm gonna do to them. I couldn't believe it, when I came out of physics and started walking across the field. And there it was in foot-high letters.

Tara   Maybe it was Roxanne.

Stacey   Roxanne can spell. Lesbian with a 'z' in it. It's gotta be one of the girls. I can't imagine any of the guys doing it. But it was in spray paint. And I don't know any girls who are into the tagging thing.

Tara   The point is it doesn't matter who wrote that you're a lesbian. What matters is proving them wrong. After tonight they'll be the laughing stock, Stace, not you. Yesterday at school was fucking awful, I know. I felt so embarrassed for you. It was humiliating for me too . . .

Stacey   Yeah, alright, Tara. But that's over now. By Monday they'll have found something new to talk about.

Tara   You and Shaun, that's what they'll be talking about. But with envy and respect. You'll never hear or see the word lesbian connected with your name again. Or virgin, either.

She passes **Stacey** *the joint.*

Tara   Look, I know you're nervous, right . . . everyone is the first time. I was shitting bricks.

Stacey   I just don't . . . I mean he means nothing to me.

Tara   Look, I'll let you into a secret . . . Some of them haven't meant anything much to me. I know at the time I always go on about how great it is. But that's cos you have to. You have to talk it up. Otherwise people start talking, saying you're a shit shagger or you're frigid and stuff.

Stacey   You lied to me. You're my best friend and you lied about that? When you were like with Jordan and Ben and Lee . . . you told me how great sex was . . .

Tara   Sometimes it was. But sometimes it was shite. Like everything else, I suppose. The thing is, if the guy's really cool, he's got a reputation for being a lover man, you don't let on if it wasn't so good. Cos he'll have to trash your reputation . . . tell everyone you were crap, to save his own credibility, see?

Stacey   I don't care if he's any good or not. I don't expect I'll know the difference . . .

Tara   You will.

Stacey   I just don't want to do this . . . I don't know why I don't . . . just that I don't. (*Beat*.) I mean I'm not bothered about it hurting and that . . .

Tara   Against when we had our tummies pierced, it's nothing.

Stacey   It's not that . . . it's just that . . . I know I'm not gonna have an orgasm or anything. I just know it. Cos I'm not in love . . .

Tara   You don't have to be 'in love', Stacey!

Stacey   You know what I'm saying. I don't fancy Shaun. I just feel . . . kinda funny about it.

Tara   Well, for fuck's sake, whatever you do, don't laugh.

Stacey   I don't mean that kind of funny . . . (*Beat*.) Have you ever been . . . like properly in love?

Tara   Yeah. Remember Finley . . . I was really in love with him . . . didn't I used to go on and on about him?

Stacey   He was a prat.

Tara   I couldn't see that at the time. That's why sometimes it's better if you're not in love. That way you don't get made a fool of.

Stacey   He better not try to make a fool of me.

Tara   He won't dare.

Stacey   I'll smack him down. I'll smash him up. (*Beat*.) And . . . what if nothing happens . . . I mean what I don't want to . . .

Tara   I thought you'd made your mind up.

Stacey   Yeah . . . yeah, alright.

Tara   Come on.

Stacey *takes a last drag on the joint, puts it out, before following* **Tara** *out onto the dancefloor. The music gets louder. Lights flash.*

Tara   Where is he? Shit.

Stacey (*hopeful*)   Maybe he's gone.

Tara   The bastard. He better not 'ave. No, look over there.

Shaun *is not looking their way.*

Tara   Dance.

Stacey   What?

Tara   Don't just fucking stand there!

Stacey *and* **Tara** *dance.* **Shaun** *sees them.*

Tara   Here he comes.

Shaun *comes over.*

Shaun   Alright, girls.

Tara   Hi, Shaun. Stace, it's Shaun!

Stacey   Hi.

Shaun   It's crap here tonight, innit?

Stacey   What? . . . Yeah, not a good vibe.

Tara   I've had about enough. We're about to shoot off, aren't we, Stacey?

Stacey   Er, yeah.

Shaun   Where you going? Somewhere good? A party?

Tara   No, I'm not feeling that well actually . . .

Shaun   I'm sorry to hear that, Tara.

Tara   Yeah, think I might call it a day, have an early night y'know.

Stacey   What? You're going?

Tara   Yeah, I'll go get a taxi.

Shaun   I could drive you home.

Tara   No, it's alright Shaun. I'll be okay. Maybe you can keep Stacey company for me. I mean otherwise I'll feel a bit guilty about going home. I mean there's no one else here we know tonight.

Shaun   Yeah, we'll keep each other company, won't we, Stace?

Tara   Great. Well I'll give you a call tomorrow, Stace. See you, Shaun.

Shaun   Yeah, later.

Exit **Tara**.

Shaun   She's a bit of a lightweight, isn't she? So, Stacey, what do you want to do? We could have another drink . . . or go on somewhere else. Up to you.

Stacey   I . . . I don't know . . . maybe we should go somewhere else . . . . another club I mean.

Shaun   Yeah. Yeah, that's just what I was thinking we should do. Are you a mind-reader, eh?

Stacey   Eh?

Shaun   Better be careful I had if you can like read thoughts and that . . . So . . . have you ever been to Oriana's?

Stacey   Yeah, it's cool.

Shaun   Let's go there then. See if it's a bit more lively than this.

Shaun *and* **Stacey** *leave the dance floor. Outside the music of the club is muffled, though the bass thump is still loud.*

Shaun   Nice to be out in the fresh air, eh Stace? So how's Joleigh? You did say she's your sister right?

Stacey   Yeah.

Shaun   Top bird, she is.

Stacey   So we're going to Oriana's?

Shaun   In my car, yeah.

Stacey   But you've been drinking.

Shaun   I've only had the one. Well, one or two. Yeah, the car's starting to look really good now – got the alloy wheels, next up's the paint job. I'm thinking metallic gold, what you you think?

Stacey   Oriana's isn't far. We could walk . . .

Shaun   Yeah, alright then, let's walk.

As **Stacey** *goes to start walking,* **Shaun** *touches her arm, turning her to face him. He touches her face.*

Shaun   You're very pretty.

Stacey   Oh, er thanks. (*Beat.*) Shall we go then?

Shaun   Yeah. (*Beat.*) I really like you. Since I saw you dancing last week, I've kept thinking about you and that.

Stacey   Oh. I've . . . been thinking about you too.

Shaun *kisses* **Stacey***, begins caressing her, hands burrowing under her clothes.*

Stacey   Don't!

She pulls away.

Shaun   Ow. Watch your nails. What's the matter?

Stacey   I want to go home.

Shaun   Oh great. (*Beat.*) Okay . . . well do you want me to give you a lift or –

Stacey (*interrupting*)   No.

Shaun   Look, I'm sorry . . . for whatever it is I've done, okay?

Stacey *walks away. She stops.* **Shaun** *rubs his hand where she scratched him.*

Shaun (*softly*)   Jesus.

He takes out his fags. **Stacey** *looks back at* **Shaun***. He doesn't look up. For a moment she is undecided, then walks back to him. Together they move into the darkness. The music from the club fades away.*

Act Two

Scene One

Tara *is sitting on* **Mr Kelsey***'s desk, kicking her legs.*

Tara   You're late, Jon.

Mr Kelsey   Have you finished your essay, Tara?

Tara   I thought I'd talk to you about it first.

Mr Kelsey   We've already talked about it, Tara.

Tara   When?

Mr Kelsey   Last Monday.

Tara   Last Monday you had to go rushing off to your wife. How is she?

Mr Kelsey   She's fine, Tara.

Tara   So we can have a longer session tonight, Jon.

Mr Kelsey   Tara, I've been thinking about our extra-tuition sessions –

Tara (*interrupting*)   So have I.

Mr Kelsey   And I don't really think I can continue them . . .

Tara   What?

Mr Kelsey   You're not making an effort to put in the work . . .

Tara   I am. I'm gonna go home tonight and write that essay . . .

Mr Kelsey   I've heard it before, Tara. And now I've got Roxanne and some of the others asking for extra lessons too . . .

Tara   That bitch Roxanne. And how did they find out? I told you it had to be our secret.

Mr Kelsey   I can't afford to give extratuition to everyone who needs it, and it seems unfair to single out one pupil for special attention, especially when that pupil still doesn't seem very interested in studying.

Tara   You can't stop our sessions. I need them.

Mr Kelsey   I'm sorry, Tara.

He moves to leave. **Tara** *blocks his way.*

Tara   You will be.

Mr Kelsey   What's that supposed to mean?

Tara   When I tell the headmaster all about the 'special attention' you've been giving me. When I tell him what's really been going on in our extra-tuition sessions.

Enter **Shaun***, sitting on the wall, drinking a beer.*

Mr Kelsey   And what has been going on?

Tara *tries to touch him. He moves away.*

Tara   I'll tell him you've been touching me . . . and making . . . improper suggestions . . .

Mr Kelsey   Okay, fine. And let's see who he believes. A teacher, or a silly, immature schoolgirl. Good evening, Tara.

He exits.

Tara   Fuck you.

She snatches up her school bag, moves to exit, sees **Shaun**.

Shaun   Hi, Tara. How's school?

Tara   Shit as usual. Who you waiting for?

Shaun   Stacey. Not missed her have I?

Tara   No. She wasn't in school today. In fact I've not seen her all week. Maybe she's sick or something.

Shaun   Have you phoned her?

Tara   Yeah. Her mum said she wasn't in.

Shaun   So she can't be . . . well, you know, *ill* ill, can she?

Tara   What?

Shaun   If she's going out, it can't be anything serious, that's what I'm saying. (*Beat.*) You two haven't fallen out have you?

Tara   No . . . no, I'll give her another ring later. (*Beat.*) Shaun . . . Saturday night . . . I mean you and Stacey, did you . . . you know . . .

Shaun   Yeah. We did yeah.

Tara   And was it good?

Shaun   Yeah.

Tara   Stacey was a good lay?

Shaun   She was. Bit nervous . . . it being her first time like . . . and she was a bit upset, bit tearful like . . .

Tara   You hurt her?

Shaun   No, no . . . it wasn't . . . I mean I think it was you she was upset with. I gave her a lift home, afterwards like . . . and she just started saying how you'd put her up to it. That you made her have sex with me.

Tara   That's shit. I wasn't there holding her down was I? She can't really think that.

Shaun   Yeah, maybe it was just cos she'd had a few drinks. Some birds get a bit weepy with a few beers inside them, don't they?

Tara   It's not just that . . . I mean sometimes, when I'm with a guy who's . . . who's really amazing, then it makes me cry . . .

Shaun   Yeah?

Tara   As I kind of get overcome with happiness . . .

Shaun   Stacey didn't really look that happy . . .

Tara   You can't look happy when you're crying, Shaun, but that doesn't mean she wasn't. You're a real lover man if you can make a girl cry . . .

Shaun   Yeah? Well, look, if you want my number . . . (*Beat.*) or if you're gonna be phoning Stacey again . . . or you see her, er just tell her . . . she's alright . . . er . . .

Tara   Tell her you really want to see her again?

Shaun   Yeah, and tell her I've started respraying my car . . . metallic gold . . .

He takes out the paint spray, fiddles with it.

. . . see, and it's gonna look real cool.

Tara   Right . . .

Shaun   . . . So if she fancies coming out for a drive this weekend . . .

Tara   If I talk to her, I'll tell her. (*Beat.*) Shaun, I couldn't borrow that could I?

Shaun   Me paint? What, you gonna use it on your nails or something?

Tara   I'll let you have it back tomorrow okay?

Shaun   Yeah, I'll be down the garage, just drop by anytime.

He exits.

Tara *shakes up the spray can. She exits running out.*

Scene Two

Roxanne *is sitting on the wall.*

Enter **Tara**.

Seeing **Roxanne***, * **Tara** *tries to pass by, ignoring her.* **Roxanne** *gets up and blocks her way.*

Roxanne   No extra tuition tonight? What's up with you and 'Jon' Kelsey? In English, he was acting like you've a nasty smell. (*Pause.*) Going round Stacey's, are you?

Tara   What do you want, Roxanne?

Roxanne   Just wondered how she was . . . seeing as she ain't in school . . .

Tara   Yeah . . . she's not well. Got flu.

Roxanne   Oh. Oh right. But you haven't caught it . . . in spite of you two being so close . . .

Tara   Fuck off . . .

Roxanne   Make me. (*Pause, more friendly.*) So . . . did you go anywhere out last Saturday night? You and Stacey.

Tara   Yeah, course. I mean don't we always? What about you?

Roxanne   Yeah. (*Pause.*) Yeah, I was supposed to be meeting someone.

Tara   Supposed . . .

Roxanne   You went to The Escape, didn't you?

Tara   We might've . . . yeah for a while.

Roxanne   Then you went home. Left Stacey there.

Tara   Oh that's right. I felt ill.

Roxanne   Maybe it was flu, yeah?

Tara   Probably was yeah.

Roxanne   And Stacey stayed there without you . . . (*Pause.*) Shaun was with you and Stacey at The Escape wasn't he?

Tara *shrugs.*

Roxanne   Luanne and Gemma say they saw him with you two.

I was on my way there. Shaun said he'd be waiting.

Then I hear Stacey was dancing with him. My boyfriend, Shaun.

Tara   Stacey danced with lots of blokes. We both did.

Roxanne   I know what you did, Tara.

Tara   Me? I went home . . . I don't know what . . .

Roxanne   You set them up together. Luanne saw you.

Tara   Set them up? What are you on about? I don't know anything about Stacey and Shaun. I wasn't there.

Roxanne   They left together.

Tara   Did they? I don't know. I'm not responsible for what Stacey or Shaun do, am I? And I've not spoken to Stace since –

Roxanne (*interrupting*)   What are you, Tara, some kind of pimp? Making your friend sleep with my man. You wonder why nobody was speaking to you today? It's surprising how fast the news gets around, isn't it? Nobody's gonna want you as a friend anymore. Nobody's gonna wanna be seen talking to you. And you can tell Stacey, when she gets over her flu, that everyone knows she's a slag. A slag who sleeps with other people's boyfriends. (*Pause.*)

You better hope Stacey gets over her flu in a hurry. Cos without your very best friend to look after you, your life ain't gonna be worth living.

She exits.

Scene Three

Enter **Stacey** *with a pile of books.*

Enter **Tara** *behind her.*

Tara   Stacey! Hi, how are you, girl?

Tara *hugs* **Stacey**. **Stacey** *doesn't respond.* **Tara** *releases her.*

Tara   I've been so worried about you. Why haven't you been in school? It's been weeks. And things have been really bad. Roxanne's been giving me such a hard time. She's been kicking the shit out of me. You should see my bruises. You're supposed to be my friend, Stace. Where've you been?

Stacey (*flatly*)   At home. Studying.

Tara   I phoned your house loads of times. Why didn't you ring back?

Stacey *shrugs.*

Tara   So what are you doing coming into school, but not to class?

Stacey   Collecting more books.

Tara   Oh right. More books. So is that it? Is it this reading thing?

Stacey   What 'reading thing'?

Tara   Since Mr Kelsey gave you those books, you've not left your house. It's like you've become addicted to books or something.

Stacey   It's not the bloody books, Tara. (*Beat.*) I'm pregnant.

Tara   What? (*Choking back a laugh.*) You what? Oh shit. You can't be. Whose is it?

Stacey   Shaun's.

Tara   You're still seeing him? He never said.

Stacey   No, I'm not still seeing him, Tara. I haven't seen him since you persuaded me to fuck him.

Tara   Now wait a minute . . .

Stacey   Okay, I was stupid to listen to you . . . but you pushed and pushed me. You wouldn't let it go, Tara.

Tara   Are you really pregnant? I mean have you done a test and everything? I mean you just had sex the once, yeah? And he must've used a johnny.

Stacey   Just shut up, Tara.

Tara   . . . And I don't know anyone who got pregnant on their first time . . .

Stacey   Just shut your stupid bimbo mouth.

Tara   *You* shut up, you slag. (*Beat.*) Oh shit. Sorry. Stacey, I'm sorry.

Stacey   Look, just leave me alone, Tara.

Tara   Wait . . . I mean you're my friend, right?

Stacey   Not anymore. I don't want to see you. My life's completely fucked now, isn't it?

Tara   No, it's not . . .

Stacey   I can't go to college with a baby.

Tara   Well, have an abortion then.

Stacey   Will you stop telling me what to do, Tara! Listening to you is what's got me into this shit.

Tara   I didn't force you to sleep with him. You've got your own mind, Stacey.

Stacey   Look, just get out of my way, Tara. I've nothing to say to you. I don't want to see you anymore okay.

She walks away.

Tara   Stacey . . .

Exit **Stacey**.

Tara (*to herself*)   Shit.

Scene Four

Garage sounds, engines being tested. **Tara** *waits.* **Shaun** *comes out, wiping his hands on an oily rag.*

Shaun   Alright, Tara? So how's things?

Tara   Fine, yeah.

Shaun   I've been thinking about you actually . . . been thinking of giving you a ring, yeah?

Tara   Oh? What about?

Shaun   Well, you're a girl who . . . knows how to have a good time, aren't you eh? And I've got my new car and –

Tara (*interrupting*)   Look, Shaun, well, I'm really sorry to have dragged you out of work like this . . .

Shaun   No problem. Do you want to see how my car's coming along? Maybe we could go for a little drive or something, you and me . . .

Tara   Look, not right now, Shaun. Listen I –

Shaun   Didn't bring my gold paint back did you? There's a few bits still in need of a touch-up.

Tara   Paint? Oops, no sorry . . .

Shaun   I saw what you wrote on the gym wall about that English teacher. 'Mr Kelsey Fucks Goats'. I mean he doesn't does he?

Tara   Shaun, Stacey's pregnant.

Pause.

Shaun   Oh, is she? Well, that's nice for her. How is she? I've not seen her around at all . . .

Tara   It's your baby.

Shaun   My? . . . no, no way.

Tara   It is, Shaun. She was a virgin . . .

Shaun   Yeah, I know that . . . but it was . . . what, nearly a month ago?

Tara   She's not shagged anyone else . . .

Shaun   Are you sure? I mean I know what you girls are like once you get a taste for it.

Tara   Oh yeah right. She's hardly left the house since that night. She's become like a recluse or something. It's your baby, Shaun. For definite.

Shaun   . . . Right . . . .

Tara   It shows you can do the business doesn't it? I mean it proves the rumours I've been hearing are bollocks.

Shaun   What rumours?

Tara   Oh you know, that you fire blanks . . .

Shaun   Who's been saying that?

Tara   I only heard it from a friend of a friend, but this'll prove your manhood once and for all. You are Mr Virility, Shaun.

Shaun   Yeah, yeah, well, I ain't gonna start bragging y'know . . . though if you want to spread the news around a bit, can't see as it can do any harm. (*Beat.*) So I'm gonna be a dad, eh? Daddy Shaun. (*Shouts, off.*) Oy, lads, I'm gonna be a dad! (*To* **Tara**.) Yeah, it's all starting to make sense now . . .

Tara   What's making sense, Shaun?

Shaun   I phoned Stacey's house a couple of times. You know just to say hi, see if she fancied going out for a drive or something. And it was her dad that answered. I thought he sounded a bit strange like. – Hey, do her folks know it was me?

Tara   I don't know.

Shaun   Only I heard when Joleigh got up the club, Stacey's old man put the guy in hospital.

Tara   Yeah, you'd better be careful, hadn't you?

Shaun   No, I could have him. He's old – fifty if he's a day. I'll lay him out flat if he starts giving me any grief. Look, she doesn't want me to marry her or something, does she? Cos no offence but I hardly know the girl.

Tara   No, I don't think she wants that . . . but you could offer her some money . . . since you've got a job and that . . .

Shaun   I can slip her the odd fiver yeah.

Tara   Oh very generous.

Shaun   Alright a tenner maybe. And Joleigh and my sister can probably give her their old baby clothes and stuff.

Tara   I don't know if she's decided what she's gonna do yet . . . whether she's gonna keep the baby . . .

Shaun   Well, if she ain't, I can't look after it, can I? Can't have a baby crawling around here while I'm working . . .

Tara   I meant she might have an abortion.

Shaun   What, get rid of my kid? I'm not paying for that. That's my own flesh and blood.

Tara   The thing I don't get is why didn't you use a johnny?

Shaun   I thought she was on the pill.

Tara   She was a virgin, Shaun.

Shaun   I'd left them in the car. I mean I always do it in the car. The Love Machine I call it. But she wouldn't let me go. It's now or never she said. Like the song innit? It's now or never.

Tara   Shaun, I'm just going over to Stacey's now . . .

Shaun   Can you give her my . . . my regards like?

Tara   I was wondering whether you'd like to come with me . . .

Shaun   Why?

Tara   To tell her you're going to be supportive.

Shaun   I don't know . . . I mean her old man . . .

Tara   He'll be at work if we go now.

Shaun   Oh alright, look, just let me go and get washed up. We can drive over there, eh? . . . the car could do with a run.

Scene Five

Stacey *is sitting alone indoors, reading.*

Tara *and* **Shaun** *are at the door.* **Tara** *rings the doorbell.*

Tara (*off*)   Stacey!

Stacey (*to herself*)   Shit.

Tara (*off*)   Stacey, we need to talk.

Shaun (*shouting*)   We're having a baby!

Stacey   Fucking hell.

She goes out to them.

Yeah, just let all the bloody neighbours know. And what do you want, coming round here?

Shaun   Just thought I'd come and see how you were like. (*To* **Tara**.) Shit, should've bought her some flowers or something.

Tara   We thought we'd come and see if there was anything we could do for you.

Stacey   We?

Tara   Yeah, Shaun's really made up about being a dad, aren't you?

Shaun   I was a bit surprised when Tara told me like, but the idea's kind of growing on me.

Tara   Can we come in?

Stacey   Yeah, yeah, okay. (*To* **Tara**.) Did *you* tell him?

Tara   He's the father, Stace . . .

Stacey   I know that don't I?

Tara   Look, I meant he was going to find out, one way or the other.

Shaun *looks around the room.*

Shaun   Had any thoughts about names, Stace?

Stacey (*to* **Tara**)   Why did you bring him here?

Tara   I told you, he wants to help you out. Moneywise. Tell him what you want. Get some cash out of him.

Stacey   I don't want his money, Tara. I don't want him in my house. Just seeing him again reminds me . . . make him go. Tell him.

Tara   Shaun, I think maybe Stacey would like to be alone for a while.

Shaun *goes up to* **Stacey**. *He takes a tenner from his pocket, offers it to her.*

Stacey   I don't want it.

Shaun   Oh . . . oh alright. But if you change your mind and you could do with a bit of cash . . . for nappies or anything, just call old Shaun. And if you need a hand . . . you know, need someone to take him to the park on a Saturday . . .

Stacey   There's more to fatherhood than that, Shaun.

Shaun   Yeah, yeah I know. But it's a start innit? I ain't never had a kid before neither.

Stacey   It's not the same for you.

Tara   He's doing his best, Stace.

Stacey   A kid's a big responsibility, Shaun.

Shaun   Well, obviously. But you don't, like . . . want me around all the time and that, do you?

Stacey   No . . .

Shaun   I mean we're not going to be, like, a couple or anything.

Stacey   I just want you to be aware of my situation . . .

Shaun   Yeah, okay . . . and well I'm sorry it happened . . . should've been a bit more careful.

Stacey   It's not your fault, Shaun.

She looks accusingly at **Tara**.

Stacey (*to* **Shaun**) I'm sorry you've been dragged into this. (*Pause.*) And it's nice of you to offer to help . . . but your whole attitude . . . I mean it's pathetic really . . .

Shaun   Oh thanks. Thanks a lot.

Pause.

Stacey   Look, would you mind just going now . . .

Shaun   Oh. Okay.

Pause.

Right, I'll see you around then, Stacey, Tara.

He exits.

Stacey   Shit, Tara! What are you? Crazy? Why'd you have to bring him here. He's the very last person I want to see right now.

Tara   Yeah? I thought that was me. (*Beat.*) But don't you see, you can get some money off him? That's something isn't it? If you want to have a quick abortion, or need to buy some baby things . . .

Stacey   Tara, I don't want anything from Shaun, okay.

Pause.

There's nothing I want.

Pause

Look . . . Can you just go, please.

Tara   I was only trying to help. Okay, you don't want to see Shaun. I know it's my fault in some ways. But I want to help . . .

Stacey   This isn't about you.

Tara   But you've been my best friend since I was five years old . . . and I want you to know I'm here for you, girl . . . If there's anything I can do . . .

Stacey   There isn't.

Pause.

Tara   Stacey . . . I was in the wrong I know . . . but I've said I'm sorry and I really am.

Stacey   And what's that gonna do? It doesn't make a difference. You can't wave a fucking great magic wand and make everything alright . . .

Tara   But I'll help look after the baby for you . . . if you're having it . . .

Pause

Are you?

Stacey   I haven't decided anything yet . . .

Tara   Okay . . . but I'll be here for you, whatever you decide. Just tell me what to do and I'll do it. You want more books from school, I'll get 'em. We could study together.

Stacey   I can't go to college now, can I? It's all fucked.

Tara   You can. They'll have a crèche or you can leave it with your mum . . . or me. I'll be your babyminder, Stace.

Stacey   It's all so easy to you isn't it? All a game. You haven't been lying awake for nights worrying about this. You need to grow up, Tara.

Tara   Alright, okay. I'll try, Stacey. I'll try to be a different person . . . and we can share the responsibilities, share it all the way we've always shared things. It'll be our baby, Stace.

Stacey (*bitterly*)   Our baby.

Tara   Yeah, yours and mine. I fucking love you, girl.

Stacey   If *I'd* said that to you a month back you'd have run a mile. You'd have called me a lesbian . . . which I hope you've learnt to spell by now . . .

Tara   What?

Stacey   When I went into school to get some books, I had to pass the graffiti on the gym wall. 'Stacey Childs Is a Lesbian'. Well, maybe I am . . . or maybe I'll become one after all of this . . . (*Beat.*) And I saw what you'd written about Mr Kelsey.

Tara   Yeah, he's a prat.

Pause.

Stacey   . . . And I saw it was the same writing as the stuff about me. Your fucking writing, Tara. Don't bother trying to deny it. I don't know why I didn't see it was your writing before. Maybe it was because I trusted you.

Tara   Oh shit. Oh, Stace.

She sobs.

I'm sorry. I'm sorry. I'm just so . . . I was like a different person then. I'm not gonna be like that anymore . . .

Stacey   Just go, Tara. Go now.

She sits down on the floor, huddled up.

Tara   Stacey, I . . .

Stacey (*tired*)   Just go.

Pause.

Tara   Stacey, please . . . alright, okay.

She goes towards the door. She hesitates, then sits down on the floor. After a moment **Stacey** *notices* **Tara** *is still sitting there.*

Pause.

Stacey   You're not going to go are you?

Tara   *just looks at her.*

The End.

Sliding with Suzanne

A play

Judy Upton

Produced in 2001 at the Royal Court Theatre Upstairs and toured nationally by Out of Joint, directed by Max Stafford-Clark. A Time Out Critics' Choice.

Original Production Details

Date: August–September 2001

Venue: Theatre Upstairs, Royal Court

Director: Max Stafford-Clark

Designer: Julian McGowan

Lighting: Johanna Town

Sound: Paul Arditti

Cast

Josh	Danny Worters
Luka	Bryan Dick
Theresa	June Watson
Suzanne	Monica Dolan
Ned	Roger Frost
Sophie	Loo Brealey

Act One

Scene One

A 7-Eleven-type convenience shop. Brighton. Night.

Seventeen-year-old **Josh** *is on the till, reading* FHM. *Outside the window, sixteen-year-old* **Luka** *is gingerly prodding a hedgehog in the kerb with the toe of his trainer. He hesitates, crouches down to look at it, stands again and suddenly stamps on it hard, repeatedly.*

Josh *looks up from his magazine, sees* **Luka** *stomping on the hedgehog, is disgusted.* **Luka** *peels the hedgehog off the kerb, picks it up and enters the shop; he takes a can of Red Bull from the fridge, comes up to the counter.*

Luka   Bottle of Smirnoff.

Josh *is staring at the hedgehog pancake.* **Luka**'s *hand is bloody.*

Josh   Er . . . have you got proof of age? I have to ask everyone.

Luka *walks behind the counter, takes a bottle of vodka from the shelf, puts it down beside the Red Bull. He takes out a couple of crumpled notes to pay, dumps them on the counter.* **Josh** *puts the barcode reader on the Red Bull, then picks up the vodka bottle, hesitates, weighing up whether to risk a confrontation.* **Luka** *is examining the hedgehog.*

Josh   I can't let you have this, I'm afraid.

Luka *puts the hedgehog down on the counter.*

Josh That's sick. That's murder. I'm calling the RSPCA.

Luka *hesitates, then punches* **Josh** *hard in the face.*

Josh   Shit.

Luka *takes the bottle and Red Bull and leaves.* **Josh** *holds his nose.*

Exit **Luka**.

Josh *has a nosebleed, his eyes are watering.*

He exits, among the shelves.

Enter **Theresa** *(age sixty) and her thirty-five-year-old daughter* **Suzanne** *approaching the shop.*

They come in.

Enter **Josh**, *dabbing at his nose with some bog roll.*

Josh (*to himself*)   Shit.

Theresa   Grab a basket.

Suzanne *walks ahead.*

Josh . . . Excuse me.

Theresa Pick up a basket.

Suzanne *ignores her.* **Theresa** *picks up a basket, starts shopping.*

Josh Excuse me, we're closing in a minute.

Theresa Thank you, we won't be long.

Josh *shrugs. From behind the counter,* **Josh** *takes a long-handled floor brush. He uses it to knock the hedgehog on the floor.* **Suzanne** *notices, watches, puzzled. He pushes the hedgehog along the floor then, taking a swing at it with the brush, sends it flying out the door, and turns the sign on the door to 'Closed'.*

Theresa I wish you'd let me know you were coming. If you'd just thought to ring, Suzanne. I'd have gone up Safeway's. They're so much cheaper than here.

Suzanne Yeah okay, hurry up, Mum.

Theresa I don't see anything of you for months at a time and then you just turn up. Out of the blue.

Suzanne You don't want to see me? You don't want to see me, is that it?

Theresa It only takes a minute to phone. I can't just be expected to drop everything for you can I? I might have had my own plans for the evening, but oh no, that wouldn't enter your little head would it?

Josh *goes back behind his counter, takes a spray bottle of disinfectant, sprays and scrubs his counter.*

Suzanne Your own plans? Like you've started going to bingo or something?

Pause. **Theresa** *picks up a box of orange juice.*

Theresa One pound seventy – for juice?

She puts it back.

Suzanne Look there wasn't time, I told you. Had to get the last train.

Theresa You could've phoned me from the station.

Suzanne There wasn't time, Mum! Have you been listening to –

Theresa Wasn't time to pick up the phone. Wasn't time to make one little call?

Suzanne (*mutters*) Oh fuck off.

Theresa Yes, that's right. Use that language. That's all there is with you.

She continues to shop.

Suzanne What's that supposed to mean?

Theresa Beans or pasta shapes?

Suzanne   What do you mean by 'That's all there is with you'? You always say that, and it doesn't mean shit. 'That's all there is with you'. You don't even know what you're saying do you? You just open your mouth and spout rubbish.

Theresa   I'm not the only one.

Suzanne   Fuck off.

Theresa   That's what I mean – swearing, being unpleasant, all of the time. I mean that's probably why it happened isn't it? You started treating him like you treat me.

Suzanne   . . . Shit – I told you what happened. I fucking sat down and explained the whole thing to you.

Theresa   You said he told you he didn't want to live with you any more.

Suzanne   It wasn't his decision. You don't know what they do – how they operate. They poisoned him against me.

Theresa   But earlier you said –

Suzanne   Just listen to me right! For once in your life okay? They poisoned him. Joanna pretending to be my friend, and trying to turn him against me. Saying 'I'm there for you', 'I hear what you're saying' – the two-faced bitch. Saying the cooker's dangerous, last Monday, saying we need Rentokil back for the mice. Always having her little talks with him, prying and snooping into our life. 'Suzanne went where? Who was she with?' I don't know what he's told her . . . I mean he's not responsible for what he says . . . doesn't know what's going on in his own head half the time . . . crazy thoughts. Joanne says he's 'got some issues' and then won't fucking explain, when I ask her, when I say to her. "What issues?" . . . You gotta help me, Mum. I wouldn't have come if I'd thought you were just gonna say it's all my fault, my fault, my fault! I wouldn't have wasted the fucking train fare coming down here – £13.65 – fuck! – if I'd have thought all you'd be worried about was what to have for fucking dinner. And you don't have a clue do you?

Theresa   A clue about –

Suzanne   About what I should do! What should I do, Mum? I've come all the way down here to ask you. Tell me what I should do to get him back?

Theresa   Well, I . . .

Suzanne   I mean what's the time now anyway?

Theresa   Elevenish.

Suzanne   I'm not hungry, and it's too late for dinner now.

Theresa   It won't take long to prepare.

Suzanne   I've got no appetite. That train smelt like shit, like the toilet had overflowed or something. And all the windows were stuck . . . well, one of them wasn't, but every time I opened it, this bloke shut it again. I nearly fucking decked him, I told him there are people suffocating in here, and if you like the smell of shit so much, Mr-Fucking-Awkward-Bastard, then why don't you stick your head up your arse?

Theresa   I've got a tin of leek soup, which I know you like . . .

Suzanne   I don't. I've never liked it. Leek soup? I've never ate it, and never fucking will as long as I live . . .

Theresa   Well, you can suit yourself, can't you then?

Suzanne   I'm gonna page him.

She goes up to the till.

You got a phone here?

Josh   No, sorry.

Suzanne *sees the phone behind him.*

Suzanne   See that? See there? What's that? That looks like a phone to me.

Josh   Yeah, but you can't –

Suzanne *goes behind the counter, pushing him aside. She picks up the phone, dials.* **Josh** *wipes his nose, it's still bleeding a bit.*

Theresa   You still vegetarian?

Suzanne   What? Yeah. (*On phone.*) Hallo?

Theresa   You'll eat a little fish?

Suzanne   No, I won't eat a little fucking fish, Mum! (*On phone.*) Hallo? Sorry. Yeah, a message to 07699 68752. Yeah. It's . . . "Call me. Urgent.' Alright, 'Urgently' – what are you, some fucking grammar expert? 'Call me. Urgently.' That's it, yeah. He'll know. Okay, okay, put 'Love Suzanne' and some kisses. You know 'X's. About three. No put four. Four kisses yeah. Wait a minute, can you just check for me . . . I sent him another message about an hour ago. . . when I got off the train.

Theresa   Though you didn't have time to call me?

Suzanne   Shut up! I can't hear. (*On phone.*) What? You sent it? You're sure? Okay. Okay. Ta.

She puts the phone down.

(*To* **Josh**.) Thanks.

Josh (*insincerely*)   No problem.

Suzanne (*to* **Theresa**)   We've got matching pagers. His 'n' hers.

Suzanne *flashes her pager.*

Theresa   I don't understand those things.

Suzanne *goes back to the phone, slipping behind* **Josh** *before he notices her. She starts dialling another number.*

Josh   Hey, why don't you go outside and use the phone box?

Suzanne   Keep your hair on. I'll pay. I'll pay in a minute.

Josh   You can't pay, it's not a payphone.

Suzanne   See my arse? Kiss it.

She listens for a moment, then slams the phone down.

Theresa   Suzanne . . . love . . .

Suzanne   Pasta shapes.

Theresa   What?

Suzanne   Don't just stand there dithering in front of the fucking shelf. I've told you what I want. The pasta shapes.

Theresa *goes to pick a large can.*

Suzanne   Just a small one. I'm not gonna be here tomorrow.

Theresa *looks at her basket of shopping.*

Theresa   – But I've just stocked up for the whole week!

Suzanne   A week? What makes you think I'd spend a week with you? Half hour I've been back. Half hour and you're getting on my tits.

Theresa *puts the basket down. She wipes her eyes.*

Theresa   That's all there is with you!

Suzanne   What! Fuck! I can't believe you said that again. I can't believe it, Mum. God, you just do it on purpose, don't you? 'That's all there is with you' – what does it mean? Why do you always say that!

Theresa   I've had enough. I don't hear a word, not a word for three months, you don't phone, you don't answer the phone. . . .

Suzanne   Mum, listen to me –

Theresa   You don't worry about me, do you? Don't give me a thought. I might as well be dead –

Suzanne   Oh don't fucking start that –

Theresa   I could be lying dead on the floor, and you wouldn't know.

Suzanne   Okay, okay, I'll phone you more. I'll phone you every day.

– And if you're lying dead on the fucking floor, a lot of good that's gonna do. It's really gonna help, that – me phoning.

Theresa   Oh it's alright for you –

Suzanne   It's not alright for me! How can you fucking say that! You never listen do you, you stupid old bat!

Theresa   I'm not being sworn at –

Suzanne   I did not –

Theresa   I'm not being shouted at. You get what you want to eat, and you pay for it. I'm going home.

Suzanne   Mum.

Exit **Theresa**, *leaving the shopping basket.*

Suzanne *notices* **Josh** *is smiling, more out of nervousness than anything. She starts to walk over to him. He stops smiling.*

Suzanne   You waiting to close up?

Josh   Er . . . when you're ready.

She puts the shopping basket on the counter.

Suzanne   Just ring up five quid's worth. That's all I've got on me.

Josh   Up to five quid?

Suzanne   I've got five quid, forty-three. Last of the big spenders.

No . . . wait, just give me four quid's worth. Gotta leave enough for my bus fare, and most of it'll only get sicked up anyway.

Josh *starts ringing up the shopping.* **Suzanne** *looks at her pager. Still no message.*

Josh   Do you want the apples?

Suzanne   What?

Josh   I mean they're a bit pricey and they don't go with anything else do they – apples?

Suzanne   They're healthy.

Josh   I'm just saying –

Suzanne   You don't eat apples? What're your teeth like?

Josh   Fine.

Suzanne   Yeah? Show me?

Josh *continues to ring up the shopping. She tries to look at him.*

Suzanne   What happened to your nose?

Josh *rubs his nose.*

Josh   It looks really bad?

Suzanne   Like a truck hit it.

Josh   Thanks.

She bites into an apple.

Do you want the apples rung up?

Suzanne   No, I'm all done with them.

Josh   Three pounds, seventy-two then.

Suzanne   Can you put in it two bags – one inside the other.

He is about to.

Suzanne   No, let me do it, you're getting blood everywhere.

She puts her groceries in a bag. She pays, looks at her change.

Not really got enough left for a drink have I? Without breaking into the bus fare.

Josh   Wanna look in the fridge?

Suzanne   I mean a sit-down-in-the-pub kind of drink.

Josh   It's cheaper to buy it here than at rip-off pub prices.

Suzanne   Yeah, but I want to sit down.

Pause.

Can I sit down here?

Josh   I'm closing up.

Suzanne   It'll take you a minute to count the cash though won't it?

She opens a beer can, one of a four-pack.

Josh   Hey!

Suzanne *perches on the edge of the counter.*

Suzanne   I'll down it in one.

Josh *starts to cash up.*

Suzanne   Here.

She spreads her change on the counter.

I'd buy you one and all if I had enough. Don't like drinking alone. I get all morbid.

She counts the money.

Couldn't lend me 60p could you?

Josh   No.

Suzanne   I'm a pain in the arse I know.

Josh *takes 60p from his pocket, puts it with* **Suzanne**'s *money and rings it up.*

Suzanne   You're a treasure.

Josh   I've gotta make the till balance.

Suzanne   I'll borrow it off my mum and bring it in, in the morning.

Josh (*preoccupied, locking the till*)   Yeah right.

Suzanne   Nearly finished.

Josh *turns to look at the beers in the fridge.*

Suzanne   Getting tempted?

Josh   Yeah, you've made me want one myself now.

Suzanne   I won't tell.

He takes a beer from the fridge.

Suzanne   You don't have to pay?

Josh   Dream on. I'll put the money in tomorrow.

He opens his beer. Then goes and dims the lights.

Suzanne   Very atmospheric.

Josh   Just in case my boss walks by.

Suzanne   Ah.

She walks up to **Josh** *and clinks her can against his.*

Suzanne   Cheers.

They drink in silence.

Are you old enough to be drinking?

Josh   Yeah.

Suzanne   God's honest? (*Pause.*) You need to clean that up.

She wipes a little blood off his face with her finger.

Josh   Don't know if it's mine or the hedgehog's.

Suzanne   Hedgehog? . . .

Josh   Don't ask. Not got a mirror have you?

Suzanne   No. I stopped carrying a bag. I lost so many.

She takes a tissue from her pocket.

Don't worry, it's clean.

She wipes his face.

That looks a bit better.

Josh   Maybe he broke it.

She feels his nose.

Josh   Ow. What you doing?

Suzanne   Trying to feel if it's broken.

Josh   And?

Suzanne   Can't tell. It's pretty swollen though.

Josh (*sarky*)   Oh great.

Suzanne   Get your mum to have a look when you get home.

Josh *sips his beer.*

Josh   Don't live with my mum.

Suzanne   So what happened?

Josh   With my mum?

Suzanne   What? With your nose. Someone hit you?

Josh   A customer yeah. A schizoid customer.

Suzanne *reaches over and ruffles his hair. He looks at her surprised. She takes out her purse.*

Suzanne   Let's have another beer.

Scene Two

Theresa's' *kitchen. Night.*

Theresa *takes a cup of tea to* **Ned** *(aged fifty-five). They are both slightly tense and awkward.*

Ned   I saw your light was still on. So I . . . I was going to ring first.

Theresa   I'm sorry. I should've rung you.

Ned   It's okay. You don't need to explain, you know that.

Pause.

Just thought I'd check things were okay.

Theresa   I'm glad you've come round.

Ned   Maybe we were pushing things on . . . you know, faster than they were meant to go. I'd been thinking about it too . . .

Theresa   Had you? Are you . . . you don't think it's such a good idea?

Ned   I don't know, Theresa.

Theresa   I understand. Maybe it would change things too much . . .

Pause.

You know what they say about fools rushing in . . . and that . . . I wouldn't want to lose . . . how things are . . . us.

He looks up from his tea.

Theresa   Ned . . . I . . . tonight was going to be . . . really special. Even if we don't . . . if we're not, I still want . . . I don't know what I want. I was going to make a risotto. Chicken. But then Suzanne's still vegetarian and –

Ned   Suzanne?

Theresa   Yes. She's here. I don't mean right now. We had a bit of a . . . we had words, up the shop. But she'll be back in a minute.

That's why I didn't ring you. I was about to start cooking you see – for us. And then she turned up. Out of the blue.

Ned   Oh right . . .

Theresa   I was about to call you and then she arrived.

Ned   Is everything alright with her?

Theresa   The boy's run off. She's worried.

Ned   The one she brought down at Christmas?

Theresa   Yeah. He's been with her nearly six months now.

Ned   He seemed nice, and that puppy . . .

Theresa   Sweet little thing – but into everything. Chewed up my chiffon scarf . . . .Oh and flattened your roses.

Ned   They survived.

He gets up.

I should be going.

Theresa   No . . .

She takes a step towards him, hesitates.

Theresa   There's no need.

She walks up to him.

I'm glad you came round.

She touches his face. There's a possibility of a kiss but it's lost through mutual hesitancy.

I don't know where she's got to . . . and she's got the groceries so I can't start cooking until she gets here. Not that I want to eat at this time of night, and she'll probably . . . I mean I think she still has problems with food.

She sits down.

I can never really get to the bottom of it. She loved her food when she was a kid. Loved fish fingers. Used to get ketchup all round her face.

Ned *sits and finishes his tea.*

Theresa   But Andy. I mean I thought he was nice. He certainly came along at the right time . . . And I thought he was giving her some kind of stability . . . (*Pause.*)

Ned *finishes his tea.* **Theresa** *swoops on the cup.*

Theresa   There's another in the pot.

Ned   Not for me.

She looks at the cup.

On Friday . . . Michael and his wife are coming down.

Theresa   That's nice . . .

Ned   I thought maybe you might like to come to dinner.

Theresa   If I wouldn't be –

Ned   You wouldn't.

Theresa *takes the cups to the sink.*

Theresa   Ned . . . I . . . I was in that little antique shop earlier, the one at Preston Circus. I do sometimes . . . just pop in, to have a bit of a look. Not that I need any more old clutter but . . . anyway I noticed they'd got a box with a couple of maps in, old ones they looked like. One was of Exeter, I remember that, the other some place in Scotland.

Ned   Were they Ordnance Survey?

Theresa   Yeah, I think so. They'd both got paintings on the cover – like some of yours have. One of 'em was really pretty – a car I think . . . though I couldn't make out all the detail. Well you know my eyes.

Ned   What colour were the rest of the covers?

Theresa   I . . . I'm not sure I remember.

Ned   I've got all the editions for Exeter, but the Scottish one . . . I suppose you can't remember where . . .

Theresa   No I . . . it began with a 'D' I think . . . Not a place I've heard of.

Ned   Dundee?

Theresa   I've heard of Dundee.

Ned   There're a few Scottish ones I still need.

Theresa   I should've written it down . . .

Ned   No, no, it's no problem I can pop in myself on Saturday morning . . . or maybe tomorrow evening if I'm home in time . . . .Just in case . . . sometimes they tend to go pretty quick.

Theresa   You'll curse me if it's gone, won't you?

The doorbell rings.

Took her time, didn't she?

She exits. She enters after a moment with **Luka**.

Luka   Alright, Mr Bisset?

Theresa   Suzanne's been worrying herself sick.

Luka   Where is she?

Theresa   Out of her mind with stress and anxiety that's what she is.

Luka (*calls out*)   Suzanne!

Theresa   She's here.

He looks around.

Luka   Where?

Theresa   Or she was. She's up the shop.

Luka   Yeah, like she didn't bother to let me know she was heading down here. I had to go crawling round all her stupid friends, and ex-boyfriends – you know just in case . . . then I see Vicky, the gobby cow who, like, pokes her nose in everywhere and she says, 'Uh, she's gone to her mum's'. (*Sarky.*) Nice of her to tell me, you know.

Theresa   She came to ask me what to do.

Luka   Do about what? Me? It ain't me with the problem, I can tell you . . .

He sits down at the table.

Theresa   They're like that all my kids, any trouble they come running back to their mum.

Luka   Is she in trouble?

Theresa   No dear, I just meant –

Luka   I had to get a train all the way down here, hiding in the loo, cos I couldn't pay the fare. I've never got any money cos she's always borrowing my allowance before she's even given me it.

Ned *gets up.*

Ned   I really should be making a move, Theresa. Had a long day – driving a bunch of flower arrangers to Bournemouth and back.

Theresa   Oh . . . Oh alright.

She goes to him, wants to kiss him goodbye but doesn't find an opportunity.

See you on Friday . . . if not before.

Ned   Friday? Oh yes.

Theresa   Goodnight.

Exit **Ned**.

Luka *starts unlacing his trainers.*

Theresa   Are those muddy?

Luka   Bloody. I had to kill a hedgehog.

Theresa   What? You had to –

Luka   A car had hit it. It's guts were out but it was still moving.

Theresa   Oh God, Luka.

Luka   Do you ever worry about stuff like that? Or dream about it?

Theresa   What dear? Dead hedgehogs?

Luka   Disembowelment.

Pause.

Theresa   No. No dear, I can't say I do. (*Pause.*) Luka, if you don't mind me asking . . . what happened between you and my daughter? I mean did you have a bit of a disagreement?

Luka   You could say that.

Theresa   You had a row? But that's still no excuse for running off, worrying everyone –

Luka   I hadn't run off.

Theresa   Suzanne thought you'd run away. Or gone to Social Services.

Luka   I hadn't. I wouldn't, I . . . I just needed a bit of space, okay.

Theresa   You can't just go off when it suits you. That's really thoughtless, Luka.

Luka   It wasn't thoughtless . . . I'd been thinking about it for days, weeks really.

Theresa   You're not happy at my daughter's?

Luka   It's not – look it was just a stupid argument, right?

Theresa   She is argumentative, I'll give you that . . .

Luka   Usually when we argue it doesn't like mean shit, but this time I'd just had enough, right?

Pause.

Luka   I'd reached my limit.

Theresa   Can you tell me what it was about?

Luka   Coming in late.

Theresa   You stayed out 'til when?

Luka   She stayed out. 'Til 4 a.m. Drinking.

Theresa   Well, I . . .

Luka   She wouldn't say where she'd been. I said some stupid stuff – and she start yelling cos she was pissed and that. So I started breaking things – mugs and a plate. Just to make her listen. To make her shut up.

Theresa *stands up.*

Luka   It was stupid. Sometimes I just get so jealous, I don't know.

Theresa   Jealous of what?

Luka   Jealous she can do anything she wants. At her age she can like do anything. Can I smoke in here?

Theresa   I'd rather you didn't.

Luka *checks his pager.*

Theresa   You've got a pager too. Oh of course, Suzanne was trying to get you on it earlier. What does it do? Can you leave a message?

He shows her; she squints to read the messages.

Theresa   They're amazing, these modern things.

Luka   Modern – I wish. It's so out of date, I can't let people at school see it. Have to pretend I've a mobile with text messaging. Everyone else has got one.

Theresa   They're so pricey though aren't they?

Luka   Not if you get pay-as-you-go.

Theresa   So, have you called her? Paged her back or whatever it is you have to do?

Luka   No point if you say she'll be here in a minute or so.

Theresa   Shop must've closed by now. Can't think where's she's got to, unless maybe she's popped in to see one of her old friends.

Luka   Girls or?

Theresa   Girls she was at school with, yes. Women they are now of course. Maria's in the post office and Michelle's a ward sister at the Princess Alexandra. With two little ones, don't know how she manages but she seems to. Sometimes I wish Suzanne hadn't moved away. Sometimes I feel sure she'd be happier . . . not to say she isn't happy . . . it's just . . . well, she's all on her own in Cricklewood isn't she?

Luka   Alone? She's always out. The pub or parties with her *friends* . . .

Theresa   Yes, but what I mean is there's no one special in her life, is there?

She catches his look.

Or is there? Is there someone I don't know about?

Luka *shakes his head.*

Theresa   I know I'm silly and old-fashioned but I just wish she'd meet some nice young man again . . .

Luka   A nice young man.

Theresa   If there is still such a thing.

Luka   My toenail's turning black.

Theresa   Did you bang it?

Luka   Stubbed it on the bedroom door. Fucking hurt. – Sorry. Looks disgusting don't it? Did have them all varnished purple so it wouldn't show.

Theresa   You varnish your toenails? I thought only girls did that.

Luka   Me too. (*Pause.*) Suzanne did it. Most of its chipped off now though. (*Pause.*) Mrs Garner . . .

Theresa   Yes dear?

Luka   Would you mind if I gave you a bit of advice?

Theresa   Oh? No, go ahead – unless it's about painting my nails, I've always thought it looked tarty.

Luka   Mrs Garner, if you want to screw that bloke from next door –

Theresa   Luka! Oh nonsense, I don't –

Luka (*interrupting*)   You've gotta tell him. Tell him or he'll never know. You can't expect him to, like, read your mind.

Theresa   Look I don't think –

Luka   He's probably thinking, 'I can't ask her, cos maybe she thinks she's too old for all that. Maybe she'll be, like, so shocked, she won't want to see me anymore, and that's gonna be kinda difficult with living next door and all. I'll have to, like, creep outside and only take my washing in after dark' –

Theresa   Will you stop it.

Luka   Tell him. Cook him a nice meal and tell him. God, I'm knackered. Must be the train journey or something.

Theresa   You can go to bed if you like. There's still a bed made up in the spare room. First right at the top – where you slept at Christmas.

He stands up.

Luka   Thanks. Where'll Suzanne sleep if I have the bed?

He picks up his trainers.

Theresa   In the double with me.

She stands, hesitates, then gives him a little kiss on the forehead.

Theresa   Goodnight, Luka.

Luka   Are you going to wait up for her?

Theresa   No . . .Well actually, I probably will . . . but don't tell her that will you? It always used to annoy her, and the boys when they were teenage – didn't like their mother still being up when they came in at all hours. And if I happened to move the curtain and look out the window, well, woe betide me. I know it's stupid, I don't worry when she's not sleeping under my roof . . . but when she is . . . old habits . . . I've got a few things to do down here. A few little jobs. When I hear the gate creak, I'll creep upstairs.

Exit **Luka**.

Theresa *looks at her watch. She starts to fuss about the room.*

Scene Three

The sound of eerily subdued sobbing. A shit-heap of a teenage boy's bedroom. **Josh**, *in his pyjamas, is asleep sprawled across the split and beer-stained duvet.* **Sophie**, *his younger sister (age fourteen, also in pyjamas), is trying to rouse him.*

Josh *wakes.*

Sophie   Josh!

He sits up, rubs his nose.

Josh   Shit.

Josh *looks at* **Sophie**.

Josh   What . . . what's. . .?

Sophie *goes to the top of the bed, pulls the duvet back a bit.* **Suzanne** *is there, crying.*

Sophie   Josh! A girl. You've got a girl in here! And she's crying.

Why's she crying?

Josh   Shit . . .

Sophie   Been crying for ages. Woke me up.

Josh   Shit.

He crawls across to look at **Suzanne**.

Sophie   Didn't know what it was. Thought maybe you'd smuggled another dog in. Not a girl. Fucking hell, Josh.

Josh   Shut up. Just shut up, right.

Sophie   She can't hear me, she's crying.

Josh   I know!

He nervously pats **Suzanne***'s shoulder.*

Josh   Hey . . . hey . . .

Suzanne *curls up, tries to move away.* **Josh** *holds his head.*

Josh   My head's fucking killing. . . Like eight beers I had.

Sophie   Eight – yeah right. You'd be dead. Or on a drip like Connor at school, after twelve Bacardi Breezers.

Josh *nervously shakes* **Suzanne** *slightly.*

Sophie   Hope she don't wake Dad.

Josh   Fuck – he's in?

Sophie   Yeah. And conscious.

Josh   Shit. (*To* **Suzanne**.) Shhh. Shhhh. Not so loud.

Sophie   What you do to her?

Josh   Shit. Fucking hell.

Sophie   You must've done something.

Josh *gingerly pushes* **Suzanne***'s shoulder.*

Sophie   Oh my God, its like 'hallo' – nobody at home. It's like she's crying in her sleep or something. Did she take anything? Pills.

Josh   It's a nightmare.

Sophie   You think she's having –

Josh   I'm having a nightmare, man.

Sophie   Did you fuck her?

Josh   Sophie!

Sophie   Did you fuck –

Josh   Course I – Oh fuck . . . I hope she's not, you know, thinking it was rape or something . . . I mean she was all over me, fucking ate me alive. Look at these scratches. Shit.

Sophie   You didn't hurt her?

Josh   Course I didn't . . . Well, I don't think . . .

Sophie   Not by accident . . . or something.

Josh   No . . . least I don't see how.

Sophie   You said that Kelly cried. Afterwards, didn't she?

Josh   Cos she was crap and I told her so. That's different –

And Kelly can't hold her drink.

Sophie   Maybe this one can't either. Was it her first time or something . . .

Josh   She's not . . . I mean she's . . .

Sophie *bends over* **Suzanne**.

Sophie   Nice perfume.

Josh   What you doing?

Sophie   Gonna tickle her.

Josh   Don't touch her. Keep away from her. I've gotta think what to do.

Pause.

This is a dangerous situation, right.

Sophie   Maybe you should tell Dad.

Josh   Shit! Are you out of your fucking –

Suzanne *stops crying.*

Sophie   Well, he brings women back and this don't happen.

Josh   She's stopped

Sophie   Maybe she's dead.

Josh   Shit.

He checks on **Suzanne**.

Josh   She's asleep.

Sophie   Maybe she was just crying in her sleep. Maybe it was just a bad dream then.

Josh   Hope to fuck I wasn't in it.

Sophie   Where did you meet her?

Josh   The shop.

Sophie   Tonight?

Josh   Yeah.

Sophie   You just picked her up? And you're always saying you're too shy. You're outrageous, Josh. Do I know her? From school or anything?

Josh   I don't think so, Soph.

Sophie   Let me look at her.

Josh   No.

Sophie   Just her face. I won't wake her. Move the sheet.

Josh *moves the sheet, a little, just off* **Suzanne**'s *face.*

Sophie   Shit! She's a woman! . . . She's like twenty-five or something.

Oh my God, Josh.

Josh   Shhh.

Sophie   A woman . . .

Josh   She's beautiful.

Sophie *looks at* **Suzanne** *critically.*

Sophie   Yeah, I suppose so. Is she naked?

Josh   I . . . I can't remember.

Sophie   *pulls the sheet down, a little, exposing* **Suzanne**'s *shoulder.*

Josh   Sophie! Leave her.

Sophie   I'm just seeing if she's okay. We did like first aid at school last term.

Josh   She doesn't need first aid, Sophie.

Suzanne *stirs.* **Josh** *and* **Sophie** *jump back,* **Sophie** *cries out,* **Suzanne** *wakes.*

Suzanne   Huh? Luka . . .

Josh   You were having a bad dream.

Sophie   A nightmare.

Suzanne *sits up, wide-eyed, startled. Recognition dawns.*

Josh   You alright?

Suzanne   No.

Josh   Fuck . . .

Suzanne   Oh no.

She holds the sheet around herself. She stares at **Sophie**.

Suzanne   Oh, no, no.

Pause.

Sophie   Er, hi.

Suzanne (*confused, to* **Josh**)   This is your place, er . . .

Josh   Josh. This is my sister.

Sophie   Sophie.

She holds out her hand. Still slightly dazed, sitting up in bed **Suzanne** *shakes it.*

Sophie   Are you okay?

Suzanne   Mmmm. Are you?

Sophie *looks at* **Josh** *for help.*

Josh   Suzanne . . . last night, do you remember . . . we got a bit wasted didn't we? And you wanted to come home with me. You wanted to, didn't you?

Suzanne   What? My eyes are burning.

Sophie   Cos of all that crying.

Suzanne   Crying? What? I'm sorry, I'm still . . . I need a drink . . .

Josh   Another one?

Suzanne   . . . of water.

Josh (*to* **Sophie**)   What're you waiting for?

Exit **Sophie**.

Suzanne   Oh my God, look at you. You're a . . .

She laughs, shocked.

Josh   Maybe we shouldn't have drunk so much.

Suzanne   You're a kid . . .

Josh   No I'm not.

Suzanne   You look like my son. Oh fuck . . . I'm really sorry.

Josh   Don't be. It was great.

Suzanne   No, no, I don't want to know . . . I shouldn't be here. I must go.

She gets up, still holding the sheet around herself. She sees her shoes on the floor, and bends to pick them up. She staggers. **Josh** *helps her sit back down.*

Josh   Steady there. Take it easy. Everything's okay. Sophie's getting your water.

Suzanne *holds her head.*

Suzanne   Sorry . . . your name . . .

Josh   Josh.

Suzanne   I'm sorry, Josh. I'm really sorry. I don't know what I was thinking of.

Josh   You wanted to.

Suzanne   It's no excuse.

Josh   I didn't . . . I mean it was like I raped you or . . .

Suzanne   No, no, I didn't mean that, I . . .

Josh   Just cos I'm young, well to you, I suppose . . . but I've had lots of girlfriends.

She puts her Doc Martens on.

Suzanne   It's stupid, so stupid . . .

Josh   I won't say anything . . . I mean I fucked my best mate's girlfriend once, kinda by accident. I'd never let on. Neither would she. Are you, like, married or anything . . . if you don't –

Suzanne   No. Not now.

Josh   But you were? Wow.

Pause.

Bet you've got a boyfriend though?

Suzanne   Look a sight don't I?

She tries to dress discreetly. **Josh** *turns away.*

Josh   If you want me to, like, wait outside. . . .

Suzanne   It's okay, love. My knickers . . .

Josh   Oh . . . oh yeah . . .

He looks in the bed and on the floor.

I keep meaning to have a tidy-up. You can borrow a pair of mine . . . if they'll fit.

Suzanne   I woke up . . . looked at you lying there. And I saw my son.

Josh   Fuck . . . I mean, yeah . . .

Pause.

That was why you were crying? Cos I look like your son?

Suzanne   The bastards.

She stands up, clenching her fists, body hard.

They've got him.

Josh   What!

Suzanne *turns on* **Josh**.

Suzanne   My son! They've got my son. Fucking socials.

Josh   Social services have, like, got your kid?

Suzanne   My son. They must have. Where else could he be?

Pause.

Josh   You better sit down.

Suzanne *wipes her eyes, looks at the make-up on her fingers.*

Suzanne   What a night, eh? What a night. I'm sorry. I'm really sorry.

Josh   For what?

She ruffles his hair.

Suzanne   For this – everything. And you're so sweet. Really sweet.

Enter **Sophie** *with the water.*

Josh   At fucking last. Bring it here.

Sophie *hands* **Suzanne** *the cup.*

Suzanne   What's the time?

Josh *cranes over to look at his clock.*

Josh   7.34 a.m.

Suzanne   Oh.

Sophie   Shit, my paper round!

Suzanne (*to* **Josh**)   Look, love, I ought to be going. Can I use your bathroom?

Sophie   Just don't wake Dad.

Suzanne *looks at* **Josh**, *alarmed.*

Josh   S'alright, he's a heavy sleeper.

Suzanne *pauses, unsteady in the doorway.* **Sophie** *joins her.*

Sophie   Gonna be long? I need to piss.

Josh   Sophie. Let the lady use the bathroom. Use the fucking paper bin.

She exits.

Sophie *tips out the contents of the litter bin, takes it behind the bed.*

Sophie   Don't watch, Josh. I'm not gonna piss with you watching.

Josh *turns away. Behind the bed,* **Sophie** *squats over the litter bin.*

Josh   I can't breathe through my nose . . . does it look really bad?

Sophie   Yeah. Is she feeling better?

Josh   Social services have got her baby.

Sophie   That why she was crying?

Josh   We should help her get it back.

Sophie   Us?

Josh   Someone should help her. She's a beautiful woman, isn't she?

Sophie *pulls back the curtains.*

Sophie   Shit, it's raining.

Sophie *opens the window, tips the bin of piss out.*

Josh   Mind the fucking begonias.

Sophie   Already getting pissed on ain't they?

Sophie   I'm going to get dressed. See you later.

Josh   Sophie, if you say a word to Dad . . .

Sophie   Course I won't.

Enter **Suzanne**.

Suzanne   Bathroom's free.

Sophie   I'm fine now thanks. See you later.

She exits.

Suzanne   How old's your sister?

Josh   Fourteen.

Suzanne   And you're. . .?

Josh   Seventeen.

Suzanne   Shit.

Josh   It's okay.

Suzanne   Your sister . . . she wasn't in here earlier when we were . . .

Josh   I'd locked the door. I'm not stupid. Anyway Sophie sleeps in the attic. In a sleeping bag. Got her bedroom too full of computers and stuff.

Suzanne   Where are we? What street's this?

Josh   Middle.

Suzanne   Middle of what?

Josh   Middle Street. Where you gotta get to?

Suzanne   Off Lewes Road.

Josh   That's near where Dee-Ann lives. She's . . . er she used to be my girlfriend, sort of.

Suzanne   Could I borrow an umbrella? I'll bring it back . . . er, drop it into the shop later.

Josh   Look, I could walk you home . . . if you wait a minute while I put some clothes on.

Suzanne   Okay.

She sits back down on the bed. **Josh** *starts unbuttoning his pyjamas, gets self-conscious, stops.*

Josh   There's some cornflakes downstairs. Or toast.

Suzanne   I'm fine.

Josh   You could make yourself a black coffee . . .

Suzanne   Yeah? Yeah, I think I'll do that.

She exits.

Josh *still can't really believe what's happened. Suddenly he grins to himself. He continues to get changed*

Enter **Sophie** *with her cycle pads.*

Sophie   Lucy's across the road. You know she works at the same place as Dee-Ann now?

Josh   Yeah, yeah.

Sophie *looks out the window.*

She's out there doing something to her car. You better take the woman out the side door in case she sees. If Dee-Ann finds out –

Josh   Fuck Dee-Ann.

Sophie   You can't treat her like that. You've no respect.

Josh   You'll understand when you're older.

Sophie   I understand now. Men are shits. (*Beat.*) So what about the baby? You're gonna try and help the woman get it back?

Josh   Yeah . . . though I don't see how I can do / anything . . .

Sophie   You're so defeatist, Josh! You could kick up a fuss, go to the papers . . . oh fuck, I should be like long gone. At least make sure she gets home safely, right?

She exits.

Scene Four

Theresa's *kitchen.*

Theresa *and* **Luka** *are having breakfast.*

Luka *is reading the paper.* **Theresa** *yawns.*

Theresa   Excuse me.

Luka   You didn't go to bed?

Theresa   Can you pass the milk?

He does. **Theresa** *stops to look at one of several photos on the wall.*

My two youngest grandchildren – Fern and Jamie.

Jamie's so like his dad and he's musical – don't know where he gets that. I feel so proud when they call me Gran. Wish I got to see more of them . . .

Luka   I didn't sleep either.

Theresa   Does Suzanne still drink milk?

Luka   Soya milk.

Theresa   Oh. Soya milk . . . made from beans or something is it? (*Pause.*) Is she eating properly? I can never ask her and get a straight answer.

Luka   She eats. Then she spews.

Theresa *stops eating.*

Theresa   She insists she's not bulimic.

Luka   Says she's sick cos life makes her feel like that.

Theresa   When she was at school she'd be sick every morning. Once the head sent her home with a letter cos he thought she was up the club.

Luka   She's getting so thin . . .

Theresa   I noticed . . .

Luka   And she won't see the doctor. Not after she had a row with her. She just buys all these pots of vitamins and shit from the health shop in Kilburn. And then she never takes them.

Theresa   Does she cook for you?

Luka   If I'm really unlucky. It's okay, cos there's McDonald's up the road. Course she hates me going there – I don't tell her. But it's better than, like, dying of malnutrition.

Theresa   When she was little she used to love to help me in the kitchen. She used to love doing the washing-up. Playing with the bubbles.

Luka   Wish she still did.

Enter **Suzanne**.

Suzanne (*coming in*)   Look, sorry, Mum I . . . (*Sees* **Luka**.) Oh fuck . . .

Luka *gets up.*

Suzanne   Oh my God . . . What the fuck are you doing down here?

Luka   Looking for you, Suzanne.

Suzanne   Luka! Shit, you can't imagine. I've been so worried!

She hugs him fiercely. He struggles free.

Suzanne   How did you –

Luka   I got the train down. Had to come looking for you, didn't I?

Suzanne   No, no. . . I was looking for you . . .

Luka   Where've you been? Your mum waited up all night . . .

Theresa   I . . .

Suzanne   . . . I've been to a café.

Theresa   All night?

Suzanne   An all-night café. (*To* **Luka**.) But I wouldn't have . . . wouldn't have sat there all night if I'd known you were here. Why didn't you page me? Why did you let me . . . why did you make me so worried, Luka?

Luka   So you were worried. I was out of my fucking mind, Suzanne. You'd disappeared. Then I get here and your mum says you're here but you don't come in.

Theresa   I thought you might be with your friends.

Suzanne   Friends?

Theresa   Maria and Michelle.

Suzanne   God no. Not seen Michelle for years and Maria's married to a dickhead.

Theresa   He seemed alright to me.

Suzanne   When did *you* meet him?

Theresa   At your wedding.

Suzanne   Oh yeah. My wedding. Enough said. (*To* **Luka**.) So what did Joanna have to say?

Luka   About what?

Suzanne   Does she know you're here?

Luka   Course not.

Suzanne   But that's where you've been?

Luka   When?

Suzanne   When you stormed out.

Luka   No.

Suzanne   You didn't go to the socials?

Luka   No I didn't go to the socials. Jesus, Suzanne, you're so paranoid. I sat up by B and Q and I did some thinking. By myself.

Suzanne   I didn't know where you were.

Luka   So you pissed off down here, and sat in a café? (*Sarky.*) Yeah, makes sense.

Theresa   Do you want some cereal?

Suzanne   Just a coffee.

Theresa *pours her one.*

Theresa   I'm afraid I don't have any soya milk.

Suzanne   I'll drink it black.

Luka   How many did you have? Coffees in the all-night cafe?

Suzanne   Six or seven.

Luka   I'd have spewed after three.

Suzanne   Lightweight.

Theresa   They just let you sit there all night?

Suzanne   Why shouldn't they? That's what people do in all-night caffs.

Luka   You look like you've been doing more than drinking coffee.

Suzanne (*sarkily*)   Well, yeah now let me see, I might just've smoked a little crack . . .

Theresa *looks at her daughter disapprovingly.* **Suzanne** *sits down next to* **Luka**.

Suzanne   Mum been looking after you has she?

She ruffles his hair.

Luka   Get off.

Suzanne   When are you gonna do something about your hair?

Luka   When are you gonna stop wearing those stupid Doc Martens?

Suzanne   You look tired . . .

Luka   And whose fault is that?

Suzanne   Would you like anything else to eat? Some toast with marmite.

Theresa   I got a new brown loaf . . . Oh . . . Suzanne? What happened to the groceries?

Suzanne   Oh fuck! I forgot all about . . . I did buy the stuff for you. Must've left it up the shop.

Theresa   You'd lose your head if it wasn't screwed on! Do you think there's much chance it might still be there?

Suzanne   It was only three quid's worth.

Theresa   Still worthing checking though isn't it?

Suzanne   Yeah, yeah, leave it to me.

Luka   And can you phone school – tell 'em I've like a bad cold or something?

Suzanne   Yeah, remind me in a bit.

She helps herself to a spoonful of **Luka**'*s breakfast.*

Theresa   That's real milk.

Suzanne (*to* **Luka**)   So what do you fancy doing? We might as well make a day out of it while we're down here. We could go up on the cliffs have a picnic . . .

Theresa   Like we used to when you were small. That'd be nice.

Luka   I'm still waiting, Suze.

Suzanne   What? For an apology? Why should I be the one to apologise? It wasn't me who ran away.

Luka   I didn't run away. (*Pause.*) Just say sorry, Suzanne.

Suzanne   After you had me so worried? You wouldn't answer my messages.

Luka *shoves bag his chair and stands up.*

Suzanne   Oh no. Don't you sulk.

She tries to put her hand on his shoulder; angrily he moves aside. Pause.

Talk to me. Don't you sulk again.

Theresa   Leave him be.

Luka *tries to pass her.*

Suzanne   Don't go walking out on me.

She blocks his way.

Look at me. Hey.

She catches hold of him.

Look at me.

Luka   I'm not getting into an argument.

Suzanne   Then talk to me! Don't give me this silent shit. You don't know how wound up that makes me.

Theresa   Leave him alone, love.

Suzanne   Shut up, Mum.

Theresa   Don't you start on me.

Suzanne (*to* **Luka**)   What is your problem?

Theresa   Don't you start / raising your voice . . .

Luka   / Guess. Take a big fucking guess, Suze.

Suzanne   Oh, it's all my fault is it? As per usual. Suzanne's gone and fucked/ it all up again, has she!

Theresa   / Suzanne! Keep it down. Ned doesn't want to hear this.

Luka   Don't you fucking shout at me. Get out of my face.

Suzanne *slaps him.*

Theresa   Oh / my God!

Luka   / Stupid bitch. You wanna be my mother? Do you? My fucking bitch of a mother? Getting pissed and bringing home psychopaths who just want to drink and beat up on her, and get her kids put in care . . .

Theresa   Luka –

Luka   You wanna hit me over the head with my fucking skateboard.

Theresa *stands up but isn't sure what to do.*

Suzanne   She never . . .

Luka   You're just like my stupid fucking mother. You drink more than she does, you smoke more fucking dope than she does . . . Just like her but with one big difference. One really big difference.

Suzanne   Luka, listen to –

Luka   I don't give a shit where you were, okay? You're just so fucking immature, can't deal with anything can you?

Can't keep a job, so you think looking after fucked-up kids is easier. / Easier cos you can just go and fuck 'em up worse.

'Stability', that's what they said I needed. Stability – don't even know what it fucking means do you?

Theresa   / Stop this. Please Luka!

Suzanne   It wasn't me that ran. You always run. That's what the socials said.

Luka   I came to find you! I thought you were cutting your wrists or under a fucking train or something.

Suzanne   None of the others were trouble like you. They warned me . . .

Luka   And you didn't listen . . . didn't care cos you looked at me and you thought –

Suzanne   I thought I could help you have a better life.

Luka   In your shitty flat? / Like no one bothered to ask me what I wanted.

Theresa   / I'm not gonna put up with this.

Suzanne   So what did you want? The fucking earth as usual?

Luka   An old foster mum, so'd there be no confusion, y'know. I wouldn't start forgetting what she was there for.

He realises **Theresa** *is present.*

Luka   A rich foster mum. One who'd give me twenty quid a week pocket money – not force to me go out and get a job . . .

Suzanne   Force you to get a job? You came home and told me you were working.

Luka   Yeah, cos I need to live, I need money . . .

Theresa   Is anyone listening to me?

Suzanne   And where am I supposed to get it?

Luka   You could get a job, 'stead of sitting around on your fucking arse. I wanted to live in a nice fucking neighbourhood, not another rubbish flat . . . so my mum has to look after my dog 'til we move, then we don't move and she kidnaps the fucking dog.

Suzanne   / We'll get Scully back, I told you –

Theresa   That poor little puppy . . .

Luka   Yeah, you told me. Told me you'd stop going out, stop holding stupid parties, hanging with your stupid friends . . . I was like the poorest kid at school and everyone dissing me about it, so I told 'em just you wait and see where I'm gonna end up . . . cos I thought my socials had, like, lined up this rich family and then I end up in your skanky flat with you going fucking crazy on me.

Suzanne   You think the rich people would've put up with you? – Think they'd mind you setting their carpet on fire?

Luka   Rich people don't have carpet, Suzanne. And it was an accident, right? I only started using paper cups as ash trays cos you did. Then you, like, total the fucking car . . .

Suzanne   So I can't even write off my own car / without you judging me.

Theresa   / You've had an accident?

Luka   I'm just sick of waiting for the bus, y'know. I'm a better driver than you and I ain't had any proper lessons. / When I take my test I'll pass first time. How many goes did it take you. Eleven. Eleven, Suze.

Theresa   / Oh my God.

Suzanne   I drove you everywhere – I was your fucking taxi service. I put myself out for you. I cook, I clean . . .

Theresa   / Suzanne . . .

Luka   Where? Where do you cook and clean? Not in our fucking flat, that's for sure.

Suzanne   And . . . and . . . when the school caught you truanting, I said I'd kept you home –

Luka   And you want a medal for it? When some guy at school was bad-mouthing you, saying you look like a slag, I split his face. Even though now him and his mates are like just waiting their chance to cut my guts out.

Theresa   Honestly, I've completely had it / with you two.

Suzanne   / What do you want? Do you want to leave me? Do you?

Pause.

Theresa   I'm sure he doesn't want that dear, he –

Suzanne   Shut up.

Theresa   I won't / shut up in my own home . . .

Suzanne (*to* **Luka**)   / You can leave me can't you? Any time you want. It's easy enough. It's not working out, you can go can't you?

Luka   I just want you to change, Suze.

Suzanne   Into an old rich woman who pays for you to have driving lessons?

Luka   I just don't want to have to look out for you the whole time, I don't want the responsibility.

Suzanne   Alright, okay. I'll change. I'll change into somebody else. I'll be what you want me to.

Luka   You always say that. You don't change. You can't.

Suzanne   And, like, you're perfect are you? The perfect foster son. Never give me a moment's fucking worry do you!

Luka   Just . . . just get out of my life, bitch.

Theresa   Well, honestly . . .

Exit **Luka**.

Suzanne   Yeah, go and sulk. Like you always do.

Theresa *puts the kettle on again.*

Suzanne   What're you looking at?

Theresa   I'm not saying any more.

Suzanne   You're giving me that judgemental look. Like you're the perfect mother . . .

Theresa   Oh I know I'm not perfect. Unlike some people.

Suzanne   Yeah, right. Blame me. He's so . . . he can be so bloody difficult. You don't have to live with him.

Theresa   Neither do you if it's not working.

Suzanne   It's not his fault. He's had a hard time . . . and he's at that age he thinks he knows it all.

Theresa   You were like that. And still are.

Suzanne   If I'm fucked-up, it's how you made me. You and Dad.

Theresa   We stayed together for your sake.

Suzanne   And made us all fucking miserable.

Theresa   If you didn't swear so –

Suzanne   Oh yeah, it would make everything alright wouldn't it?

Theresa   At least you'd be setting that boy some kind of example.

Suzanne   I swear a lot more since he's been around . . . maybe he does too. But so what? Luka and me – we swear and spit and scream, so what? We've got a lot to be pissed-off about.

Theresa   You don't know when you're well-off.

Suzanne   Well-off! Why don't you ever listen to yourself, Mum?

Theresa   You've got a roof over your heads.

Suzanne   Have you seen it? My roof? No, you haven't. You haven't cos it's three floors up and there's two of them floors between it and me. One with a fucking demented cow who plays her fucking Steps CDs all night and the other with a mad bloke who just screams and cries . . . leaves his windows open and screams blue fucking murder, night and day.

Theresa   You should move.

Suzanne   Yeah right. Go down the estate agents and say yeah I'll have that one – the nice semi, with conservatory and reception rooms. What the fuck's a reception room? Somewhere where you listen to your neighbour's bloody radio reception all fucking night?

I even went and got a job, Mum. Another one. You'd think I'd have learnt by now, wouldn't you? Course I lost my benefits, and no contract, no minimum wage, but what can I expect? What use are fucking A levels anyway? They've never done me any good have they? So there I am in a city coffee bar, making coffees, all kinds of bloody coffees – as quick as possible. And you've got to make them just right – just a drop too much milk and a macchiato becomes a latte and you can bet your life the customer's gonna notice and give you hell. First day I scald my wrist so bad the skin just peeled off like it was plaster. The supervisor says I'm working too slow, starts standing right behind me . . . and pressing his fucking little dick against my arse. I tell him he's looking to get a premium expresso burning his beans. But if it wasn't him, it was the hordes of city tossers, trying to tug my thong every time I reached over to wipe a table. But I put up with the verbal, the groping, the whole fucking lot, cos I needed the money, needed to move from that shitty flat. Then Joanna says Luka's not going to school. 'Maybe you should try to be there for him a little more", "or maybe his needs don't fit in with your new career". "Career", yeah that was their word – my coffee-making career. So I cut down my hours, and then it wasn't worth the tube fare in.

Theresa   Perhaps after Luka's moved on –

Suzanne   Moved on? He's not moving on.

Theresa   I don't mean right now, love. I mean later on . . . you'll have the chance to get another job, a better job using your A levels –

Suzanne   Shit, Mum, no one wants my fucking A levels. If you've never had anything but shit jobs you'll never get anything but shit jobs. You know that if anyone does.

Theresa   I enjoyed my job . . .

Suzanne   Even though it's left you doubled up with sciatica and blind as a bat.

Theresa   It was the people . . . being with the other girls, having a gossip and a giggle. Plus we got the seconds cut-price, and halfway decent knickers aren't cheap. But it was the women that made the job, the friendship. That's where you miss out. I think you're a bit isolated in London really. . . .

Suzanne   I've got my friends.

Theresa   I just think . . . it'd be nice if you met someone again. Someone special.

Suzanne   Special? Oh I've met some really special guys, Mum. So special, you've no bloody idea.

Theresa   Maybe you're just not looking in the right place.

Suzanne   I'm not looking at all. They find me. Like fleas find a fucking dog.

Theresa   You just need someone nice . . .

Suzanne   Nice like Andy?

Theresa   You thought he was Mr Right at the time . . .

Suzanne   I married him cos I wanted to get away from . . . from here.

Theresa   That's not true. You were in love. You were, Suzanne.

Suzanne   When he saw me struggling to pitch my tent, came to help and made a complete fucking cack of it cos he was so stoned, I thought he was wildest man at Glastonbury. Two years later he's like software sales bore of the century. I'm waking up next to Mr Floppy Disk and wanting to press eject.

Theresa   And now there's no one?

Suzanne   Not at the moment, no. I'm picky.

Theresa   Well, nothing wrong with that I suppose . . .

Suzanne   Shame you weren't a bit more picky yourself.

Theresa   If you mean your father . . . we weren't so badly suited . . . we made the best of what we had . . .

Suzanne   Even if that wasn't very much.

Theresa   If he hadn't had that crash, and hit his head . . . if that hadn't changed him . . . I'm sure we'd still be together.

Suzanne   Well thank fuck for black ice.

Theresa   Suzanne!

Pause.

Look, don't jump down my throat, but have you ever thought at all about joining a dating agency?

Suzanne   You're a loopy old bag sometimes.

Theresa   Think you'll always be young?

Suzanne   I'm not young, Mum. (*Pause.*) So what about this picnic then? A picnic at Beachy Head.

Theresa   I didn't think you were very –

Suzanne   Come on. Are you gonna get ready? Put your best frock on like you always used to, so you can get grass stains and dog shit on it and moan all the way home. We should buy a football on the way. And have you still got my kite! Let's take the kite.

Theresa   I . . . I gave it to Help the Aged.

Suzanne   Fucking hell.

Theresa   It'd got the moth anyway. But I think we've got a football . . . and I could make some sandwiches if you do really want to go . . . cucumber sarnies . . .

Suzanne *runs from the room, to shout up the stairs.*

Suzanne   Luka! Luka, we're going for a picnic!

Luka (*shouts down*)   Fuck you!

Scene Five

The shop.

Josh *is at his counter.* **Sophie** *is lounging in the doorway, playing a Craig David CD on her stereo.*

Sophie   It's a cool job, bro. Well at least you don't have to wear a poncey uniform, like Calum does at the Co-op. And you don't have a boss breathing down your neck most of the time.

Josh   Yeah, but how long before they catch him out?

Sophie   How can he spend his whole life in the bookies? That is so monotonous. And like totally irresponsible. He must be losing so much money . . .

Josh   – Just to get the girl behind the counter to speak to him – that's *so* lame. Still at least he gets free coffee. What do I get here?

Sophie   You eat the pic 'n' mix.

Josh   Only the raspberry and coconut truffles. Otherwise I just stand here all bloody day.

Sophie   You get paid for it. If you want a really shit job you should try the morning paper round.

Josh   I used to do the free paper.

Sophie   Stuffing, like, the whole lot under a shrub in someone's garden. That's not, like, work.

Josh   All this standing around is, I don't know, it's starting to bug me.

Sophie   You get to read all the magazines. You can just stand there looking at Gail Porter in a thong and get paid for it.

Josh   Badly paid for it.

Sophie   So why don't you leave school then? Get a full-time job . . . though nobody'll pay you very much cos you're not interested in anything that pays.

Josh   It's not just computer programmers that get rich, Soph. But I wasn't talking about leaving school – just getting a job with more social hours . . .When I think I could be out there . . . Friday night, Saturday . . . My life's drifting away.

Sophie   Girls come in sometimes . . .

Josh   When you're not standing in the doorway, squeezing your spots.

Sophie   Fuck you. And you met that woman last night.

Josh   I told you that's, like, a non-subject.

Sophie   Yeah but –

Josh   A non-subject.

Sophie   You think she'll come in again today?

Pause.

A quid says she won't.

Pause.

You really want to see her again, don't you? Your older lady.

Pause.

She's got a kid she said. She's probably, like, married.

Josh   She's divorced. Anyway, I told you I'm not discussing it.

Enter **Luka**, *approaching the shop.*

Josh   Shit. It's the homicidal hedgehog killer.

Sophie   You what?

Josh   A psycho, Sophie. If he comes in, don't look at him, right?

Avoid eye contact.

Luka *comes in.* **Sophie** *looks intently at her stereo.* **Luka** *walks up to the counter.*

Luka   Did my mum leave some shopping here last night?

Josh *stares at him.*

Luka   About three quid's worth. She says she'd paid for it, then forgot it. It'll be in two carrier bags, one inside the other, cos she always thinks they're gonna split.

Josh   Oh . . .

Luka *wanders to the fridge, takes a can of Red Bull.*

Josh   The police are looking for you. This shop takes assault on its employees very seriously.

Luka   Come here.

Josh   I'll press the panic button.

Luka   Have you got the shopping or not?

Josh   I have . . . but you see, there's a rule . . . there's a rule isn't there, Sophie?

Sophie   Like, how would I know?

Luka *looks at* **Sophie**, *she looks at him.*

Josh   The customer has to claim it herself. In person.

Luka *looks under the counter.*

Josh   It's not there. It's in the safe.

Luka   Open it.

Josh   I can't do that unless she signs for the goods in person.

Luka   I can do her signature.

Josh   There's like this alarm on the safe, isn't there, Sophie?

Sophie   Uhuh.

Luka *looks at* **Sophie**.

Josh   It alerts the police.

Luka   Your nose looks like shit, man. Like a fucking squashed tomato.

Luka *wanders to the door, walks past* **Sophie**.

Luka   Want Craig David to fill you in, huh?

Luka *beckons to someone off outside.*

Luka (*shouts*)   Mum! The kid says you've gotta, like, come in and sign for it.

Turn the fucking stereo down.

Sophie *does.*

Luka   Not you, sweetness. (*To* **Suzanne**, *off.*) Turn the fucking car stereo down, if you can't hear me.

He exits.

Sophie *goes to* **Josh**.

Sophie   Do you know him?

Josh   It was him that gave me this.

He indicates his nose

Sophie (*a little impressed*)   Yeah?

Enter **Suzanne**, *in a summer dress (and still wearing those DMs).* **Josh** *is visibly affected.*

Josh (*to* **Sophie**)   Beat it, Soph.

Sophie   Josh . . .

Josh   Disappear.

Sophie *smiles at* **Suzanne**.

Sophie   Hi ya.

She saunters off among the shelves.

Josh   I'll . . . just get your shopping.

He scurries off to the back of the shop. **Suzanne** *picks up a bag of jelly babies, then goes behind the counter to take a packet of cigarettes. She hesitates, then pockets them. She looks at the front of her dress, hesitates, checks* **Josh***'s not watching and puts them down her front.* **Josh** *comes back with* **Suzanne***'s shopping.*

Suzanne   Your nose looks like shit.

Josh   Thanks.

Pause.

Josh   He . . . he's your son?

Suzanne   Foster son.

Josh   Oh.

Suzanne   Does this pay?

Josh   What?

Suzanne   I oughta try and get another job.

She presses a couple of buttons on the till.

Oh, how does this one open?

Josh (*smiling*)   Are you gonna rob it?

She smiles.

It's like this.

He opens the till.

Suzanne   Yeah, like in the coffee shop. That's what I used to do. Sell coffee. Boring as shit. I wouldn't mind working in a pet shop . . . or a florist maybe. Arranging bunches of flowers for people, that would keep you cheerful, wouldn't it?

Josh   And wreaths for funerals?

Suzanne   Oh yeah, that'd be a bit of a downer. Perhaps that's not the job for me. What about a CD shop?

Josh   They're still called record shops.

Suzanne   Thanks, Mr Fucking Know-all. Whatever happened to trade descriptions?   How can they call it a record shop if it only sells CDs? I just gotta find some kind of job. Something that's not all stress or heavy lifting. You sell books in here?

Josh *gestures to a rack.*

Josh   Bargain ones. Shite mostly.

Suzanne   Is there any of those 'Change Your Life' ones?

Josh   There's one on learning to look into the future I think. We've had that for years.

Suzanne   I don't want to know about the future, not at the moment. Not 'til I've done something about making things right for him.

Josh   Him?

She gestures towards the door.

Suzanne   Him.

Uneasy pause. **Josh** *goes back to the till, closes it.*

Suzanne   I paid you last night, didn't I?

Josh   What? – Yeah. You did.

He hands her the shopping.

Suzanne. (*Pause.*) Can I see you again?

Suzanne   No. No, I don't think so.

A car horn. She hesitates. Then leans over the counter to kiss **Josh**. *She means it just to be a little one, but it doesn't work out that way. They part, she leaves.*

Exit **Suzanne**.

Sophie *looks out from behind the shelf.*

Sophie   Wow.

Josh   Shut it.

Sophie   Romance.

Josh   Yeah? Fuck off.

Sophie   He's blushing. Got an erection?

Josh   Don't you have some place to go?

Sophie   He has. He's hiding it behind the counter.

She goes to the window.

Crap car they've got.

Josh   Get away from the fucking window.

Sophie   I'm not nosing. They've gone now anyway. (*Beat.*) There was a message for you on the machine.

Josh   . . . from her?

Sophie   From Dee-Ann.

Josh   Right.

Sophie   You've so many girls, Josh. Such a *stud.*

Josh   Just fuck off, right?

Sophie   I could tell 'em some stuff about you – like that you have to spray your trainers with deodorant, and you never clean your teeth . . .

Josh   You're such a child, Sophie.

Sophie   And like how old do you think you are, Mr Maturity? Just cos you've been to bed with a *woman*. (*Beat.*) But you can't really go out with her if she's that guy's mum, can you?

Josh   She's not his real mum.

Sophie   If she's his step-mum then.

Josh   Foster mum.

Sophie   She's loads too old for you anyway. And if she didn't say she wants to see you again . . . and she didn't, did she? (*Pause.*) Then I don't see there's anything you can do.

Josh   When I want advice I won't ask a fucking virgin.

Sophie   What makes you think I'm still –

Josh   Because nobody'd ball a spotty geek girl.

Sophie   I'm not spotty. Okay, it was a problem, but I tackled it.

Josh   Fuck, you sound exactly like Mum sometimes.

Sophie   Better than sounding like Dad.

Josh   Why don't you go back to live at Mum's?

Sophie   Just so you can take over the attic? I ain't having you up there. And I've passworded the whole system now.

Josh   Like I'm oh so interested in American boys who e-mail and tell you they look like Brad Pitt. – Like Brad Pitt after his billionth burger.

Sophie   He's not the only guy I chat online with. There's Cody, who's from Tampa, and he scanned in these pics of him surfing . . .

Josh   So why don't you piss off to America then?

Sophie   I might do. I might go to college there or something.

Josh   Yeah, right.

Sophie   Mr James says I could. With the extra tuition he's giving me.

Josh   Swot.

Sophie   You only think that's an insult cos you're so under-motivated, Josh. Swot is the new cool.

Josh (*not convinced*)   Yeah, right.

Sophie   The thing is to stay focused. That's what Mr James says.

Josh   Did him a lot of good didn't it? Teaching at our school – he's really got a long way in the world.

Sophie   He says he thinks it's really worthwhile, helping us get on.

Josh   He doesn't help me.

Sophie   Cos you're a dreamer. You're beyond help, Josh.

Josh   Dee-Ann had ambitions. And what is she – a secretary.

Sophie   At least she's got keyboard skills. She can build on those later if she wants to . . .

Josh   'Buil on those later' – hello, it's the mobile careers lesson, coming to a convenience store near you.

Sophie   You've just got to make the most of your opportunities haven't you? (*Beat.*) What're you gonna do if Dee-Ann finds out about the woman?

Josh   She won't.

Sophie   I'm saying what if she does?

Josh   I'll finish with her.

Sophie   The woman?

Josh   Dee-Ann.

Sophie   I can see all kinds of problems, if you get involved with the woman.

Josh   Yeah, well why don't you go on Jerry Springer and tell everyone all about it?

Sophie   It'll all end in tears, Josh . . .

Josh   Yeah, yeah, just cos you can't get laid.

Sophie   It's not you she wants, she's just desperate for it.

Josh   What?

Sophie   Women need sex more as they get old. I read a survey.

Josh   She's not *old*. And she's not desperate. It's no good talking to you about it, you won't understand.

He takes a beer from the fridge, opens and swigs from it.

Sophie   Drinking the stock again. (*Beat.*) Look, just admit it's never gonna work out. You and the woman.

Josh   Her name is Suzanne.

Sophie   I'm just saying it won't work, so it's no good getting in a state about it.

Josh   I'm not getting in a state about anything.

Sophie   You're drinking and it's not, like, afternoon yet. (*Pause.*)

Why did he hit you? Her foster son.

Josh   He's a psychopath.

Sophie   What did you say to him?

Josh   Nothing. I told you.

Sophie   You must've said something to make him hit you.

He swigs the beer.

Sophie   You'll end up an old piss-head like Dad.

Josh   Oh just fuck off out of it, Soph. Go and bother someone else. Go back to your lardy yanks on the internet.

He walks off among the shelves, still drinking.

I've work to do.

Sophie *turns to leave.*

Sophie   Fine. Enjoy your life in Loser-ville.

She exits.

Scene Six

Beachy Head.

Ned *and* **Theresa** *are sitting on the grass, looking at the sky.* **Ned** *wears sunglasses.* **Theresa** *is in a summer dress and cardi.*

Theresa   I can hear a lark but I can't see him.

Ned   There. Look.

Theresa   You can see him? The sun's in my eyes.

Ned *puts his sunglasses on her face.*

Ned   There.

Theresa   Can't see a bleedin' thing. Your eyes are much better than mine. Too many years spent squinting over a sewing machine.

She hands him his sunglasses back. **Suzanne** *and* **Luka** *race by, kicking a football between them.*

Theresa   Keep away from that edge!

Exit **Suzanne** *and* **Luka**.

Theresa   That takes me back. We'd always come up here with the kids in the summer. A car full of little boys – ours and their friends. Even Suzanne's friends were mostly boys. We'd set up cricket stumps, play rounders . . . I could never hit the bloody ball . . . Did you ever use to come up here?

Ned   Once or twice maybe. We used to play cricket on the beach though. On Beach Green. You know, along by Goring.

Theresa   Oh course, you were living out that way when yours were small. A bit of a long drive out here wasn't it?

Ned   And Helen was nervous of heights.

Theresa   Was she? I thought you used to go mountaineering.

Ned   No. Hill walking.

Theresa (*laughing*)   I used to imagine the pair of you scaling the heights with ropes and what are those things? Cramp ons? I used to think you were so intrepid.

Ned (*smiling*)   Well, I'm sorry to disappoint you.

Theresa   Hill walking sounds nice though. Where'd you go?

Ned   Oh all over. The Pennines, Cumbria, North Wales . . .

Theresa (*laughing*)   Anywhere with hills basically? I wish we'd had a hobby like that – something we could do together as a family . . . Your three must've love it.

Ned   Well . . . they did when they were very small. . . Later the girls used to say they'd rather go to a holiday camp – for the discos mainly, I think, and then it was, 'Why can't we go to Lanzarote, Dad?'

Theresa   But Michael, he must've loved it . . .

Ned   He was never an outdoors type really. Always whining that his feet hurt, he was cold or something had bitten him.

Theresa   Still it was doing them good. All in the fresh air.

Slightly awkward pause. She offers him a jelly baby from the packet.

Ned   No thanks.

Suzanne   Not got much of a sweet tooth, have you?

Enter **Suzanne** *and* **Luka** *(carrying the football).*

Suzanne   Ow! Something's stung me. Look.

Theresa *shares a smile with* **Ned**. **Suzanne** *and* **Luka** *flop down.*

Suzanne   A wasp's stung me.

Luka   It's nettle rash.

Suzanne   No, it fucking hurts. Look, Mum.

Theresa   I can't see anything.

Suzanne   You might if you wore your bloody glasses.

Theresa   Can't see with 'em, can't see without 'em.

Suzanne   Well, you need a new pair don't you?

Theresa   Can't afford 'em can I? Not every couple of years.

Ned   They do some quite good two-pairs-for-the-price-of-one offers now.

Theresa   Be alright if I could afford the price of the one pair to start with.

She gets up.

Well, I don't know about you lot but I'm about ready for the picnic.

Suzanne *is rubbing her leg.*

Luka   Don't rub it.

Ned   I'll help you carry it over shall I?

Theresa   Shall we sit here, or is the grass a bit wet?

Suzanne   Sit here.

Ned   We can always sit on our coats.

Exit **Theresa** *and* **Ned**.

Luka *slaps* **Suzanne***'s hand off her leg.*

Luka   Leave it alone. Do you want to get blood poisoning?

Suzanne   Kiss it better.

Luka   Kiss my arse.

Suzanne   Nah. Mum might see.

She lies down.

Come here. Be my pillow.

She uses **Luka***'s chest as a pillow.*

Luka   Don't start talking about the clouds.

Suzanne   Why?

Luka   You always say look at that one, doesn't it look like this or that. When it just looks like a fucking cloud.

Suzanne   I thought you liked me talking about the clouds.

Luka   Well, now you know I don't, don't you?

Pause. He strokes her hair. She relaxes a bit.

Suzanne   I'd like to move back down here.

Pause.

Are you listening?

Luka   Don't have to answer you all the bloody time do I?

Suzanne   Would you like to live down here?

Pause.

Would you?

Luka   I don't care.

Suzanne   But if I did, right? Moved back to Brighton. Would you come? Or would you want to stay near your brother and sister?

Luka   And my friends.

Suzanne   You'd rather I didn't move then?

Luka   I didn't say that.

He moves away from under her.

It's up to you, Suzanne. You do what you wanna do. I don't know what I want. It's complicated. It keeps changing. I'll say 'yes' and then tomorrow it'll be 'no', and you'll want to give be a hard time about it.

Suzanne   I want to be with you.

He squirms back beneath her so she's leaning on him again.

Luka   You are.

Pause.

It's no good just like moving somewhere else and thinking things'll be different. I mean you move from your shitty little flat to a shitty little flat down here . . . so what? What's gonna change? How're things suddenly gonna be like wonderful? I don't get it.

Suzanne   Maybe a change would . . . change things.

Luka   What about getting a caravan? Be better than living in a flat.

With a caravan like the whole world's your garden, isn't it?

Suzanne   You want us to become travellers?

Luka   I mean a caravan in a caravan park. A big one with a proper loo and shower.

Suzanne   In a caravan park all your neighbours are old.

Luka   But you don't share walls with nobody – so you could play the Chili Peppers all night if you wanted. Leave the door open and dance in the fields.

Suzanne   Dance in the fields . . . That'd be so cool.

Luka   But not in those fucking boots.

Suzanne   Okay, so I'll rent us a caravan. Down here? Or where?

Luka   It's only a dream. You take everything so seriously.

Pause.

Suzanne   Things are serious, Luka. Things are more serious than you can know.

She reaches behind her to feel where he is.

Where are yer?

She touches his leg.

Luka   Don't.

Suzanne   Why?

Luka   You know why.

Suzanne   No I don't.

Luka   They'll be back in a minute, and I'll be lying back here with my dick pointing straight at the fucking clouds.

Suzanne   Now's who's talking about clouds?

Luka   Oh, like, pardon me a minute, Mr Bisset, while my foster- mum sucks me off.

Suzanne   When I wanted you to call me Mum, you wouldn't, would you?

Luka   Sorry, Mum.

Suzanne *gets up.*

Suzanne   Don't.

Luka   What? What is it? Mum.

Suzanne   I've been trying to pick my moment . . . or maybe I've been trying to avoid it . . . Fuck it there's never gonna be a right moment.

Luka *gets up, starts kicking the football around.*

Luka   A right time to tell me what? You love me? I know, I know. Say 'I love you, motherfucker.' 'I fucking love you.'

Suzanne *kicks the ball violently away.*

Luka   What the –

Suzanne   I'm having your baby.

Pause.

Luka   Wow.

He stares at her. Pause.

Suzanne   Is that all you're gonna say?

Luka   Yeah. Yeah it is. Shit.

Blackout.

Act Two

Scene One

Beachy Head.

After the picnic. The picnic cloth is spread with paper plates and other debris.

Ned *and* **Theresa** *are walking along the cliff edge.*

Luka *and* **Suzanne** *are drinking beers.* **Suzanne** *is smoking a spliff.*

Suzanne   You're so . . . I don't know . . . philosophical about it. I'd been going crazy wondering how to tell you, whether to tell you . . . trying to imagine what you'd say.

Pause.

I was scared you'd leave me.

Luka   It's one of those things . . . that's both good and bad at once.

Suzanne   Can you imagine what it's gonna be like, being a dad?

Luka   Pushing a three-wheeled buggy down the Broadway? Unless you move back down here that is.

Suzanne   I move? Not we move?

Luka   We move. As long as it's a caravan, not a shitty flat.

Suzanne   I don't know how it happened . . .

Luka (*sarkily*)   Really?

Suzanne   I should've been more careful . . . I mean I never got pregnant by my husband, so I thought –

Luka   Was he shite at sex?

Suzanne   No, no . . . it was okay.

Luka   I'm better than okay aren't I?

Suzanne   Yes, dear.

Luka   Three times a night. I'm superb.

Suzanne   Wait 'til you're thirty.

Luka   I'll keep fit. Keep in practice. (*Pause.*) Were you faithful? To randy Andy?

Suzanne (*looking away, i.e. lying*)   Yeah.

Luka   I don't think I could be.

Suzanne   You're young.

Luka   You don't like it when I look at girls.

Suzanne   Can't stop you though, can I?

Luka   Nope.

Suzanne   I wish I was still sixteen.

Luka   I wish I was your age.

Suzanne   Do you? No, you don't . . . it's not much fun.

Luka   I won't be poor like you. I'm gonna make a success of myself. Run a business. Sell mobile phones or something. I saw a bloke who'd done that on 'Working Breakfast'. He was raking it in.

Suzanne   You see me as a failure don't you?

Luka   No . . . not really.

Suzanne   How're you gonna become a businessman? Without money?

Luka   I'll go to college.

Suzanne   I went to college. It didn't get me anywhere.

Luka   Maybe you took the wrong things then. Took exams in things nobody wants.

Suzanne   It's people like us nobody wants. Look at people in top jobs – are they like us? Do you actually know anyone in a top job?

Luka   I've met my social worker's boss. He's got a Mercedes . . . .Someone at my school's brother plays for QPR.

Suzanne   I'm not saying you shouldn't be ambitious. When I came out of college I really tried. I didn't know exactly what I wanted to do . . . work in a museum or an art gallery, that would've been nice. Looking after the exhibitions and answering people's questions. But there's only one museum in Brighton and they didn't want me. So I tried for office jobs. Got taken on at the Inland Revenue. A rewarding career, they said. 'With us the sky's the limit' they told me at the interview. But when I asked about promotion it was: 'Oh we don't need any more administrators right now.' You couldn't even get to the second rung. To get to the top you needed to come in much higher up. Unless you can afford to go to university, unless you have contacts, you're fucked. I did apply for some other jobs where they ask for A levels but didn't get past the interview. You're up against the posh kids – dressed up to the nines, taught to be confident and how to behave in interviews. You don't stand a chance . . .

Pause.

If I can do anything to help you get a good a start in business I will – anything. But at the moment I can't see how it's gonna happen.

Luka   Least you'll get kid's allowance won't you? (*Beat.*) Have you been thinking about names? It's really important we pick something good. Not one every other bloody kid's got, and nothing embarrassing.

Suzanne   I've not really started to think . . . of it as a him or a her.

Luka Well, you got to.

Suzanne I'm still finding it really difficult to believe it.

Luka The doctor's certain?

Suzanne Yeah, I know it's for real . . . I just don't feel . . . like a proper mother. I know I've fostered a few kids, but only bigger kids . . . the youngest was twelve, I've felt more like . . . a big sister I suppose. . . . That's how I saw you to begin with . . . like a younger brother really. There was nothing sexual at all . . .

Luka Not from your side . . .

Suzanne I know you say you fancied me from day one, but I didn't have any inkling. Didn't feel it. It wasn't until you had a friend from school round – that girl with the short black bob . . .

Luka Melissa?

Suzanne . . . And the big nose . . .

Luka Melissa.

Suzanne You were flirting with her . . . sitting on the sofa watching *Gladiator* I was shocked to realise I was jealous. But I still think nothing would've happened . . . I'd have been able to fight it . . . if I hadn't got wasted a couple of weeks later and you had to put me to bed. If you'd then gone to your own bed . . .

Luka . . . And I would've if you'd have shut up, not kept going, 'Stay here', 'Don't leave me' . . . But then you were out like a light anyway.

Suzanne Yeah, but the next morning . . .

Luka Weren't nobody's fault. It just happened.

Suzanne I still feel kind of maternal towards you. I know it's fucked-up but there it is.

Luka I'd be in trouble if people knew?

Suzanne You wouldn't. I would.

Luka I know you would. You're a very bad girl. They might lock you up.

Suzanne I'd leave the country.

Luka To go where?

Suzanne I don't know. Somewhere warm. Brazil.

Luka I wouldn't let you. I don't want my baby growing up in Brazil. (*Pause.*) You'll have to stop drinking and smoking, Suze.

Suzanne This is my last spliff.

Luka You're getting our kid stoned.

Suzanne It's not big enough yet. This is my last boozing session.

Luka   You'll have to wear tent dresses.

Suzanne   I will not. I'm not gonna be that big.

Luka   You should tell your mum. I don't mean tell her it's mine – just tell her.

Suzanne   Make up a boyfriend?

Luka   Say he was someone you're not seeing anymore. Same as you'll tell the socials.

Suzanne   They won't suspect anything will they?

Luka   Course not.

Suzanne   You sure you won't just let it slip out?

Luka   I'm not stupid. I tell 'em as little as possible about my life y'know. They ask me about drugs and I'm, like, 'no, never', and they know I've never been nicked for anything . . . except breaking my mum's windows, so I mean I'm the least of their worries. I mean there's other guys Joanna has to deal with doing all kinds of shit.

Suzanne   Joanna's always been really friendly to me. Sometimes I almost forget and want to tell her things. You know when she asks how everything's going.

Luka   She says, 'How're you finding things at Suzanne's? Is that still working out for you.' I go "fine, yes", she goes like, 'Is there anything you want to talk about?' and I'm like 'no'. That's how you gotta be.

Suzanne   When you're eighteen, I guess we can be open about things if we want.

Luka   We're probably have another two kids by then.

Suzanne   We fucking won't! I'm going back on the pill. The extra-strong variety.

Luka   Yeah, you're going out to work. I don't want my baby living in your crummy flat. You gotta afford to live something nice.

Suzanne   What about you?

Luka   I've already got a job.

Suzanne   A Saturday job.

Luka   Yeah, that's all I can do if I'm going to college, innit. You should work, Suze. What's the problem with that? Even if you don't get promoted, Least we'd have some money – for nice stuff for the baby. You could get another office job. You've experience.

Suzanne   It's all changed though. I was just doing filing. Now it's all on computer. And I don't know one end of a computer from t'other.

Luka   You must've done that at school.

Suzanne   They didn't have computers when I was at school.

Luka *laughs.*

Luka   Yeah right. Like they hadn't been invented.

Suzanne   I don't mean that – I mean we didn't have lessons on how to use them.

Luka   I can show you. We can get one.

Suzanne   If we could afford it.

Luka   Get a cheap one. It's worth it if we're gonna get you a job.

Suzanne   While you're stopping home with the baby?

Luka   While I'm at college. If we move back down here your mum can look after it. Your mum and Mr Bisset.

Suzanne   That's not gonna work out.

Luka   She must like babies, she brought up you and your brothers didn't she?

Suzanne   I mean her and Mr Bisset's not gonna work out.

Luka   Give 'em a chance. Why don't you think it'll work?

Suzanne   He's nice. I like him . . . But I think they're both very different.

Luka   So?

Suzanne   I think he still misses his wife. Like big-time.

Pause. **Luka** *gets up, plays with the football.*

Luka   Scully would love it up here. I'm gonna get her back. Even if I have to go and, like, break in to me mum's when she's out.

Suzanne   When your mum rang up, I told her I'd sue her if she didn't give her back.

Luka   It's too slow. I've had enough with courts. It's pathetic. They'd like say Mum's got a garden and we haven't. Like that's what matters. Mum never takes Scully out, never fucking walks her. Just leaves her to shit in the garden then sticks flower pots over it.

Suzanne   Your mum could do with the exercise.

Luka   Fat bitch. – You're gonna be a fat bitch too soon.

Suzanne   Fuck off.

Luka   And don't swear in front of the baby. We'll be there at the clinic or whatever and everyone else's baby'll be going goo, goo, Ma Ma, and ours'll be, like, 'Fuck you, arsehole'.

Suzanne   I'm not being the one changing all the nappies.

Luka   No, your mum is.

Suzanne *suddenly jumps up.*

Suzanne   Mum! – Get away from the edge!

Theresa (*off*)   I'm not at the edge.

Suzanne   Famous last words. It can crumble you know. Lots of people have been caught out and gone over. (*To* **Luka**.) Dozy old cow.

Luka   Can you like survive it?

Suzanne   Only if you get stuck on a ledge or something. If it breaks your fall. I suppose as Mr Bisset's a mountaineer he could rescue her.

Luka   Thought he was a coach driver.

Suzanne   Mountains are his hobby. That and collecting maps.

Luka (*sarcastic*)   Collecting maps? Wow, how exciting.

Suzanne   Shhh. He can't help it.

Ned *and* **Theresa** *come over.*

Theresa   I could stay up here all day.

Luka   If there wasn't the football on telly at seven.

Ned   You had enough of the great outdoors?

Luka   It's not the same without my dog.

He gets up.

Theresa   Ned and I have got something to tell you two. Haven't we?

Pause.

Suzanne   Have you?

Theresa   We've decided to go on holiday together . . .

Suzanne   That it? Thought you were gonna tell us you were getting married or something.

Theresa   Suzanne. That . . . that would be a bit hasty wouldn't it . . .

Suzanne   Least I won't have to buy a bloody hat.

Luka   You'd have to be bridesmaid.

Suzanne   I would not!

Luka   Bridesmaid in fucking DMs.

Theresa   We're talking about a holiday, that's all.

Suzanne   Where you going?

Ned   Snowdonia.

Luka   Been there.

Suzanne   Have you?

Luka   School field trip. For geography. It was all map reading and stuff.

Suzanne *gives* **Luka** *a nudge.*

Theresa   Was it nice? Snowdon.

Luka   S'alright. Mountains and that. Are we gonna go back to yours now then?

Theresa   You're in a bit of hurry aren't you?

Luka   Too much fresh air always gets me depressed.

Theresa *and* **Ned** *walk back towards where they've parked the car.* **Luka** *hesitates, kicking the football.* **Suzanne** *waits for him.*

Suzanne   Depressed?

Luka   Just thinking of my responsibilities.

Suzanne   The baby?

Luka   The baby, you and Scully.

Suzanne   Is Scully alright with kids?

Luka   Yeah . . . well, I guess so. . . I mean she's never been around a baby . . .

Suzanne   So what – neither have I. My older brother's got kids but I didn't see much of them when they were really tiny.

Luka   But you've like fostered other kids.

Suzanne   Big kids. There's a lot more can go wrong with a baby. It's scarey – the responsibility. I mean you can't just like go out and forget to feed it.

Luka   You won't forget – it'll cry when it's hungry. Complete idiots manage to bring up babies, Suze.

Suzanne (*sarkily*)   Well, thanks for the vote of confidence.

Luka   They're waiting for us.

He starts to walk off.

Suzanne   Luka . . . . . .if I was ill or something . . . you'd look after the baby?

Luka   Yeah, stop worrying, Suzanne. Come on.

He exits. Still thoughtful, **Suzanne** *follows.*

Scene Two

Theresa'*s kitchen. Morning.*

Theresa *and* **Ned** *stand close together looking at a glossy coffee-table book with pictures of Mount Snowdon. An open map is beside them.*

Ned   3560 feet above sea level.

Theresa   How high's Beachy Head?

Ned   Only 500 or so feet.

Theresa   How come you remember stuff like that? You must have a head like an encyclopaedia.

Ned   I've always been interested in general knowledge. And it's useful if we're stuck in traffic. You can tell the passengers some facts and figures about the scenery we're no longer passing. If you don't they all suddenly decide they need the loo. Old ladies are the worst.

Theresa   I'm glad that map was worth having, the Dunoon one.

Ned   Ellis Martin's one of my favourite illustrators. He often featured a car and used his family as models. Must of been a nice day out for them, while he was painting. Little works of art his map covers were – mini-masterpieces for three shillings.

Theresa   My parents used to holiday in Scotland, before the war came along and stopped all that. Suppose they must've had a drawer full of maps, but I never saw them. Maps aren't something you ever chuck away though are they? You always think you'll go back to a place, even if you never do.

Enter **Luka**.

Theresa   You're up early.

Luka   So are you two.

Theresa   When you get older it's harder to sleep. Too much going on in your head.

Ned   Yes there's no point in just lying around worrying . . . remembering what you used to have . . .

Theresa *looks at him.*

Ned   . . . just got to get on with it, haven't you? (*Pause.*)

He checks his watch.

Thanks for breakfast, Theresa.

Theresa   Not got to go already have you?

Ned   Afraid I have. Unless I want a load of irate WI ladies gunning for me. Should be home around fourish though.

Theresa   Oh, oh right. Well, pop in then if you want, er . . . safe journey.

He hesitates then goes and kisses her. They enjoy it, oblivious to **Luka** *who is amused. As they part, he applauds.*

Ned   I'll be back for the encore later. See you, Theresa.

He exits.

Luka   Result. You finally got a shag!

Theresa   Shhhh.

Luka   Good was it?

Theresa *turns the pages of the book, pretending to be engrossed in the mountain pictures.*

Luka   Okay, okay, we won't go there.

He puts some cornflakes in a dish. He sniffs the milk.

Theresa   Everything's fresh. You're not at Suzanne's.

Luka   Where you like unleash a plague every time you open the fridge.

Theresa   I keep saying I'll come up and stay for a couple of days but I don't know if I could stand it.

Luka   When I have kids I'll teach 'em to clean up after themselves.

Theresa   I did. Suzanne didn't used to be so . . . you know . . . before she was ill . . .

Luka   Ill? Oh her breakdown. She was a tidy girl before that?

Theresa   She told you about what happened?

Luka   I've had a breakdown too. When I was twelve. I was back at my mum's and she had this really weird boyfriend. I got all paranoid about him. Thought he was gonna like try to kill me. I joined all these self-defence-type classes, bought big knives and stuff. Even started digging a pit in the garden to put him in.

Theresa   Oh my God . . .

Luka   So now he's under the patio, with geraniums sprouting from his brains.

Theresa   Don't talk daft.

Luka   No, I rang the socials and said get me out of here before I, like, kill the bloke. So they put me in a home – I'd been there about a week and I get stabbed by some headcase. Fourteen stitches and a ruptured spleen. You should've seen the huge great fucking hole and the kind of yellow bits inside. Now that's my worst nightmare, having my guts cut out.

Theresa   You're putting me off my breakfast.

Luka   I couldn't be a woman . . . having a baby . . . in case I had to . . . you know, when they cut it out.

Theresa   A Caesarean. Two of mine came into the world that way.

Luka   Suze?

Theresa   And Jonathan. It's much the best way in my opinion.

Luka   Was your husband there? At the births.

Theresa   No. It wasn't so usual in those days.

Luka   I'd die. I couldn't watch. Disembowelment.

Enter **Suzanne**, *huddled in her dressing gown. She looks rough.*

Theresa   You're up early.

Luka   Mr Bisset finally did the business, didn't he, Mrs Garner?

Suzanne (*flatly*)   Yeah? Congratulations, Mum.

Theresa   Coffee, love? With soya milk?

Suzanne   No.

She sits down.

Theresa   You should have something . . .

Suzanne   You know I don't do breakfast.

Theresa   Every healthy living article you read . . . every one says the meal you should never miss is breakfast.

Luka   Miss breakfast – you die.

Suzanne   I'm just not hungry okay? Jesus, why do you have to get at me all the time?

Theresa   Nobody's getting –

Suzanne   Just leave me alone.

Theresa   Suzanne . . .

Pause.

Suit yourself.

She exits.

Luka *puts his hand on* **Suzanne***'s arm.*

Suzanne   Not got a fag have you?

Luka   You can't smoke anymore.

Suzanne   Shhh.

She checks **Theresa** *is out of the room.*

Suzanne   I feel a bit rough, y'know? Shaky.

Luka   You look it.

Suzanne   Look my age? Thanks. Didn't sleep at all last night.

Luka   Thinking of me?

Suzanne   Yeah.

Luka   So why didn't you come in? Your mum was round Mr Bisset's getting a shag.

Suzanne   Don't.

Luka   What?

Suzanne   It's kind of gross thinking about it . . . I mean she's my mother.

Luka   And you're my mother. And my baby's mother.

Suzanne   Don't, Luka.

Luka   Was that what was keeping you awake? Thinking about the baby.

Suzanne   No. No, I was thinking . . . but about other things . . .

Luka   Me too. 'Bout what Mr Bisset was saying to me last night . . .

Suzanne   Yeah, what were you two nattering about?

Luka   College. Business courses. NVQs. He said you can, like, phone up a lot of different colleges and they'll send you details. I was thinking about that . . . thinking where I might go.

Suzanne   . . . Right.

Luka   His son Michael did this business course and now he's got a top sales job – He's like flying off to meetings in New York all the time.

Suzanne   Would you like that?

Luka   To go to New York? And like all over the world – flying business class.

Suzanne   Nice work if you can get it.

Luka   And I can, if I get the right qualifications. It's not like trying to get a job in a museum, Suze, that maybe employs five people. There's always work in business. Lots of well-paid work. I can see myself at college, I was just lying back and imagining it. (*Beat.*) So you were thinking of me, were you? Thinking horny thoughts . . .

Suzanne   Not really . . .

Luka   So, what were you thinking? Come on. Tell me.

Suzanne   I . . . I really do need to smoke. I'm going up the shop.

Luka   It's raining.

Suzanne   So. I'll get wet.

She fetches her jacket.

Enter **Theresa**.

Theresa   It's raining out.

Luka   She doesn't care.

Theresa   You can take my umbrella. It's by the door. Only don't lose it, it's a good one. Would you like to borrow a raincoat?

Suzanne   No, Mum, I wouldn't.

Theresa   But that jacket of yours isn't waterproof, and so thin. Couldn't get us a bag of Jelly Babies could you love?

Suzanne   What? Yeah, yeah.

Luka   And a Red Bull.

Suzanne   Mum? Can you –

Theresa   Lend you the money? There's nearly a quid's worth of change on the corner of the what-not.

Suzanne   Okay. Ta. (*Beat.*) Bye.

She exits.

Theresa   I heard her being sick in the night.

Luka   What's new? I'll look after her, Mrs Garner.

Theresa   You'll make someone a good husband one day.

Luka   Me? I don't think so.

Theresa   Do you have a girlfriend yet?

Luka   Yeah.

Theresa   Is she nice?

Luka   Mrs Garner . . . could you lend us some money?

Theresa   Well, I . . . how much do you need, love?

Luka   I mean me and Suzanne. We want to get a caravan.

Theresa   A caravan? But she don't even have a car now . . .

Luka   A live-in caravan. Down here. Suze wants to move back down here to be near you.

Theresa   She's not said anything to me.

Luka   That's cos she doesn't want to worry you . . . You see it's our flat . . . there's been a lot of break-ins in the block. It's making her really like stressed and ill. She'd like to come back down here where it's safer. (*Beat.*) Could you lend her a couple of grand?

Theresa   Oh, I don't know. I have got a little bit put by, like, but that's for when I get old . . . in case I have to go in somewhere.

Luka   You can come and live with us when you're old.

Theresa   . . . And if I gave Suzanne money, I'd have to give the boys the same amount. To be fair, see?

Luka   She needs to move somewhere nice. It's so shitty where we live. It's not just the burglars. It's damp, it stinks, there's rats, the paper's peeling, we've live fucking wires sticking out the walls . . .

Theresa   Can't the council –

Luka   They don't give a shit. If she lived somewhere nice, she'd eat properly. She wouldn't be so stressed out the whole time and I could get her to eat her breakfast. If it was quiet – no neighbours-from-hell – she wouldn't wake so early and she wouldn't be sick so much. We could go outside when we were getting on each other's tits, instead of screaming the place down. We could dance in the fields . . .

The doorbell rings.

Theresa   It'll be the milkman. He didn't call for his money last week.

Luka   You still have a milkman. Doesn't he get mugged?

Exit **Theresa**.

Luka *helps himself to more cornflakes, almost overflowing his dish. He mashes at them.*

Enter **Theresa** *carrying a bag of shopping.*

Theresa   The boy from the shop. Said we'd forgotten some more stuff. Said he must be mistaken, but he insisted. Must've been Suzanne. She'd forget her head if it wasn't screwed on.

Luka   Did he make you sign for it? He's such a wanker.

Theresa   Would you like any more . . .

She clocks the cornflake mountain.

Theresa   You must be hungry. A growing lad, eh? How about a coffee – wash it down?

Luka   No thanks, Gran.

Theresa   'Gran' is it now?

Luka   Don't you like it?

Theresa   No . . . I mean call me what you like . . . within limits of course. I'm just gonna see if I've still got that hat Suzanne left last time. She might be glad of it, weather stays like this.

Luka   When it stops, you could go to the building society, Gran.

Get us the money.

Exit **Theresa**.

Luka *gets up. He opens the bag of groceries, takes out a box of chocolates. He is surprised. In the bottom of the bag is a coloured envelope addressed 'Suzanne'. He takes it out and opens it. It contains a card. He opens it and reads it. He pockets the card and puts the chocolates back in the bag. He puts his jacket on. He goes to the kitchen drawer, takes out a carving knife. He tries it out on a (wrapped) loaf of bread. Hearing* **Theresa** *approach, he hides the knife inside his jacket.*

Enter **Theresa**.

Luka   If Mum comes back, I've just popped out a minute, okay?

Theresa   Do you want to borrow . . .

Exit **Luka**.

Theresa   . . . an umbrella?

Scene Three

Josh's *bedroom.*

Luka *barges into the room, followed by* **Sophie**.

Sophie   Hey you can't . . .! (*Shouts out the door.*) Dad!

Luka *looks around the room.*

Sophie   I told you . . . he's not here. He should be at the shop.

Luka   He's not. I been there.

Sophie   Why did you hit him?

Luka   What? He pissed me off. Looking down his fucking nose at me.

He laughs.

His fucking nose . . . the state of it.

Sophie   What do you want with him?

Pause.

I'm getting Dad to throw you out. I can't believe he let you in. Stupid pissed bastard.

Luka *takes out the little card.*

Luka (*reads*)   'Suzanne, I must see you again. I'll be at the shop all Saturday morning –'

Sophie   See?

Luka '– or you could drop by my house later maybe. In case you can't remember the address, it's . . .' – what a fucking wanker.

Pause. He puts the card away.

Did you know?

Sophie My brother and your mum? I was so shocked.

He swings round to face her.

And you know what? I think he's in love with her.

He sits down on the bed.

Sophie What're you gonna do?

Luka Wait.

Sophie *leans on the wall.*

Sophie Well you can't wait here.

Pause.

Why do you have such a problem with it anyway?

Pause.

I think it's sweet.

Pause. There is a crash, off. **Sophie** *looks out the door.*

Sophie Dad's fallen over.

She comes in and sits down on the edge of the bed. He doesn't look up.

You're crying. Are you?

She moves closer to **Luka**.

Sophie Hey . . .

Pause.

Do you wanna talk about it?

He reaches and feels the beads of the bracelet on her wrist. He looks up at her, discovering her watching him intently.

Luka You've got your brother's fucking nose.

Sophie No.

Luka And in a couple of years you'll be like your old man – too fat to get up the stairs.

Sophie Fuck off. I'm really fit.

Luka A fit girl.

Sophie   I work out. After school. See.

She flexes her (small) muscles.

And . . .

She pulls up her top, flexes her stomach.

Luka   Who do you think you are – Jennifer Lopez? Wait 'til you have to have a Caesarian.

She pulls her top down.

Sophie   A what?

Luka   Show me your tummy again.

Sophie   No.

Luka   You're shy.

Sophie   Me?

She shakes her hair back, sits back. He puts his hand under her shirt, strokes her tummy with a finger.

Luka   Your tummy's really soft.

Sophie   You've cold fingers.

He breathes on his fingers; she giggles. He brushes her cheek with them.

Luka   Warmer?

Sophie   Warmer.

He strokes her face, then kisses her. She responds eagerly. They kiss hungrily. He starts to undo her trousers.

Sophie   Don't.

Luka   What? I'm not doing anything.

He strokes her face.

Luka   Trust me.

Sophie   This is Josh's bed . . .

Luka   Did he bring her here?

Sophie   Your mum? No, no . . .

*She turns **Luka**'s face back to her.*

Sophie   I don't think so.

Luka *lifts* **Sophie**'s *t-shirt again, kisses and rubs his cheek against her tummy.*

Sophie   Dad'll go ballistic.

Luka   He'll never get his fat arse up the stairs.

*She giggles, strokes his hair. He lies her back on **Josh**'s bed and climbs on top of her.*

Sophie   We can't . . . no, I mean . . . we can't!

Luka   Can't we?

Sophie   No . . . we shouldn't . . .

Luka   It's meant to be.

Sophie   I'll get pregnant . . . hey!

Luka   Yeah, I'll use a condom, okay.

Sophie   You've gotta . . .

Luka   It'll be good, it'll be fine . . .

Sophie   You will? You better?

They continue kissing and caressing.

Luka   That's great . . . really great . . . oh hang on . . .

*Astride **Sophie**, **Luka** unzips his jacket and pulls out the carving knife. **Sophie** looks up and sees. She screams.*

Sophie   Fuck! Oh my God, no . . .

Luka *chucks the knife on the floor.*

Luka   Don't want to go disembowelling myself do I?

Sophie   Jesus. I don't believe . . .

Luka   S'alright, I'm not Jack the Ripper. I brought it to cut your brother's dick off.

Sophie   Dad'll have heard me . . .

Luka   He won't. It's okay.

He kisses her.

Sophie   If he comes up here I'll die.

Luka   Relax. There . . . You're beautiful, you're really very beautiful.

Sophie *puts up her arms to embrace him. They start making out, rather uncomfortably.*

Sophie   Luka . . . it's . . . ow . . .

Luka   It's okay, baby . . . it's fine . . .

Scene Four

The shop.

The sign on the door is turned to 'Closed'. **Suzanne** *paces outside the shop with her umbrella up.*

Enter **Josh** *with the keys.*

Suzanne   You're supposed to be open. Where've you been?

Josh (*flatly*)   Walking.

He opens the door, holds it for her. He watches her pass him and go to the shelves. He turns the shop sign to 'Open'.

Suzanne   Gotta get one or two things. Provisions.

Josh *goes behind his counter.* **Suzanne** *takes a basket and starts shopping.* **Josh** *watches.*

Josh   So? – How's it going?

Struggling with her resolve, **Suzanne**'*s thoughts aren't on shopping. She takes a loaf of bread, then another, then discards them.*

Josh   Everything okay?

Suzanne *puts a pack of sandwiches in her basket, then another, then another.*

Josh   How was the picnic? Having another one are you? – All those sandwiches.

Moving out of **Josh**'*s sight,* **Suzanne** *starts filling her basket, just picking up anything and stuffing it in.*

Josh   It's a bit rainy for picnicking today. Might clear up later, I suppose.

Pause.

Okay, you don't want to talk. Okay. But if you're trying to pretend I don't exist, if you're pretending we never happened . . .

Suzanne *emerges from behind the shelves with an overflowing basket of shopping. She staggers to the counter with it and plonks it down.*

Josh   You want all of this?

Suzanne *takes another basket and goes back to the shelves.* **Josh** *hesitates, then follows her.*

Josh   . . . Suzanne.

Suzanne *starts pulling things from the shelves, causing a massive box and can avalanche.* **Josh** *rushes over to her.*

Josh   What are you doing?

Suzanne *gathers up a handful of groceries defensively.*

Josh   You don't need all this. Three Fairy Liquids?

Josh *tries to take them, she holds on. He gives up.*

Josh   What's the matter?

Suzanne *drops the bottles in the overflowing basket she has discarded on the floor.*

Suzanne   Nothing is the matter.

She picks up some more bottles of washing-up liquid.

Josh   And I suppose I'm gonna have to put all this back.

Pause.

Is that it? Are you angry with me? Have I upset you? Was it my note?

He walks away from her.

I don't know what it is you want.

Suzanne *drops the bottles into the basket.*

Josh   What is it, Suzanne? Is it me you want? If it is, I sure fucking wish you'd tell me. Tell me one way or the other.

Pause.

What do you want?

Suzanne *takes a packet of biscuits from the shelf.* **Josh** *grabs hold of it, they struggle over it, he pulls it away from her.*

Josh   Do you want Hobnobs?

He thrusts them back at her, takes another packet of biscuits from the shelf.

Josh   Or Rich Tea Fingers?

She reaches for it. He continues to thrust packets of biscuits at her, pulling them away and trying to take those she's already clutching.

Josh   No, no you can't have them both. Or would you rather have Malted Milks?

Large or small packet? Chocolate covered or plain? Decision time, Suzanne.

How about digestives? Digestive creams? Our own brand or . . .

She grabs hold of him, shakes him.

Suzanne   I don't know what I want! You bastard, don't do this to me! I want to be happy. What's wrong with that? Mum brought me up to believe you could be poor and happy. But that's a big fucking lie. Or else there's some secret to it that I don't know. I'm thirty-five years old and I'm sliding.

She releases him.

I'm on the fucking slide.

Josh   And you what? You want me to catch you? I'll catch you, I'll stop you . . . If you tell me that's what you want. Look me in the eye and –

Suzanne   I wanted a husband, a job, a flat, a son . . . a lover . . . a baby . . . a caravan by the sea, a dog called Scully, me and Luka playing the Chili Peppers and dancing in the fields . . .

Josh   Okay, I thought you'd come here this morning because you wanted me. Okay, I was wrong.

He walks away from her.

You better go. Leave all that. I'll put it back later.

Suzanne *crouches down, looking at the basket. Pause.*

Josh   Suzanne . . .?

She ignores him. Reluctantly he returns to her. She looks up. She's crying.

Suze . . .

Suzanne (*shaky*)   Help me. I'm not going back. I'm no good for him . . .

(*She looks at* **Josh**.) I'm no good for anybody . . .

Josh   No . . . no . . .

Awkwardly he cuddles her.

It's okay . . .

Suzanne   I need to be strong. Help me be strong.

Josh   You are strong, Suze . . . You're the strongest girl . . . woman . . .

Suzanne   . . . If I stay, there's the baby – the expense, the work . . . Luka . . . he'll end up just like me – he won't get to college, or if he does – the noise, the baby crying, the looking after it, looking after me – he won't be able to do his homework, he'll have to get a job to buy all the things the baby needs, he'll fail his exams, he'll have to drop out. You don't get many chances . . . and I'm taking his chance away. Josh, don't let me go back.

She gets up.

Will you come to the station with me? Will you see me off?

Josh   Wait a minute . . . where are you going? Back home . . .

Suzanne   No. No, I know some people in . . . no I'm not gonna say. In case he finds out. I mustn't see him again. I . . .

She sobs. **Josh** *comforts her.*

Enter **Luka** *with* **Sophie**

Luka   Mum.

Suzanne   *She starts, pulls away from* **Josh**. **Luka** *catches hold of* **Sophie** *and snogs her. He stops and looks at* **Suzanne**. *For a moment she just stares, then slowly she gets up and walks towards him.*

Luka   You slag.

She slaps him.

Suzanne   I . . . I'm . . . giving up everything for you. You bastard. Bastard!

Luka   Giving up everything? What exactly have you got? Or do you mean shop boy here? You've had him haven't you bitch?

Josh   Don't call her / a bitch!

Suzanne (*indicating* **Sophie**)   / How old is she?

She looks towards **Sophie**, *then grabs* **Luka** *by the hair.*

Suzanne   She's just a kid you stupid bastard.

Luka *pushes* **Suzanne** *away from him, just holding his temper.*

Luka   Don't you. Don't, Suzanne.

Suzanne   I love you.

Josh   Oh / shit.

Sophie   / Gross.

Luka   Fuck you! Fuck you, bitch!

Sophie *goes over to* **Josh**.

Sophie   My God, Josh . . .

Suzanne   Look at me, you little shit. You're all I think about. Living with you and dancing in the fields.

Luka   Jesus.

Suzanne   . . . A caravan by the sea . . .

Luka   Did you fuck him?

Josh *is about to say something.*

Sophie   Leave it, Josh.

Suzanne   Are you listening to me?

Luka   Did you –

Suzanne   Did you fuck her? You little cunt. Why do I love you? (*Beat.*) It was never gonna work, Luka. Was it? Tell me it was never gonna work. Give me that at least.

Josh *returns to his counter.*

Suzanne   Admit that somewhere inside you knew it. . . knew that we've both been so . . .battered, so disappointed. . . and fucking shat on from the day we were born. . . that it was never gonna work. It couldn't work, no matter how hard we tried . . .

Luka   You tried? When did you try, Suzanne? It's like hallo did I miss something? When did you try to make things better? When did you try to get us some money?

Suzanne   It's not about fucking money!

Luka   You're a loser.

Suzanne   And what exactly are you?

Luka   I'm a cunt, I admit it.

Suzanne   We're both cunts. And we're having a baby. When we can't even be good to each other. What would it feel like having us as parents? Would you want to be our kid?

She walks away from him.

Would you? I know I sure as hell wouldn't. It's gonna be hell for that baby. (*Beat.*) It's not right. I shouldn't have it. I'm not having it.

Luka   You are.

Suzanne   It probably hates me already. It's probably listening right now.

Sophie   Shit . . . / you're having his . . .

Luka   / Stop it Suzanne. You're having it.

Suzanne   No, I can't, not now –

Luka   I'm not letting you get rid of our baby.

Suzanne   'Our baby' – our baby while you're out there shagging someone else's little girl? Christ, Luka, you make me sick. I must have been crazy, like really, really stupid . . .

She starts to leave.

Luka   Where are you going?

He blocks her way.

You're not killing my baby.

She tries to move past him. He pulls out his knife.

Sophie   No, Luka!

Josh *moves in front of* **Sophie** *protectively.* **Suzanne** *laughs.*

Suzanne   Whoa, that makes sense. You'll kill me and save the baby.

She rolls up her shirt, exposing her belly.

That's where it is, right there. Our little boy or girl. Why don't you cut it out and rescue it from me. You want the baby? You want the fucking baby . . . come and get it . . . come on.

Josh   Suzanne, for fuck's sake . . .

Suzanne *advances on* **Luka***, takes the knife blade in her hand, tilts it to her belly.*

Suzanne   You want to hurt me, fucking do it. You want to be the one that breaks this thing – do it, Luka.

Sophie (*to* **Josh**)   Press the alarm!

Suzanne   Gonna spill my guts? Come on.

Sophie   Josh!

Luka *is shaking. He can't look at the knife, nudging* **Suzanne***'s belly. She snatches it from him by the blade, cutting her hand. She wipes the blood on* **Luka***'s face. He is frozen in shock. Pause.*

Suzanne   A vow in blood. It's the end. I swear.

Suzanne*, looking at* **Luka***'s horrified, frightened face, drops the knife.*

Suzanne   Oh. Oh God.

She wipes **Luka***'s face.*

Suzanne   I'm sorry, baby.

She kisses her hand and plants it on her belly.

And I'm sorry, little baby.

Josh *edges forward and picks up the knife. He takes it back to the counter, takes a cloth and goes back to* **Suzanne***.*

Josh   Look – your hand.

He wraps the cloth around her hand.

You should sit down.

Sophie *brings a chair over.*

Suzanne   Luka . . .

She reaches out to him. He doesn't look at her. **Suzanne** *sits.*

Suzanne   . . . It's gonna be okay.

Josh   That's right.

Suzanne   I know what to do.

Pause.

Josh   We could have a beer.

Sophie *gives the other three a beer each. They open them and drink, in their own space and time, silent, introspective, no one wanting to break the truce.* **Suzanne** *looks at her belly, puts her hands on it.* **Luka** *snatches a glance at her while she isn't looking.* **Suzanne** *stands up.*

Suzanne   You might have a chance . . .

Luka *wipes his eyes on his sleeve, doesn't look at her.*

Suzanne   Some kind of a chance.

She walks to the counter.

I won't hurt the baby. I didn't mean . . . I couldn't. I'll look after your baby, darling. I promise.

She opens the till. **Sophie** *looks at* **Josh.**

Suzanne   I'll do the best I . . . I'll do better.

She takes out a big wad of notes.

You're right. Money matters.

She puts the money in her pocket. **Luka** *doesn't look up.*

Exit **Suzanne.**

Sophie *picks up the phone.* **Josh** *stops her.* **Luka** *looks up, watches* **Suzanne** *go. She falters but doesn't look back.*

Scene Five

Theresa's *kitchen.*

Ned *is in his coach driver's uniform, making tea.*

Theresa   You don't think I'm being a fool?

Ned *is engrossed in what he's doing.*

Theresa   You do, don't you? I know it's a lot of money . . . and it was what I'd been saving up . . . you know in case I need an op or something later. And it doesn't feel right . . . to give it all to her . . .

Ned *brings her the tea.*

Ned   Have I put too much milk in?

Theresa   No, that's lovely.

Ned   Both your boys are doing well, aren't they?

Theresa   Yes. Oh yes.

Ned   Well, I don't suppose a couple of thousand would make such a difference to them . . .

Theresa   No, but there's being fair, especially when there's my grandchildren to think of. I don't know what her father would've said . . . well, I do. He'd have expected her to fend for herself, to be independent, 'stand on her own two feet'.

Ned   I don't think Suzanne's doing so badly. In fact I admire her.

Theresa *is about to sip her tea, but stops, surprised.*

Ned   She looks after that boy, that can't be easy. And the previous ones . . . that very quiet girl who used to eat her hair . . .

Theresa   Zoe. Poor little thing.

Ned   Kids like that who would've probably been in care if they weren't staying with Suzanne.

Theresa   Yes, but it's not a proper job . . . she doesn't earn –

Ned (*interrupting*)   But it's doing some good isn't it?

Theresa   Yes . . . I suppose –

Ned   You should be proud of her.

Theresa   Yes . . . (*Pause.*) I suppose I am . . . in some ways. She's just . . . different that's all. Always has been. Different. But this idea of living in a caravan. I mean it's all very nice . . . but I don't really see . . . it'll be cramped, miles from anywhere, what do you do for your washing, God only knows, and how you heat the place, let alone cook . . . Plus most of those caravan parks are full of retired couples looking for a bit of p and q – they're not really going to appreciate my daughter as a neighbour . . . It's just not really practical, is it Ned? It's just a pipe dream. I really don't see it working . . .

Ned (*thoughtful*)   Oh I do . . .

Possible projection of **Suzanne**'s *caravan. Red Hot Chili Peppers soundtrack.*
Theresa *and* **Ned** *are joined by (pregnant)* **Suzanne** *and* **Luka**.

Caravan vision fades. Sound of the wind over the cliffs.

Suzanne *is left on stage alone.*

The End.

Gaby Goes Global

A play

Judy Upton

Original Production Details

Date: February 2009

Venue: New Wimbledon Theatre

Director: Kirrie Wratten

Designers: Nick Somerville and Becky Warrilow

Lighting Designer: Jacob Mason-Dixon

Sound Designer: Nela Brown

Cast

Gaby	Lynda Bazely
Matt	Samuel Collings
Jed	Joel Mellinger
Debra	Corin Campbell Hill
Larry	Paul Coldrick
Kay	Abigail Longstaffe
Marjorie	Jennie Lathan

Act One

Scene One

Jobcentre Plus, Brighton.

Enter **Kay** *and* **Gaby**. **Kay** *is the needle-sharp manager,* **Gaby** *an employment adviser, new to this office.* **Gaby** *is unfashionable and a little awkward.*

Kay   This will be your desk while Tammy is recuperating.

Gaby   Excuse me . . . I wasn't told. What exactly is she recuperating from?

Kay   She was involved in a hostile situation.

Gaby   A client assaulted her?

Kay   Well, yes . . .

Gaby   They didn't tell me that at Worthing. Said I was being transferred here to cover for holidays.

Kay   Well, Tammy *is* taking a holiday. While her ribs heal. (*Beat.*) But you needn't worry yourself unduly. There's a pepper spray in the top desk drawer and a mailing tube stuffed with paperclips, which I'm told makes a remarkably heavy cosh.

Gaby   Right . . .

Enter **Matt** *and* **Jed**. *They queue behind the 'Queue Here' sign for* **Gaby**'s *desk; both have bulging carrier bags.* **Matt** *is the older brother, late twenties, confident, swaggering;* **Jed** *his thin, rather intense younger sibling.* **Gaby** *regards* **Matt** *and* **Jed** *warily.*

Kay   Plus we do have a direct line to the police station and their response times are improving. By the way, you do need to lock all your valuables in your locker. Otherwise the crackheads will be down your pockets while you're still asking for their JSP booklet. If you found life at Worthing Job Centre a little challenging at times, remember how longshore drift works – eventually all the scum from everywhere else washes up in Brighton.

Gaby *takes out the tube stuffed with paperclips, holds it like a truncheon.*

Kay   Now we're very proud of our record here for finding our clients gainful employment. As of course you'll be aware there is a small bonus for every long-term claimant found a useful place in the working world.

Gaby   At my previous office I won the prize for finding the most clients employment, three years in a row.

Kay *is less than impressed.*

Kay   Really. (*Beat.*) Look, haven't you noticed you've a queue building up?

Here we don't keep the clients waiting.

She goes to her own desk at the back of the room. **Gaby** *stands up a sign on her desk. It says 'Employment Adviser'. She prepares herself for combat.*

Gaby (*calling to the first in queue*)   Yes?

Matt   Good luck, bruv.

Jed *goes up to* **Gaby**'s *desk.*

Gaby   Do take a seat.

He sits, hands her his dole card.

Gaby   Have you worked at all in the last two weeks?

Jed   No.

Gaby   Are you taking steps to actively seek work?

Jed   Yes.

Gaby   How many jobs have you applied for in the last week?

Jed   I don't know.

Gaby   One? Two? (*Beat.*) None at all?

Jed *tips the contents of the carrier bag out on* **Gaby**'s *desk. It contains a huge pile of letters.*

Jed   Rejection letters. All recent. Do you want me to count them?

Gaby *starts looking through the letters.*

Gaby   Gas company . . .

Jed   Sales job – didn't want me.

Gaby   Though it does say they're keeping your name on file in case of future vacancies.

Jed   They always say that. Rubbish, innit?

Gaby   Well, you never know.

She continues to look through **Jed**'s *pile of rejection letters, nodding approvingly.*

Gaby   Electricity board, water board, council – all large employers and worth a try . . .

Jed   That's what I thought, but I tried lots of smaller ones too.

He indicates some more letters.

Gaby   Eurotherm, Crowhead Mortimer . . . letter from Mr Mortimer himself, Skincladding UK . . .

Jed   . . . Just general office jobs.

Gaby   Is that what you did before, Mr Haines?

Jed   Well, no . . .

Gaby   So in what area did you work previously?

Jed   I didn't.

Gaby   You've never worked? At all? Since leaving school.

Jed   I went to art college. Studied photography.

Gaby   And you've tried –

Jed   – Local papers, police, estate agents – no one needs a photographer.

Digital cameras mean everyone can take a passable photo these days.

Gaby   Mmmm . . . I can see that's a problem, plus you do appear to be making a good effort to find work. Okay, that's it, see you in two weeks.

Jed *stands, not quite believing his luck.* **Gaby** *hands him back his dole card.*

Jed   Right . . . Er, thanks.

Jed *picks up his rejection letters and leaves.* **Gaby** *fills in the paperwork.* **Jed** *passes* **Matt** *on his way out.*

Jed   She's a push-over, bruv.

Gaby *'s phone rings.*

Gaby (*on phone*)   Hello?

She pushes some buttons on the phone.

Gaby   Bloody thing. Hello?

Debra (*heard amplified*)   Hello. Is that the Job Centre Plus?

Gaby (*on phone*)   It is. And you are?

Debra   Debra Wallis. You sound far away and echoey.

Gaby   Because now I've accidentally put the wretched thing on speaker phone.

Debra   Other people are listening to our conversation?

Gaby   Not deliberately I assure you.

Debra   It still infringes my civil liberties and the Data Protection Act.

Gaby   Well, you do have the option of terminating this call and attending the office in person.

Debra   Actually I don't. I'm agoraphobic. So I can't sign on.

Larry *comes into the office, in motorbike leathers, takes off his helmet. He queues behind* **Matt**.

Gaby   No show, no dole. I don't make the rules, just enforce them.

Debra   I can't leave my flat.

Gaby   Okay, get a medical certificate from your doctor.

Debra   I can't get to the doctor's, can I?

Gaby   Call him out.

Debra   My doctor is a she and doesn't do call-outs.

Gaby   Not my problem. You need a medical certificate or you need to come down here. Goodbye.

She puts the phone down.

Next.

Matt *approaches the desk.*

Gaby (*to* **Matt**)   Please take a seat.

Matt   You're new aren't you?

Gaby   Only to this office.

Matt   Well, if you'd worked here very long, you'd know there's no point in me taking a seat. I give you this.

He gives her his JSP booklet.

Matt   You give me the thingie to sign . . .

She passes him the form. He signs.

. . . and while I'm signing it, you ask if I've done any work at all . . .

Gaby   . . . during the last fortnight.

Matt   I say 'no', and we're all finished.

He goes to take back his card. **Gaby** *keeps hold of it.*

Gaby   Not so fast, Mr . . . (*She checks her notes.*) Haines. Common name in these parts?

Matt   Is it? You tell me.

Gaby   I see in your notes that you're eligible for both the Job Club and the Fresh Start Scheme . . .

Matt   What!

Gaby   In fact you have been for some considerable time . . .

Matt   Yeah? My usual clerk . . . she don't reckon the Job Club or Fresh Start would suit my particular requirements . . .

Gaby   I'm your usual clerk from now on, Mr Haines.

Matt   Call me Matt.

He offers her his hand. She does not shake it.

Gaby   Please do take a seat, Mr Haines.

Matt   I'm a bit pushed for time actually . . .

Gaby   Because you're working?

Matt   No. I wish.

Gaby *checks his details.*

Gaby   And have you been applying for many jobs whilst you've been in receipt of benefit?

He tips the carrier bag out on the desk. It contains lots of letters.

Gaby   Rejections from electricity, gas, Crowhead Mortimer . . . Why do I get a sense of déjà vu?

Matt   Could be because me and my brother tend to go for the same jobs.

And you just saw my brother.

Gaby   Now it all starts to make sense. How are your literacy skills?

Matt   Fine. I've been to college.

Gaby   Studying?

Matt   Of course.

Gaby   What did you study, Mr Haines?

Matt   Art. There's no money in it.

Gaby   Are there a lot of artists here?

Matt   Every second person you meet.

Gaby   And do any of them make a living at it?

Matt   If so I've not met them.

Gaby   But if you're never likely to make money from your art, why do it?

Matt   If you were an artist you'd understand.

Gaby *makes some notes.*

Gaby   Okay, now I'm reasonably satisfied that you've made a decent effort to find employment so I shall let you off Fresh Start or the Job Club this time. See you in a fortnight.

Matt *can hardly believe his luck.*

Matt   Right. Thanks. Very nice to meet you. Hope you *are* my usual clerk from now on.

He leaves, taking his rejection letters. **Gaby** *looking bemused.*

Gaby   Next.

Larry *comes and sits down. He's rather shy and nervy, but to* **Gaby** *he's a vision in his leathers.*

Gaby   Name?

Larry   Larry Rust.

Gaby *flicks through her file.*

Gaby   I don't seem to have a Rust down for today.

Larry   I'm not here to sign on.

Gaby *leans back, eyes him with curiosity.*

Gaby   Then to what do we owe this pleasure?

Larry   Thought I'd see if you've any jobs, like.

Gaby   There're plenty on the screens near the door –

Larry   I know. But most of those will have gone by now, won't they?

Gaby   It's possible, but I'd still have thought it worth having a look, Mr Rust . . .

Larry   I have looked. I came in yesterday, 'bout the same time, talked to your friend over there.

He indicates **Kay**.

Gaby   She's not my – (*Stops herself.*) I see. And was there nothing suitable?

Larry   No, nothing that fits in with my hours.

Gaby   Your hours?

Larry   I'm a nurse at the General. But it don't pay the bills, know what I'm saying? I couldn't give it up . . . helping people, putting something back – that's what really matters, isn't it?

Gaby (*gazing at him admiringly*)   Yes . . . I'm sure it is. But have you really enough spare time to take on another job?

Larry   Providing it fits in with my shifts.

His mobile bleeps.

Excuse me a minute.

He takes out his mobile.

Oh sorry, I, er, gotta go.

Gaby   The hospital need you? An emergency?

Larry   No, Pizza on the Pier.

Gaby   You mean you already have a *second* job, Mr Rust?

Larry   Yeah. Catch you later, yeah?

Gaby   Yeah . . .

Exit **Larry**. **Gaby** *watches him go. Her phone rings. She picks up.*

Debra (*on phone*)   Hello.

Gaby (*on phone*)   Job Centre Plus, how may I help?

Debra   I called earlier but the person I spoke to was extremely unhelpful.

Gaby   I'm sorry to hear that – how may I help?

Debra   You see I'm agoraphobic . . .

Gaby   Oh you again.

Debra   You! I want to speak to someone senior.

Gaby   Out of the question. How have you been managing to sign on previously if you can't leave your flat?

Debra   . . . Well it comes and it goes . . . the anxiety and panics.

Gaby   I see.

Debra   But last time it was bad, someone from your office visited me.

She'd pop round to my studio at the end of her shift so I could sign.

Gaby   Studio?

Debra   I'm an artist.

Gaby   Why doesn't that surprise me?

Debra   But I have been looking for home-based computer work – I could email you my rejection letters if you require evidence.

Gaby   How far is your studio from this office?

Debra   No more than a couple of blocks.

Gaby   Okay then, I'll come over. I have your address here on file.

Debra   I'll have the kettle on.

Gaby *stands and puts her jacket on.* **Kay** *notices and approaches.*

Kay   You've another hour before your first official tea break, Gabriella.

Gaby   Actually I'm visiting a client. An agoraphobic woman.

Kay   Debra Wallis. She always tries it on if she's lucky enough to speak to someone new.

Gaby   She said my predecessor used to visit her.

Kay   And when exactly did you start believing anything a client says?

Ms Wallis will come down here soon enough if you tell her you won't stand for any nonsense.

Gaby *sits back down.*

Kay   May I ask how many clients have you signed off so far today?

Gaby   Well, none yet. . . .

Kay *looks at* **Gaby***'s paperwork.*

Kay   I see you encountered the brothers Haines. Both ripe for the Job Club and Fresh Start. Please don't tell me you let those hoodlums slip through your fingers?

Gaby   Actually they'd both been applying for a considerable amount of jobs. I couldn't fault either of them.

Kay   Where's the proof?

Gaby   They took their rejection letters with them, but I did check them thoroughly. – It's a shame there're so many talented artists out there, having to apply for ordinary office jobs.

Kay (*sarcastic*)   Isn't it just? Didn't it cross your mind that the Haines brothers took their rejection letters with them because that saves them a lot of work next time? I assumed you'd have come across it before. It is after all an elementary dodge. The clue to look for is that the firms they seemingly applied to are all companies that would be sending them bills – council, water board, gas, electricity. They put the bills in a scanner – then delete the letter but keep the company letterhead. They type their own letter in its place making it look as if it from the personnel department. Simple.

Gaby   But they had some letters from private companies . . . Crowhead something . . . and some others.

Kay   There is a Yellow Pages under your desk. Check the companies in front of the client and, if they do exist, phone them. It's a small perk of the job – watching the client squirm when the firm deny all knowledge of their application.

Gaby   I see . . . And I suppose none of them are really struggling artists either?

Kay   Oh, they're struggling alright. How many famous Brighton artists can you name? (*Beat.*) Exactly. I'm only telling you this for your own good. If you're a soft touch who lets herself be taken in by any tall tale, then you won't be taking home any bonuses. Do I make myself clear?

Blackout.

Scene Two

Jobcentre Plus, Brighton. Day.

Kay *is using the computer on* **Gaby***'s desk.* **Matt** *is standing behind the 'Queue Here' sign.*

Enter **Gaby***, clutching a gardening magazine.* **Kay** *pounces on her, sadistic smile on her face.*

Kay   Thought you'd take an extra-long lunch today, Gabriella? I don't know what it's like at Worthing, but we thrive on punctuality here.

Gaby   I've only had forty-five minutes. I didn't finish 'til quarter past.

Kay   Did you try the sandwich place in Churchill Square I suggested?

Gaby   Er, no . . .

Kay   Pity. They've such a wonderful selection of low-calorie things . . .

She moves out of **Gaby***'s seat.* **Gaby** *puts her magazine down on the desk, sits down.* **Kay** *swoops on the magazine.*

Kay   Oh, *Amateur Gardening*! Got green fingers have you?

Gaby   Not really . . . well, I don't actually have a garden.

Kay (*interrupting*)   Oh, what a shame. I wouldn't be without mine. Nothing like a spot of digging to keep you fit.

Gaby   I . . . (*Beat.*) I won the competition.

Kay   I'm sorry?

Gaby   In the magazine . . . a few months back, there was this –

Kay   Competition? And you won a prize? How clever of you . . . And without even having a garden. So what did you win?

Matt *looks at his watch, fiddles with the 'Queue Here' sign.*

Gaby (*flatly*)   A holiday.

She resignedly opens the magazine on the appropriate page.

Kay (*reading*)   'A holiday for two in romantic Venice'. Mmm, I see. And who're you going to take?

Gaby   I . . . dunno yet . . .

Kay   You mean you don't have a boyfriend . . . or anyone? That must make you feel so bad about yourself . . .

Gaby   I've plenty to occupy me . . . I like taking photos . . .

Kay   Then you must join a photography group. Even if, as is quite possible, you don't meet anyone who finds you attractive, you might make new friends . . .

Gaby   Thank you for your constructive advice, Kay. It's good to learn from someone else's experiences . . .

Kay   Yes . . . Eh? What do you mean?

Gaby   You're single aren't you? And you don't let it make you feel on the shelf . . . Or past your sell-by date?

Kay *glares at her.*

Kay   If your clients this morning look slightly familiar, it's because, with my line-manager's approval, I've invited back a few of those you saw yesterday. Perhaps this time you will manage to enrol them in the Job Club . . . which incidentally, while Ritchie is off with lumbago, you will be supervising.

Matt *walks up to the desk.*

Matt   You're supposed to start at two.

Kay   That's very true. This is an extremely busy office, Gabriella . . . and we don't have the time to sit around gossiping. Try to remember that in future. And if you can avoid dropping your Twix wrappers in your confidential waste bin, it would make life so much easier for everyone.

She walks off.

Matt   I can't imagine why you want to see me again so soon.

Gaby   I checked out the sources of your rejection letters, Mr Haines – the council and the utility companies had never heard of you . . .

Matt   Isn't that typical, eh? Large faceless organisations, just lose your application – probably goes straight in the shredder.

Gaby   Forgery is a criminal offence, Mr Haines.

Matt   If you are going to accuse me of something, then you better be one hundred per cent sure you are right. Remember I'm on the dole – I'll get legal aid to defend my case.

Gaby   Perhaps so, but the evidence is stacked against you. I've checked in the phone book – Crowhead Mortimer and Skincladding UK do not exist.

Enter **Jed**. *He is clutching a digital video camera. He stands behind the sign, starts filming everything.*

Gaby   I'm afraid the filing system here leaves something to be desired. Do bear with me.

She takes a huge wodge of forms from her file, stuffs them in her confidential waste bin, using her foot to stamp them down.

Matt   You've got quite nice legs.

Gaby   What?!! Look, I don't have to deal with this . . . this . . .

Matt   Deal with what? That was a compliment. You don't have to deal with compliments. You just accept them.

Gaby *checks in the filing cabinet by her desk.*

Enter **Debra**, *posh, bohemian-looking, but nervy. She queues behind* **Jed**. *He ushers her in front of him. She's not keen, he insists.* **Gaby** *finds the pile of leaflets she wants. Triumphantly, she hands* **Matt** *one.*

Gaby   Since you're unable to prove to me that you have been making any effort to find work, you will, from tomorrow morning, nine o'clock sharp, be attending the Job Club . . .

Matt   Oh God . . .

Gaby   . . . presided over by yours truly. No show – no more Jobseeker's Allowance – do I make myself clear?

She dismisses him with a flap of the hand.

Gaby   Next.

Matt *walks out, passing* **Jed**.

Matt   Good luck, bro, you'll need it.

He exits.

Debra *approaches the desk.*

Debra   Excuse me, I'm an hour later than my signing time I'm afraid.

Gaby   You know the rules. More than twenty minutes later, you have to make another appointment.

Debra   I had to drink a bottle of Chablis and take two diazepam before I could even take a step outside . . .

Gaby   Ah, you're the agoraphobic.

Debra   I could have a panic attack – would you know what to do?

Gaby   Yes. . . . unless it triggered me to have one myself.

Enter **Marjorie**, *seventies, immaculate. She queues behind* **Jed**. *He ushers her in front of him. She is not keen, he insists.*

Gaby   Look, come in again, tomorrow morning. Er . . . It's a special artists' seminar. 9 a.m. sharp.

Debra   It sounds suspiciously like the Job Club to me.

Gaby   Doesn't it just? (*Beat.*) Next.

Jed   That's you.

Marjorie   But you were definitely here first. You were standing there when I came in, weren't you?

Jed   It's alright, love, you go first. I'd rather wait all day than talk to an employment adviser.

Marjorie   Very well . . . if you insist . . .

She approaches **Gaby**'s *desk.*

Marjorie   Do you mind if I sit?

Gaby   It's what the chair's there for. How can I help?

Marjorie   U3A.

Gaby   I'm sorry.

Marjorie   University of the Third Age. I want to sign up. Oil painting, intermediary.

Gaby   This is the Jobcentre.

Marjorie   I know, dear. In my day it was the labour exchange.

Gaby   What you need is the community centre.

Marjorie   Yes, that'll be it. A good painting class. Oils. I used to use water colour but a change is as good as a whatever . . .

Gaby   Okay, Mrs . . .

Marjorie   Marjorie Alice Miller.

Gaby   Mrs Miller, I suggest you head over to the community centre and enquire there about the possibility of art classes.

Marjorie   Thank you for your help and assistance. I'll let you know how I get on.

Gaby   Eh?

Marjorie   Art class, dear. Oils.

Gaby   Bye. (*Beat.*) Next.

Jed *comes and sits down.*

Jed   Look . . . I'm sorry, right. Forgot my card.

Enter **Larry***; he queues behind the 'Queue Here' sign.*

Gaby   Jed Haines . . . let me see, you've been unemployed for coming up to six months now.

Jed   I can't do another Fresh Start Scheme. I mean I'd love to and everything, but I just won't have the time . . .

Gaby   You've got a job since yesterday, Mr Haines?

Jed   I've got this.

He flourishes the digital video camera.

Gaby   Very nice – top of the range model with power zoom.

Jed   You've got one?

Gaby   Well . . . I've seen 'em in Dixons window. Only I couldn't afford to buy one . . .

Jed   Oh. Er, neither could I really . . . what with being on the old Jobseeker's. Had to save up for weeks I did. . . . Well, months really . . . you know and my gran died . . . after a long illness . . . and left me a few quid . . .

Gaby   But not enough to put your savings over your personal capital allowance, I presume . . .

Jed   No, no it was just a few hundred like. (*Proudly.*) And it's all gone now. Not got a penny to my name.

Gaby *offers* **Jed** *a booklet.*

Gaby   This explains how your Fresh Start scheme will help you . . .

Jed *looks at her through the camera, zooming in.*

Gaby   . . . though I don't suppose much has changed since the last time you were on it . . . Stop filming please.

Jed   I wasn't. The disc won't fit. It must be faulty.

He takes the disc out of his pocket and shows her it won't fit.

Gaby   It goes the other way up.

She takes the camera and looks at it.

Jed   Are you interested in film-making too then?

Gaby   Well . . . actually I did have a video camera when I was a kid. I made a little film, used plasticine . . . made little models. It was about the survivors of a nuclear war . . . set it in my little brother's sand pit. Burnt a few plants with my dad's lighter, to create an apocalyptic landscape.

Jed   Do you still have the film?

Gaby   No. My teacher reckoned I should send it in to the BBC and they'd show it on the telly.

Jed   And did they?

Gaby   No. I never saw it again. My only copy. All that work . . . I could've been the next Steven Spielberg but, well, you know how it is, people trample on your dreams . . .

She hands the camera back.

Jed   You're not very positive for an employment adviser. Aren't you supposed to be inspiring and motivating me?

Gaby   I'm doing my best, Mr Haines. But I'm afraid we don't have any schemes or placements featuring film-making as a component.

Jed   Can't you just give me a break. I'm an artist.

Gaby   So are the majority of claimants here it seems.

Jed   Yeah, but I've seen the light. YouTube is the new medium.

Gaby   But whether you make videos or paint pictures, you still have to sell them to make money, don't you? And I can't see many people wanting to pay for something they could do themselves. Anyone can make a video and stick it on the internet for people to download for free.

Jed   I'm not talking about any old video. I'm talking about something original and creative . . .

Gaby   Like?

Jed   Fly on the wall documentaries are really big right now. Choose the right subject, get interest from the BBC . . .

Gaby   Well, I suppose they can't lose your only copy if it's on the internet . . . So what did you have in mind? Subject-wise?

Jed   Well, I thought . . . maybe if I filmed in here, just a few hours in the everyday life of the Jobcentre Plus.

Gaby   I don't know about that. And it'd be dull as dishwater believe me. (*Beat.*) Hang on, wait a minute . . . Do you ever watch *The X Factor* or *Britain's Got Talent*?

Jed (*thinking she's joking*)   'Claim Academy'. Instead of signing on, we'd get voted off?

Gaby   There seem to be a lot of artists signing on here. In fact I've press-ganged a couple of them into attending my Job Club. If I made a little documentary about *them* and their struggles to make the big time . . .

Jed   If *I* did you mean?

Gaby   No I don't. My office, my rules.

Jed   My camera.

Gaby   If *we* made a video documentary . . . then that might be a promotion in it for me, and you'd have something practical to put on your CV.

Jed   Okay. Let's do it. Er, when do we start?

Gaby   Tomorrow's Job Club, 9 a.m.

She takes the camera before he can complain and locks it in her desk.

Jed   Hey!

Gaby   Just to ensure you're an early riser. See you at 9 a.m., Mr Haines. Next.

Larry *approaches. To* **Gaby** *he is a vision of loveliness.*

Exit **Jed**.

Larry   Thought if I kept coming down, you'd remember and give me first pick of any jobs that come in.

Gaby   Unfortunately nothing new has come in yet . . . However, if you don't mind working on a casual, cash-in-hand basis, I could do with a little help here myself. Here, tomorrow morning, 8.45 a.m.

Larry   You're a star.

Gaby   . . . Well you never know . . . See you tomorrow, Mr Rust. (*Beat.*) Next.

Blackout.

Scene Three

Jobcentre Plus.

Larry *is setting up a whiteboard in front of a group of chairs.* **Kay** *is snooping around.*

Kay   Do I know you?

Larry *shakes her hand. She finds him enchanting.*

Larry   Larry Rust, conference co-ordinator – as of today.

Kay   A pleasure. If you want anything, anything at all, don't hesitate, just ask.

Enter **Gaby***, emerging from the ladies loo.*

Kay   Oh, you are here. I was presuming you were late.

Gaby   I was in the toilet. Something I ate last night disagreed with me.

Kay   Spare me the details. By the way, the stationery delivery's arrived. I know unpacking it probably wasn't in your job description at your previous office . . . but here unfortunately our admin assistant Ritchie has a medical certificate exempting him from heavy-lifting duties, due to his recurrent lumbago . . .

Gaby   So I have to do it? I suppose having a stomach upset . . .

Kay   . . . Is inadequate grounds for exemption? Yes I'm afraid so.

She exits.

Larry   I'll get the stationery shifted for you.

He starts shifting boxes. She looks at him admiringly.

Gaby   You're very fit aren't you?

Enter **Jed***. He has a couple more video cameras with him.*

Jed   Where's the camera?

Gaby *points – it's pointing towards the seating area.*

Jed   Reality TV isn't just shot on one camera. So I hired these. Who do I give the invoice to?

Gaby   Invoice?

Jed   Well, when I say hired . . . actually I had to buy them.

Gaby   What!

Jed   But as long as you take 'em back within twenty-one days and get a refund, it's the same as hiring them. But for free.

Gaby   Just you make sure they are taken back – or you'll be on Fresh Start schemes for the rest of your natural.

She turns to help pile **Larry** *up with boxes.* **Jed**, *after a furtive look round, disappears into the female toilet with the other camera.*

Enter **Debra**, *carrying an artist's portfolio.*

Debra   Not early am I?

Gaby   No, in fact, you're five minutes late.

Debra   Really? I don't see any other people here. Are you expecting anyone else to turn up?

Gaby   Count on it. The threat of benefits being withheld tends to ensure good attendance.

Debra   Are you proud of what you do?

Gaby   At least I'm not painting pictures nobody's gonna buy.

Debra   How can you say –

Gaby (*interrupting*)   I presume these are yours?

She indicates the pictures visible through the polythene cover of the portfolio. She looks through them, she's not impressed.

Debra   You don't like them?

Gaby   I *quite* like them. The question is would I or the public at large buy them, and the answer to that you've no doubt discovered for yourself.

Debra   So what would you suggest?

Gaby   Please take a seat.

She writes with a felt-tip pen on the board the word 'marketing'.

Gaby   Right, Ms . . . Er . . .

Debra   Debra Wallis.

Gaby   What sells?

Debra   I don't know.

Gaby   Then the key word is 'research'.

She writes it up.

And where do we do research?

Debra   Er . . . local galleries?

Gaby *writes it up.*

Debra   They're all full of pretty, pretty chocolate boxy stuff. Cats in windows, teddy bears . . .

Gaby *writes it up.*

Debra   I'm not doing that – before you ask. My work is instinctive, spiritual, from my soul.

She shows one of her pictures.

This one's called 'The Earth Goddess Greets Her Creations.'

Gaby   The Earth Goddess doesn't sell, Debra. Now I did quick survey of internet art sites and prices last night . . . and people like nudes . . .

Debra   My Earth Goddess is virtually nude . . . .

Gaby   She's wearing a wispy veil thing that somehow covers her modesty . . .

Debra   I could paint it out.

Gaby   . . . And possibly the majority of the Goddess with it . . . It's close-ups of genitalia that are selling well and commanding the best prices.

Debra   If you think I'm going to abuse my talents –

Gaby   Work by painters without your obvious talent is making three or four grand a time.

Pause.

Debra   Was it male or female parts?

Gaby   Either and both seemed to sell equally well.

Debra   My husband's . . . er . . .

Gaby   Not well-hung?

Debra   Divorcing me . . . so for the male ones I will need a model. And they don't come cheap.

Gaby   They might if I threatened to withhold their benefit.

Enter **Matt**. *He looks at the whiteboard.*

Matt   Cool. Marketing. Someone speaks my language.

Gaby   Have you marketing experience, Mr Haines?

Matt   I can sell anything saleable.

Gaby   You told me you were an artist.

Matt   Yeah, that's my other line of work . . . when I am working, which of course, I'm not, or I wouldn't be signing on.

Gaby (*sarkily*)   It goes without saying. And have you brought along any of your work today to show us?

Matt   That wouldn't be very practical. I paint murals.

Gaby   On walls. Graffiti I presume.

Matt   No figurative paintings. Like this young guy down the road died in a knife fight, his friends wanted a tribute . . . So I painted him on the side of his house, wearing his Albion shirt and holding his dog. After that I got other commissions – a cat that got run over, a bloke wanted his Lotus Esprit painted on the outside of his garage so people could be envious without damaging the car . . .

Debra   You just copy from photos?

Matt   Yeah.

Debra   That's not real art. Just copying.

Matt   You don't reckon? Well look at your goddess there – legs all out of proportion, and excuse me but I never saw a woman with breasts up there.

Debra   It's a stylised interpretation of femininity.

Matt   It's always the ones that can't paint for toffee who get all pretentious.

Debra *stands.*

Debra   I don't have to sit here and take this!

Gaby   True, but if you don't it may have an adverse effect benefit claim.

Debra *sits abruptly.* **Jed** *comes out of the ladies loo. Everyone looks at him.*

Gaby   Mr Haines, that is the ladies.

Jed   Yeah, sorry. Easy mistake to make eh? (*Beat.*) I'll sit at the back, I don't want to be in the film.

Debra   Are you filming us? Without our permission. Doesn't that infringe my civil liberties?

Gaby   No. We always film claimants with CCTV for their safety as well as that of our staff. But I've decided to make a documentary publicising the artists who visit this office, in order to bring their work to a wider public, and therefore generate sales and commissions for you all. What's not to like? (*Beat.*) Excuse me.

She rushes into the loo.

Matt   What do you reckon? Does she know what she's doing?

Debra   And what's to say this film of hers will help my career? I mean I'm not sure I want prospective customers to know I sign on. I don't want to look like a charity case who can't make a decent living from her work.

Matt   So what are you then?

Enter **Larry**.

Matt   You look familiar.

Debra   Yes . . . I've seen him before too. Unless he's just got one of those familiar faces. No wait a minute . . . Didn't you bring me a pizza – last Friday night?

Larry   I . . . I'm sorry I couldn't stay for the glass of wine . . . I had a lot of deliveries to make.

Jed   You invited him in for a glass of wine?

Debra   I did say I'm getting divorced.

Matt (*to* **Larry**)   Now I can remember waking up and seeing you looking at me . . . but I've certainly never invited you in for a glass of wine.

Larry   Last week – you were brought into casualty sparko from a fight outside a club. I was the nurse you threw up over.

Matt   Whoops, sorry. Very worthwhile job, nursing . . .

He draws **Larry** *off to one side.*

Matt   And presumably you have access to the drugs trolley . . .

Larry *gives him a card.*

Larry   Call for a list of what's in stock, and the price.

Gaby *comes out of the loo.*

Gaby   My apologies. Dodgy tummy. Larry, I don't suppose you have anything appropriate?

Larry   Not on me. I could pop to a chemist.

Gaby   Later will be fine. Now I thought I would begin the project today by explaining my aims. Then, I intend going to the local papers and regional TV channels to get them to run with the story . . .

Jed   We're going to be on YouTube and Facebook too . . .

Gaby   Then, having created a bit of a buzz, we'll auction your art on eBay . . .

Matt   And what about creating our own website? One showing live webcam footage of us as we work?

Gaby   Could you design one?

Matt   Of course.

Debra   I could have a camera in my studio. People could watch me create a painting.

Gaby   If it wouldn't infringe on your civil liberties too much.

Debbie *gives her a black look.*

Matt   So I'm designated website designer then?

Gaby   Absolutely.

Matt   Cool. Just one small thing. I'll need a Crisis Loan of about 200 quid.

Gaby   Why?

Matt   Need to buy my computer back from Cash Converters.

Gaby   We've a computer here you can use. (*Beat.*) But what are *you* going to exhibit, Matt? Murals aren't very portable.

Matt   I also sculpt. When I can afford the materials.

Gaby   Anyone come up with a material Matt can sculpt with, see me.

Debra   And I need a male model . . .

Larry *is about to volunteer.* **Gaby**'*s glare stops him.*

Matt   Look no further, lady.

Gaby   Well, this looks like a very successful morning's work. Jed, can you get a webcam rigged up at Debra's?

Jed   No problem

Gaby   Well, that's it, meeting over.

Debra, **Matt** *and* **Jed** *get up.*

Gaby   However, the Job Club runs until midday, so I suggest you each take a local paper from the rack, and circle at least five jobs that you could realistically apply for. Stamps, paper and envelopes are on the front desk and the phones are at your disposal. No making of personal calls of course, mobiles will remain switched off.

They all sit down again.

Any questions? (*Beat.*) Good, excuse me.

She heads for the toilet again.

Gaby   Larry, I think you better pop over the chemists now. Quickly.

Jed *smiles.*

Blackout.

Scene Four

Jobcentre Plus. Two oddly coloured paintings of male genitalia are propped up on desks.

Matt *is sprawled naked over a desk. He seems pretty relaxed about it. His modesty is protected by the local paper he is reading.*

Debra *is at an easel painting him.*

Matt   If you're divorcing, why don't you move out?

Debra   I've just got the flat how I like it. I'd always wanted a Paula Rosa kitchen. It was the very last shaker style available in rustic pine in the south of England.

Matt (*sarcastic*)   I can see how leaving that would be a wrench.

Debra   And I've just had all the floors stained.

Matt   They'll clean. When I had my pitbull it pissed everywhere –

Debra   Staining is an effect. I had the floor in the lounge stained a deep russet, and then covered the suite in white muslin. Not expensive or over-dramatic, but pure, minimal and classically modern.

Matt   I think I've got a splinter in my arse.

Debra   Oh, I'm sorry. Shall I have a look?

She does.

Matt   Not one to get embarrassed are you?

Debra   I had quite a bohemian upbringing.

Matt   Parents walked around the house naked?

Debra   Yours too?

Matt   Only my step-dad when he was pissed.

Debra *is still looking for the splinter.*

Debra   In some ways I'm glad Giles threw us out. The office setting makes a much more interesting backdrop . . .

Matt   You did explain to your husband that we weren't lovers?

Debra   Oh yes.

Matt   It must've been obvious to him that I was posing.

Debra   Yes.

Matt   And you have painted nude models at home before?

Debra   All the time.

Matt   So why did he react like that?

Debra   Perhaps because I can't seem to stop myself, it's part of absorbing the subject's being, getting close to understanding them . . . whatever . . . (*Beat.*) I do have the absolutely infuriating knack of ending up sleeping with my models. Does that shock you?

Matt   No. (*Beat.*) No, it makes me wonder about other possibilities.

Debra   Possibilities?

Matt   If our friend Gaby is keen for you to paint meat and two veg because they sell, then she isn't going to take the moral high ground over the website is she?

Debra   I still don't really understand how the website will work . . .

Matt   The object of the exercise is to get as much publicity for our art as possible, and to make as much money as possible. Now what makes a website with live webcam footage get the maximum number of hits from punters logging on?

Debra   Well, I've only looked at Africa-cam and there it tends to be when elephants or lions visit the waterhole.

Matt   You might get your kicks from watching zebra shagging but that's not what most people wanna see.

Debra   No, it's people shagging.

Matt   Or failing that, a nice bit of nudity would probably draw the crowds. I'll leave the site free to log on to for a couple of days then make it pay-to-view. We could make a fortune.

Debra   But what about your art? Have you found something to sculpt in?

Matt   That Larry guy, the nurse . . . I called him last night . . . he has access to all kinds of amazing substances . . .

Debra   Must make sure he comes to my next soiree.

Matt   And the guy has sky-high debts, he'd sell his own grandma for cash.

Debra   Well, you can't make a sculpture out of his grandma.

Matt   No . . . but someone else's grandma perhaps.

She looks at him quizzically, but he's pulling his jeans on. He goes over to the computer on **Gaby***'s desk.*

Matt   Jed said he'd connected the cameras up to this one, so we should be able to see what's already been filmed.

He presses some keys.

Matt   There. There we are, at the Job Club yesterday morning.

Debra   Oh no. Look at the bags under my eyes. I must detox this week. Nothing but parsnip juice until Friday.

Matt   Now let's try 'camera two'.

Debra *leans on his bare shoulders, as he double clicks the mouse.*

Matt What the hell is that? See if I can improve the focus . . .

Debra *starts laughing.*

Debra   Don't you know what it is?

Matt   Wait a minute . . . pull back and increase definition . . . (*Beat.*) Fucking hell! It's . . . it's Gaby . . .

Debra   She appears to be on the loo.

Matt   Jed! Jed you dirty little monster. He's stuck the camera in the ladies.

Debra   It's the most interesting bit of the film so far.

Matt   Yeah. (*Beat.*) It's the only interesting bit . . . That'd pull in the punters.

Debra   You can't use that!

Matt   I didn't hear any objections to putting the footage of me naked on the website.

Debra   She won't let you use it anyway.

Enter **Jed**.

Matt   It's always the quiet ones.

Jed   What?

Matt   Putting camera two in a cubicle of the ladies' crapper!

Jed   Oh that. That's not part of this project! It's my video entry for this year's Turner Prize. 'Scenes from an office toilet'.

Matt   Are you serious, bro?

Jed   How many times has something non-controversial won the Turner?

Matt   Fair point.

Jed   It could be huge.

Debra   You mean Gaby could be. *If* she lets you use it.

Jed   Right . . . I can see that might be the problem . . .

Debra   She might sue you.

Matt   Nah. If it came to that, she wouldn't have a leg to stand on. I mean you also recorded her telling us all to be enterprising and that nudity is what sells. What are you doing but taking her advice?

Jed   Yeah . . . you're right. . . . Still don't know how I'm going to tell her though.

Matt   The Turner Prize judging is months away. You'll think of something by then, bro. I'm sure you could bribe her with a share of the £25,000 first-prize money. Let's face it, who'd object to being filmed on the loo for some serious dosh?

Debra *doesn't look entirely convinced by* **Matt***'s argument.*

Jed   Er, do you think she'll settle for 500 quid?

Matt   That is a bit stingy, bro.

Jed   It *is* my idea.

Debra   It *is* pretty explicit, Jed.

Matt *is studying the webcam footage with enjoyment.*

Matt   You've certainly caught her at just the right angle. Oh look at her face –
straining.

Debra, *though, is thoughtful.*

Debra   I suppose it's not so different from Stanley Spencer painting himself and his
wife on the loo, or Duchamp signing a urinal.

Jed *nods enthusiastically, without really knowing what she is talking about.*

Jed   See? You might find it hilarious, bro, but I think you'll find the art
establishment will take my work *very* seriously.

Blackout.

Act Two

Scene One

Jobcentre Plus, Brighton. Night. **Debra**'s *paintings are hanging on the wall.*

Gaby *is laying out a tray of glasses of wine.* **Larry** *is following her around.*

Larry   Just checking whether any of the other local Jobcentres have anything for me.

Gaby   Sorry, Larry, I've not had time to call them yet.

Larry   I've debts, creditors, loan sharks, bailiffs, court fines . . . No furniture left in my flat, and pretty soon, I won't even have a flat.

Gaby   I've a spare room. I mean it's a one-bedroom flat, but I tend to sleep on the sofa . . . honestly.

Pause. **Larry** *doesn't seem keen on pursuing this offer.*

Gaby   Larry, can you paint?

Larry   No.

Gaby   Pity. If you did, I could market your work. Do you take photos?

Larry   No.

Gaby   You don't happen to stuff sharks in your spare time?

Larry   No.

Gaby   What exactly do you do in your leisure moments, Larry?

Larry   Sleep.

Gaby   Anything else?

Larry   Buy lottery tickets and eat stale pizzas.

Gaby   Right . . . I see . . . unless . . . maybe that's it . . . Yeah! . . . maybe. I have to go out now – forgot the twiglets and canapés. Go and bring me a pizza – preferably a stale one that's been left on your floor . . .

Larry   I could get you a fresh one . . . I get a staff discount.

Gaby   No, no, just get on your way. I'll call your mobile in a bit to explain exactly what I want.

Exit **Larry** *and* **Gaby** *as* **Matt** *and* **Debra** *enter carrying a big cardboard box.*

Debra   It feels really cold.

Matt   It's been in my freezer.

He opens the box. He takes out a sculpture of an arm, the hand sticking two fingers up.

Debra   Wow, that is brilliant. It feels so real.

She touches the arm.

Matt   It is real.

Debra *recoils.*

Debra   Tell me you are joking?

Matt   I've given it a coat.

Matt   I got Larry stoned last night and he helped me steal it from the hospital. Even if they find out, they won't admit to losing it because it would cause a scandal. I won't exhibit it as real, but as 'looking real'. People can make their own minds up.

He goes over to the computer. **Debra** *follows.*

Matt   Time to upload the website to the server, then I'll stream all our recorded footage . . .

Debra   Except for the bit where Gaby is on the toilet.

Matt   Actually . . . I've left that in . . .

Debra   Are you mad?

Matt   I've already put it on YouTube. It's the kind of thing that'll draw people to our online gallery space.

Debra   You can't do that to Gaby . . .

Matt   Why not? There's no way she'll ever find out. Well, as long as I just leave it up for tonight – while Gaby is here at the party.

Debra   And supposing she logs on and sees herself?

Matt   She won't. We'll keep her distracted. Look, hits on the site mean money, Debs. I've got some pay-by-click ads on there that could earn us a good few hundred quid, even if no one buys our art. So we need as many visitors as possible.

Debra   No, I won't let you do this – it's immoral.

Matt   You could put the money towards a new Paula Rosa kitchen when you leave your husband.

Debra   Well . . . I can't really see how I can stop you. On your head be it then.

Matt   Thank you for your understanding and support, Debs.

Enter **Kay**.

Kay   Saw you two on the TV news earlier. Very risqué and all that.

She helps herself to a glass of wine.

I wasn't convinced of course. You can't fool me with tricksy camera work. You both had clothes on, below what we could see, didn't you? Clever though. Good for publicity.

She sips the wine.

Shouldn't really drink you know, goes straight through me. (*Beat.*) Even though it's Saturday I've had a call from area management, congratulating me on this initiative. Naturally I didn't take all the credit, Gabriella's done a wee bit in terms of administration.

Debra   Oh, Gaby gave us the impression that it was mainly her idea.

Kay   Really? I suspect modesty isn't her strongest quality. Personally, I think it's linked to self-esteem issues . . .

She starts to looks at the paintings.

Very accurate depiction. I suppose you painted it last Saturday, down the horticultural show?

Debra   Horticultural. . . .

Kay   The courgette and Brussels sprouts here. Or do you grow them yourself? Gabriella won a prize in a gardening magazine, you know. A romantic holiday, though she's no one to go with of course . . .

She sees the arm.

Not to my taste, but very realistic.

Debra   Isn't it? Made of resin.

Matt   Upload complete. The Job Club Artists' Website is now online.

Kay   To the website.

She downs her drink.

Let's see it then.

Matt (*panicked*)   Er, no, not yet.

Kay   But as the project's senior supervisor and development officer, I should surely be allowed a sneak preview . . .

She approaches **Matt***. He stands in front of the computer screen.*

Matt   It would spoil the surprise. You wouldn't thank me.

Kay   Oh, you are a tease, aren't you? What time will people start arriving?

Matt   It says eight o'clock on the invites.

Kay   Then I'm almost two hours early!

Matt *and* **Debra** *want* **Kay** *to go.*

Debra   Well . . . never mind . . . that gives you time to treat yourself to a lovely meal, and come back later. There's a lovely little Greek place on the corner . . .

Matt   Oh, that's my favourite, Greek food.

Debra   It's exquisite. The . . . er . . . spanakopita is the best I've tasted. And I've had some spanakopita's in my time, I can tell you.

Matt   Don't, I'll be rushing down there right now. I swear I've never tasted better, er . . . what is that delicious . . .

Debra   Souvlaki.

Matt   . . . better souvlaki anywhere.

Kay   What's it like price-wise?

Matt   Cheap. Very cheap.

Debra   It's a crime to undercharge the way they do.

Kay   Well, then, I think I just might give it a try . . . but first nature calls.

She goes into the ladies.

Debra   Will that harridan never go – she'll completely poop the party. (*Beat.*) Is the camera still running in there?

Matt   Yep, and I put 'out of order' signs on the other cubicles.

Debra   You're not gonna put her on the web?

Matt   No, I think Ms vinegar pussy having a pee would put people off . . . But then you never can tell . . .

Debra   The problem with appealing to the lowest common denominator is how low you might have to go . . .

Matt   Don't see it as a problem . . .

Debra   I know, see it as a new kitchen.

He comes over to her with a glass of wine.

It's weird to think of it though . . . While we're sat here talking . . . Jed's footage of Gaby on the loo is being digitally streamed into millions of homes around the world . . .

Kay *emerges from the loo, straightening her clothes.*

Debra   Have a great meal. I can almost smell the dolmades from here.

Exit **Kay***, passing* **Jed** *who is carrying a pile of photos*

Jed   What was the point of inviting everyone we know to the party?
None of them have got the money to buy anything.

Matt   Well, Gaby won't know that. She'll see the place thronging and think we've put loads of effort into inviting art collectors and galleries . . .

Jed   Unless she recognises them. They all come in here to sign on . . . and a couple busk outside too.

The phone rings. **Jed** *looks at the others expectantly.*

Jed   Is somebody gonna get that?

He picks up.

(*On phone.*) I have a gorgeous *what*?

Enter **Marjorie**.

Marjorie   Hello. Have I come to the right place for the private view?

Jed *puts the phone down.* **Debra** *takes* **Marjorie**'s *arm.*

Debra   Why don't you peruse my pictures? All very reasonably priced.

Marjorie   Oh I haven't come to buy. I'm an artist myself see.

Matt   Oh great. Another one.

Marjorie   Oils. Intermediary. U3A.

Matt   I think I may have made a big mistake . . . Gaby . . . . That footage of her on the loo . . .

Jed   Oh my God . . . that phone call . . . you've put Gaby in the loo on the website? You bastard!

Jed *goes to attack* **Matt**, *who pushes him away.*

Matt   Actually it's worse than that. I'd forgotten that I've also put up details about us being based here. Now every pervert with a computer will look up phone numbers for Brighton Jobcentres, and call them until they reach Gaby . . .

Jed   Shit! You bloody idiot! She'll kill us!

Matt *heads for the computer, switches it on.*

Matt   Bloody hell – look how many hits we've had already – almost two million coming via YouTube alone. It's incredible. . Seems people can't get enough of Gaby's, er . . . of Gaby.

Marjorie *has come to the end of* **Debra**'s *paintings.*

Marjorie   Do you mind me being frank, dear? Personally I think the nude has had its day. Have you not thought of trying your hand at a landscape?

Debra   Well, no, not really . . .

Marjorie   I see you've still a few spaces on the walls – I could bring a few of mine along to fill up the spaces – views of the South Downs, windmills, sheep . . .

Debra   Sorry, it's a closed exhibition I'm afraid.

Marjorie   Oh that is a shame.

She sees the arm.

That's remarkably realistic. I wouldn't buy it though . . . take too long to dust . . .

Enter **Gaby** *with* **Larry**. **Gaby** *is wearing a rather horrible glittery jumper and carrying bags of nibbles which she starts to unpack.*

Matt *quickly switches off the computer.*

Matt   Alright, Gabs.

Larry *takes a pizza box from his bag.*

Debra   Great, I'm starving.

Gaby   Don't touch!

Marjorie   Thanks for sorting me out the other day.

Larry *takes out a squashed soft drinks bottle.*

Gaby   What?

Marjorie   The U3A.

Gaby   My pleasure.

Marjorie   Oh, I almost forgot . . .

She takes a crumpled flyer from her handbag.

This is for our exhibition. Me and a few friends from the WI are exhibiting at St Peter's church hall. There'll be a cake stall, bric-à-brac and a raffle. You're all very welcome of course.

Gaby *takes the flyer without enthusiasm and stuffs it in her desk drawer.*

Marjorie   Bye then, dear.

Gaby   Bye.

Exit **Marjorie**.

Gaby   Had time to get changed into something less formal.

Matt   You look fantastic.

For a moment she believes him, then her eyes narrow.

Gaby   What've you done?

Matt   Me?

She walks over to her desk, **Matt** *nervously eyes the computer.*

Gaby   I can't imagine getting a compliment unless it's a smoke screen to put me off the scent of some wrongdoing. There were three doughnuts in that drawer.

Matt (*meeting her eyes*)   There still are.

She checks the drawer.

Gaby   Okay, so what did you do? Put chilli pepper on them? Or have you been stealing my stationery? Changing my answer machine to something rude . . .

Matt   If we're going to work together, we need to trust each other.

Gaby   If you'd worked in a Benefit Delivery Centre since you left school, you wouldn't trust anyone either.

Gaby *looks at the pizza and bottle.*

Not bad . . . 'Half a Pizza and Empty Bottle' – how about that as a title?

Matt   You can't exhibit that.

Gaby   It's art.

Debra   No way.

Gaby   What about 'Two Fried Eggs and a Kebab'? Wasn't that a famous work of art?

Jed   It just looks like a limp stale pizza.

Gaby   Better title.

Debra   I'm not exhibiting next to that. I'd be a laughing stock.

She starts to gather up her pictures.

Stop my benefit if you want, but I won't have my work compromised like this.

Matt   She's right, Gaby. 'Two Fried Eggs and a Kebab' was back in 1992. No one will take copying that style seriously today. Mark Leckey won last year's Turner with a combination of sculpture, film, performance and sound.

Gaby   So I have to film someone eating the pizza and making funny noises. Not impossible.

Matt   But it's still not art. Because Larry's not an artist.

Larry   I told you it wouldn't work, Gaby. Matt's right. You have to have been to art college for your leftovers to be valuable.

He shuts the pizza box.

And anyway, this is all I've got left to eat tonight. I better get going.

I need to get home and eat while there's still enough daylight to see what I'm doing. No money for the meter.

He starts to go.

Matt   Even if you could afford to switch your light bulb on and off – it still wouldn't be art. Sorry, mate, that's just how it is.

Gaby   Larry, wait . . .

Exit **Larry**.

Matt   Shame he took the pizza with him. I hate canapés. Those little bits of fish always give me the shits.

Gaby   I hope you're proud of yourselves. All of you. You call yourselves artists – claim to be starving in your garrets – but you've never gone home to a tiny cramped room, where the light keeps going out while you fumble for another coin for the meter. You've never lived on the stale remains of fast food, sitting on the floor cos you've sold all the furniture . . . surrounded by the discarded lottery tickets that have failed once again to save you from your misery.

Debra   I didn't know. I'm so sorry.

Gaby   So you should be. Wait 'til you see the full installation.

Debra   What?

Gaby   Larry's room – it says so much about his life – And the irony is, it speaks to us all, provokes a reaction. It's a life laid bare – someone like us, with failings, suffering, and raw pain. We might not all have to survive on cold pizza but we all feel like we have . . . And with the credit crunch . . . well, only those of us working in the Jobcentre have any real financial security. People will know this could be their future . . .

Matt   But like I keep saying, as he's not an artist. It's worthless.

Gaby   That's where good PR comes in. So Larry needs to have been to college, had exhibitions, patrons, admirers, reviews . . . His fake biography needs to be available in print and online . . . Wikipedia is a must. And I can do all of that . . . Or rather you can, Matt.

Matt   Me? What makes you think I can or would write a complete load of old bollocks . . .

Gaby   The job rejection letters you showed me.

Debra   She's got you there, Matt.

Matt   Alright, alright, I'll get concocting bullshit.

He goes back to the computer.

Gaby   Larry'll need a copy of course, so he can tell people which college he went to, and where his work's been shown.

Debra   But people wouldn't buy Larry's room . . . it's worthless – An empty space and some rubbish.

Matt   I think you'll find they might actually . . .

Gaby *turns her attention to* **Jed**'s *photos.*

Jed   They're the remains of the West Pier with starlings roosting on it, the West Pier on fire, the West Pier falling into the sea, the West Pier when a bit more of it has fallen into the sea . . .

Gaby   I think a theme is emerging. Sell many usually?

Jed   Yeah, down the seafront in the summer, to tourists. About ten quid a picture.

Gaby   Profit?

Jed   Yeah. When I can get the frames for 10p at the station car-boot sale.

Gaby   There's at least three other stalls on the lower esplanade selling photos of the remains of the West Pier. You see I've done my research.

Debra   Jed's are really good though. Look at them.

Jed *looks at* **Debra**.

Jed   Thanks, Debs. I have to undercut the others to make a profit.

Gaby   You're not making a profit. Take your time into consideration, even at the minimum wage. Zero profit. You need to realise it's sex that sells. If you could picture a couple going at it in broad daylight, in front of . . . well the remains of the West Pier. With that you could sell the poster rights. Earn money from it for the rest of your life.

The phone rings. **Matt** *grabs it.*

Matt   No he doesn't live here. Bye.

Gaby   How is the website coming along, Matt? Is it up and online?

Matt   Yeah, and ready to start showing us live at eight.

Gaby   That arm's very realistic. What's it made of?

Debra   Resin.

Gaby   It's your only exhibit?

Matt   I'm working on a life-size human figure, also in resin.

Gaby   You know what . . . I've just had an idea . . . we could pretend that it's a real corpse! Wouldn't that be controversial?

The phone rings. **Debra** *grabs it.*

Debra   No, sorry no one here ordered a pizza.

Matt   And Larry just left with a perfectly good one.

Debra *puts the phone down. Another rings;* **Jed** *races to it and picks up.*

Jed   Sorry, wrong number, mate.

The phone goes. **Debra** *gets it.*

Debra   No, we already have double glazing – we're the Jobcentre.

Gaby *is getting suspicious.*

Enter **Kay**.

Kay   I couldn't find that little Greek place you recommended.

A phone rings. **Matt**, *standing near its lead, pulls it out of the wall and pretends it was an accident.*

Matt   Oops. Pulled it right out the wall. So clumsy.

Gaby   Greek place?

Kay   The restaurant. Just round the corner.

Jed   You mean that one environmental health closed down last year?

Kay *glares at* **Matt** *and* **Debra**.

Debra   It's closed down – what a tragedy. A Greek tragedy . . .

Gaby   Show Kay how the website's looking, Matt.

Matt   Er, we're currently experiencing a few technical difficulties.

Gaby *barges him aside. She clicks on the mouse.* **Matt** *tries to stop her.*

Gaby   Get off. What are you doing?

Matt   It's not quite ready . . . I don't want you seeing it before it's the best it can be, in case you're disappointed.

Gaby   I'm glad you take such pride in your work, Matt, but I really do need to check out the website before the press arrive.

Debra   Kay, I really had no idea about the restaurant. Come into the stationery office, where I've arranged the twiglets and Pringles.

With a backwards glance at **Matt***,* **Debra** *ushers* **Kay** *out.*

Exit **Debra** *and* **Kay**.

Two more phones ring, momentarily distracting **Matt***.* **Gaby** *logs on.* **Jed** *and* **Matt** *both pick up and put down the phones.*

Gaby   Things sometimes takes a minute to download on this computer . . .

Matt *and* **Jed** *watch in horror. They know what is coming.* **Gaby** *screams.*

Gaby   Oh my God, oh my God. Switch it off!

Matt *does so.*

Gaby In the toilets, my God, what lowlife scumbag hid a camera in the toilets . . . You bastards. Bastards! I'll have you all locked up! For life! Bastards!

Silence. The desk phone rings; in a state of shock, she automatically picks up.

Gaby   Hello. (*Beat.*) Yes it is. (*Beat, then bleakly.*) Yes, it is me on the loo . . .

Matt   Look, Gaby it was a mistake, a terrible . . .

Gaby *has again picked up the ringing phone.*

Gaby (*on phone*)   Beautiful? Yeah right.

She slams the phone down.

Gaby   I'll sue you for this . . . this outrage . . . you and your no-good brother.

The phone rings again. She picks up.

(*On phone.*) Get lost.

She presses a button; a woman's voice is heard on speaker phone.

Woman   I just wanted to say how courageous, how empowering, it was for me, as a woman with a negative body image to log on and and see you, proud, strong, assertively confronting us with your body . . . making us see beyond the hype, the cheap magazine glamour that enslaves us all. There you are, you're sensuous, nurturing, tender yet invulnerable. You are gorgeous and you, not some stick thin model, not some teenage nymph, you're who we all must aspire to be.

Pause. **Gaby** *is affected and embarrassed.*

Gaby   I'm sorry, you must have a wrong number.

She puts the phone down. The others look at her, not knowing what to expect.

I . . . I . . . No one ever said anything that . . . no one ever said anything that nice about me before . . .

She stumbles to her feet and exits.

Matt *and* **Jed** *look at each other.*

Matt   Gaby . . .

The door slams.

Blackout.

Scene Two

A TV studio.

Gaby *walks centre stage to sit on one of two chairs. The lights are dim. A censored pic of* **Gaby** *on the loo is the backdrop.*

The slightly mumsy female **Presenter** *enters.* **Gaby** *has her dealing with difficult Jobcentre clients expression.*

Presenter   I'm Kate. Welcome to the show.

Gaby   Thanks.

Presenter   Nervous?

Gaby   When most of the world has seen you without your knickers there's little left to be nervous about, Kate.

Presenter   You got the list of questions we emailed?

Gaby   They seem fine.

Presenter   Remember it's a family audience, no swearing or being too explicit.

Gaby   Considering the reason you invited me on here, that is quite hypocritical.

Presenter   It wasn't me that invited you. I was in favour of having Uri Geller back, but the production team vetoed it.

Gaby   I wouldn't have bothered myself, I don't really like your show – but I'm trying to buy a house.

The **Presenter** *frowns.*

Gaby   And next time you can send a car for me. I was talking to your other guests in the green room, and even the golfing dog had one sent for it.

Presenter   You're assuming there will be a next time.

Gaby   You think I'm a five-minute wonder?

Presenter   I wouldn't give you that long, sweetheart. (*Beat.*) Okay, we're about to come back from a break. (*Into her earpiece.*) Are we? Okay.

Lights become bright. Cheesy music, applause soundtrack. Suddenly the **Presenter** *becomes all sweetness and light.* **Gaby** *notices and she too smiles in a fake way towards the cameras.*

Presenter   Last week, a quiet, unassuming employment adviser cast her modesty aside in the cause of art, and became a worldwide internet phenomenon. This morning you can meet the women with the *global assets* – Gaby Johnson. Welcome, Gaby.

Gaby   Hi, Kate.

Presenter   I hear you didn't know that you had even been filmed until the footage of you on the toilet had been seen by millions . . . How did you feel?

Gaby   I was initially shocked . . . but then I got to thinking . . . Ever since I was a child I've felt awkward and somehow ashamed of my body. I've never felt confident enough to wear a bikini on the beach . . . or let anyone see me naked.

Presenter   What, nobody at all?

Gaby   At school I was teased and bullied every day for being shy and awkward, and at work I seem to be practically invisible.

Presenter   Well, I'm sure a lot of women share –

Gaby   I suppose I'm just one of those people . . . who no one wants as a friend . . . or a girlfriend.

Presenter   Not any more surely –

Gaby   Then suddenly millions of people were logging on to the internet – just to see me. I was no longer invisible. In fact I doubt whether many Miss World contestants have that amount of adulation I've had this past week . . .

Presenter   Adulation?

Gaby   My inbox is full of messages of support from other women, and I've had over two hundred emails from men who find me attractive, including six marriage proposals.

Presenter   But what about the attentions of less salubrious characters – have you not also received abusive messages?

Gaby   Far less than during a usual day at the Jobcentre.

Presenter   From midnight the website became 'pay to view'. Do you not feel at all exploited?

Gaby   Not when most of the cash is coming my way, Kate. I live in a small rented flat with no view. Tomorrow I'll be straight down the estate agents looking for something with a garden.

Presenter   Well, good for –

Gaby *gets up and addresses the camera while the horrified* **Presenter** *takes instructions from her earpiece and tries to stop her.*

Gaby (*to camera*)   If you live in Hove, and have a large semi you'd like to sell in a good neighbourhood near the beach . . . and with a garden that has decking, you can email me direct at the benefit delivery centre.

Presenter   And how do you see yourself now, Gaby? As an employment adviser, artist, stripper or what?

Gaby   I'm an entrepreneur, Kate.

Presenter   Today, on your artists' website those paying to log on can see both male and female artists painting in the nude, taking communal showers, visiting the loo, possibly so we're told even having sex. So is it really art, or pornography, you're selling?

Gaby   I think people can make their own mind up about that.

Presenter   After they've paid to view?

Gaby   Of course. And I'd advise anyone interested to buy now, as all of this publicity may have inflated the prices by tomorrow.

Presenter   You seem extremely keen to line your and your artists' pockets.

Gaby   Not just our pockets, everyone's pockets. With interest rates currently at rock bottom, and your money no longer safe in the bank, buying one of our works represents the only investment that is guaranteed to go up.

Presenter   If you don't mind me asking, how have your family reacted to the whole debacle?

Gaby   My mother's dead, and if you can't drink it, my dad's not particularly bothered.

Presenter   I take it from your earlier comments that you are currently single?

Gaby   Yes, but only as I've yet to find time to sift through my marriage proposals. I recently won a trip for two to Venice, so the honeymoon is already sorted.

Presenter   To be honest I'm really not sure whether you're advancing the cause of feminism, Gaby, or setting it back thirty years.

Gaby   Are you going to put up our website address onscreen for your viewers, like your researcher promised me?

Presenter   Yes, yes, coming right up. (*Beat.*) And I sincerely wish you luck with your hunt to find Mr Right, Gaby, as well as with all your artistic endeavours.

Gaby   Thank you Kate. (*Beat.*) I sincerely hope the rumours about your show being axed because you're getting on a bit aren't true.

Kate *is momentarily thrown, but recovers herself quickly.*

Kate   Coming up after this break, all the new season's fashion news, and the incredible story of the dog that scored a hole in one.

Presenter *gives a smile on camera, lights change, she relaxes, snarls.*

Presenter   That's it, Gaby. I suppose it's back to the daily grind of the Jobcentre for you now, eh?

Gaby   No, actually, it's the Sky News studio, then the BBC.

She leaves the set.

Enter **Debra**.

Debra   You were great! Matt sent me a text. His resin corpse and all Jed's photos on the website sold the minute you made that announcement about them being good investments. He's currently uploading some more photos and starting on a new figure. (*Beat.*) And *The Culture Show* rang. Lauren Laverne wants to interview you tonight.

Gaby   I think I can fit her in. After ITN and before Capital Radio. Could you give Larry a ring, ask him to get the train up to town? Tell him I could do with some support up here tonight.

Debra   Larry? Support? I thought I was your PA and personal stylist.

Gaby   You are – but I need you to go home and get back to your online naked painting. And Larry deserves a night out on the town . . . with me.

Blackout.

Scene Three

Jobcentre. **Kay** *is taking the paintings down from the walls. She starts to clear* **Gaby**'s *desk.*

Enter **Debra**.

Debra   You can't sack Gaby!

Kay   Yours are over there. I can hardly bring myself to look at them, now I know they're . . . they're of . . . thingies.

Debra   You can't sack Gaby.

Kay   Do you think that kind of . . . exposure doesn't give this civil service institution a bad name?

Debra   Can you think of a civil service institution that doesn't already have a bad name? And isn't it true that a number of fraudsters who your department was desperate to track down, have got in touch, hoping to part Gaby from some of her money?

Kay   Yes, but unfortunately benefit claims have also risen steeply. And whereas normally we struggle to get people along to the Job Club. Since Gaby's . . . disgusting display, there's a six-month waiting list to attend.

Debra   Which is good, surely?

Kay   It's chaos. The system can't cope with so many claimants.

Debra   But you can't make Gaby the scapegoat. She didn't know Matt had put a secret film of her on the website . . . He was using her . . .

Kay   And who was using her when she appeared on *This Morning*, *Ready Steady Cook*, *Have I Got New for You* and *Graham Norton*? Oh and that's without the rumours that she's in the new series of 'Strictly Come Dancing' and will be Doctor Who's next companion. .

Debra   If you were an underpaid, frumpy employment adviser what would you do about it? – Oh but I forgot, you are and you've done nothing but become more bitter and twisted year by year.

Kay   How dare you!

Debra   Yes, how dare I? What will you do – send me on another Fresh Start scheme?, make me wait twelve weeks to receive a cheque, stop my housing benefit unless I move somewhere so small an ant would get claustrophobia?

She gathers up her pictures.

Well you can't, because I'm no longer unemployed. All these paintings are sold – and I've been commissioned by Spearmint Rhino to redesign the décor of their clubs worldwide. I'm setting up my own design consultancy. I don't need this any more.

She tears up her dole card. The phone rings. **Kay** *picks up.*

Kay (*on phone*)   Yes, Roger . . . I suspended her yesterday . . . What . . . no . . . Roger . . . I don't see the logic in that . . . Publicity, yes, but of the wrong kind. No I don't think sacking her is the wrong kind of publicity. Well, I'm sorry, it's done. Yes, she's sacked. What? Roger! No, you can't . . . I've been with this office since . . . voluntary redundancy . . . wait . . . Roger?

He has rung off.

Kay   I can't believe . . . He wants me to apply for voluntary redundancy . . .

Enter **Matt**.

Matt   Where's Gabs?

Debra   Sacked. Thanks to you.

Matt   What?

Kay   Not any more she isn't. Unfortunately.

She dumps **Gaby**'s *things back on her desk.*

Debra (*to* **Matt**)   How's it going?

Matt   Well, I sold the second tramp from the morgue, but I can't risk my luck nicking another body, so I'm ringing round local farms trying to get hold of some dead animals. Got the offer of a sheep so far. I've been using an old water tank in my grandad's shed and gallons of formaldehyde which you can buy off the internet no questions asked. As long as Grandad doesn't pay a visit to his allotment, it's fine. Oh and I've been offered a contract to create horror film props for Hollywood.

Debra   And Jed has the Serpentine Gallery wanting him to make some more films for an exhibition in a couple of months.

Matt   Gaby's done alright for us all, I reckon.

Debra   And she's not done bad for herself either – she's been offered a four-figure advance for her biography and already sold the film rights to Working Title. That's without the percentages she makes on our work, the website and her TV appearances.

Enter **Gaby**, *wearing rather obvious designer clothes and blinging jewellery.*

Gaby   Morning all. Apparently I've been sacked and re-instated.

Debra   Yes, but you won't need to spend your life behind a desk now will you?

Gaby   It's what I do. It's all I've ever known really. I don't much like it, but I can't imagine life without it.

Phone rings. **Gaby** *answers.*

Gaby (*on phone*)   On Friday? Trevor McDonald? Fine. You'll send a car? Look forward to it. Bye. (*To* **Debra**.) Forgot to tell you, I've been offered a column in the *Guardian* – it's only weekly, shouldn't involve too much writing should it? I don't want to aggravate my repetitive strain injury.

Debra   Perhaps they'll write it for you if you ask nicely.

Phone rings

Gaby (*on phone*)   Speaking. Roger . . . who? Oh right, head office. No we've never spoken. Probably because you're an executive and I'm a pleb. Well, I was a pleb. (*To* **Debra**.) Ask Kay to come over please?

Gaby *hangs up.* **Debra** *fetches* **Kay**.

Gaby   Roger wants me to head a team setting up job clubs for artists all over the country. Unfortunately with my TV commitments and guest curatorship of the Tate Modern I'll be too busy to fully commit for a month or so, so do you think you could act as deputy . . .

Phone rings.

Excuse me a sec.

She picks up.

(*On phone.*) Hello. Haines brothers at the Guggenheim in August? Yes, I'm sure that we can set that up. You have a nice day too. Bye. So, Kay – sorry to keep you waiting. Was that a 'yes' or 'no' to the position of deputy team leader . . .

Kay   Well, er . . . it was a yes.

Gaby   Great. Only one thing. You need to show you're one of us. And appear naked on the website.

Kay   What? Absolutely no way.

Gaby   I believe the salary is in the region of 50 grand per annum. Take some time to consider the offer.

Enter **Larry**.

Gaby (*to* **Kay**)   Can you leave us for a moment?

Exit **Kay**. **Gaby** *opens her desk drawer. She is suddenly shy.*

Gaby   So Larry . . . er, how about a chocolate hobnob to celebrate selling your room for half a million?

Larry   Why not? Gaby . . . I . . . I'm just so grateful to you, I've cleared my debts, I've made a down payment on a Harley Davidson. You've transformed my life. I've been able to tell Pizza on the Pier where to stick their job, and I'm working my notice at the hospital.

Gaby   But I thought you said . . . that your art was paying for you to continue as a nurse . . .

Larry   Yeah, well I was emptying the eighth bedpan of my shift at 5 a.m. and I just thought, 'Why am I doing this? I'm rich.'

Gaby   You were doing it because you cared.

Larry   Well, call it compassion fatigue. I've quit, okay?

Gaby   You being a nurse was a good selling point.

Larry   I'm still connected with the job y'know. There's the slot on *Jeremy Kyle* and I'm on *Newsnight* next week talking about the state of the hospitals. Besides I need a bit of time for myself. It's been a lonely old life, rushing around trying to make money. I can't remember the last time I had a night out.

Gaby   Really? Well how about tonight? We could go out for a meal to celebrate your success. Er, if you'd like that.

Larry   Yeah. Yeah, I would like that.

Gaby (*smiling*)   So would I, Larry.

Blackout

Act Three

Scene One

Jobcentre.

Gaby *is at her desk with* **Larry**. **Matt** *is at a computer at* **Kay**'*s desk.*

Larry   Last night . . . the meal . . . it was really special, thanks.

Gaby (*flatly*)   Don't mention it.

Larry   I was a bit nervous . . . about bringing Anna along . . . but since things are getting serious with her now, I wanted her to met my boss, y'know.

Gaby (*not meaning it*)   She seemed very nice. Very.

Larry   She is yeah. (*Pause.*) But, Gaby . . . When the bed failed to sell . . . I mean I've been thinking about my other exhibits – 'The Contents of My Fridge', 'Unwashed Clothes', the sample jar I peed in when I had a bladder infection . . . and I want to take all the stuff off the website. It somehow feels too personal, it's like selling my soul . . .

Gaby   Hundreds of people bid thousands of pounds for the last jar of your pee.

Larry   Am I supposed to be proud?

Gaby   You could buy another motorbike.

Larry   I don't need one.

Gaby   A bigger flat.

Larry   I just want to Pause. live quietly, out of the limelight, with Anna.

Gaby   Right. Fine. (*Pause.*) You know I could have made you a billionaire? I had it all planned out, right down to the last detail.

Pause.

Larry   Right . . . Well, I suppose I better be going. Thanks for everything, Gaby.

He starts to go. **Gaby**, *stricken, watches.*

Gaby   Larry . . .

He turns.

Have you ever been to Venice?

Larry   No. Why?

Gaby   It doesn't matter. Oh and incidentally, you'll find the contract you signed means I have legal ownership of your fridge, your old clothes and your jar of manky wee – so if you really want your soul back you'll have to pay me the market price for them.

Larry   What? Gaby! . . . have a heart.

Gaby   What use would one be to me. Bye, Larry. *Love to Anna.*

Exit **Larry**.

Gaby *slumps across the desk, weary. The phone rings.*

Gaby (*on phone*)   Gaby speaking. Oh hello. (*Pause.*) What? You'd already booked someone else for tonight's show? A mistake. You're sorry. Extremely sorry. Okay. I'm sure someone else will snap me up for a prime-time chat.

Enter **Kay**. *She brings coffee and doughnuts on a tray to* **Gaby**'s *desk.*

Gaby   I asked for treble chocolate doughnuts.

Kay   They only have double chocolate.

Gaby   Well, get bespoke ones. And the stationery delivery needs unpacking.

Exit **Kay**.

Matt   The server says the visitors counter isn't stuck after all. We've actually had a big drop in hits on the website. We're losing punters in droves. People are losing interest.

Gaby   Wipe the footage of Kay stripping. It's putting them off.

Matt   Tried that.

Gaby   *The One Show* rang just now to cancel tonight's booking. Am I losing my popularity? What's happening?

Matt   Well, I've just checked our message board and people are being as complimentary to us and to you as ever. There's even a marriage proposal for Kay.

Gaby   Now that guy needs help.

Matt   It's from a woman actually. But I *have* noticed the number of messages has been steadily falling over the last few days.

He gets up and comes over. He rubs her shoulders.

Gaby   And I've just saddled myself with a huge mortgage.

Matt   For a semi in Hove, near the beach, and with decking?

Gaby   No decking.

Matt   I could come round and lay some.

Gaby   It's alright. Debra tells me decking is 'so incredibly five years ago' anyway. (*Beat.*) Like a doughnut?

Matt   No ta. (*Beat.*) So are you going to reply to any of your six marriage proposals?

Gaby   It's eight now. Two more yesterday. No, I don't suppose so. (*Beat.*) Are you and Debra getting it on?

Matt   No . . . She's buying a flat with my brother . . .

Gaby   With Jed? Oh my God.

Matt   . . . Just as soon as she sees one with a kitchen she likes.

Enter **Kay**. *She toils to and fro with boxes in the background.*

Gaby   You must be gutted?

Matt   What? Nah, she's not my type . . . unlike someone I could mention . . .

Gaby   Who? What? Oh yeah, right. Like I was born yesterday.

Matt   It's the truth. I find you very attractive, Gaby.

Gaby   Right. Okay . . .

Matt   Since the day I first met you.

She considers this a moment.

Gaby   And I . . . I'm very flattered . . . but I think, all things considered . . . that I've been a virgin for far too long to want to change that now.

Matt   Eh? You're still a . . .

Gaby   When I get in my new house and the cat has settled in, I'll do just fine.

Enter **Jed** *and* **Debra**, *carrying a newspaper.*

Jed   Anyone read the paper today?

Gaby   Only my own column. It was rather witty.

Jed *opens it on* **Gaby**'s *desk and reads*:

Jed   'The newest art world phenomenon is Joanna Mackles, who paints delicate watercolour landscapes of the rolling hills near her Tuscan home. Eminent critics such as Brian Sewell are already predicting that watercolour landscapes will be the new big thing. People are growing bored of the endless depictions of genitalia from the Jobcentre school of painters, and are ready to return to something pretty and pastoral. When Prince William was rumoured to have bought a Mackles as an anniversary present for Kate Middleton, it started a feeding frenzy, and it seems people can't get enough.'

Debra   That's us finished then.

Jed   They go on to say they also reckon it's a kind of change in attitudes. People are fed up with the harsh realities of the recession. They want to be taken back to a world of quaint little teashops, long country walks and cosy log fires.

Matt   I pray they're wrong.

Gaby   Why? Don't be so defeatist. Got plenty of green paint don't you? Surrounded by the South Downs aren't we? There's gold in them there hills – go and paint them!

Debra   But I can't. My attempts at landscapes look flat and lifeless.

Gaby *looks at* **Matt**

Gaby   Dump the body parts. Go and paint a hill on someone's wall. In watercolour.

Matt   It'll just look like a big green lump – and it'll wash off as soon as it rains.

He goes back to the computer.

Jed   Bloody hell, they also say Joanna what's-her-face is favourite to win the Turner. It's a new judging panel and they're banning videos, installations and old tat generally. It's paintings only now this year.

Debra   There was a voicemail on my phone cancelling one of my biggest design contracts. Now I'll never get my new kitchen . . .

Matt   We're over aren't we?

Gaby   Listen to yourself – 'we're over'! You just need to get over it and move on. Just do what I told you! Go out and paint me some landscapes.

Debra   I can't.

Jed   I won't.

Gaby   What's the matter? When you first came to me, you were all happy to take my advice and paint what I suggested. Was I wrong? Didn't I make you all successful?

Debra   Watercolours are fiddly. It takes years of practice just to get the first wash down correctly . . .

Gaby   You went to art school?

Debra   But I didn't do watercolours – it was considered old hat. It's Women's Institute art, the kind of thing old ladies enter for the Royal Academy's Summer Exhibition . . .

Gaby *remembers something.*

Gaby   Old ladies, eh . . .

Matt   You can pick up a decent watercolour down any church hall in the land for a couple of quid . . .

Gaby *starts rummaging in her desk. She finds the flyer for* **Marjorie***'s exhibition.*

Gaby   It finished yesterday! I missed it No contact numbers, nothing. Jed, get on the bus to St Peter's – see if you find the vicar and get him to call me. Matt, go out and get all the free papers, scan the 'forthcoming events' and look on the community centre noticeboard.

She takes money from her wallet.

Debra, go round all the charity shops. Any original watercolour landscapes, buy them! – Well go on!

Exit **Jed***,* **Matt** *and* **Debra***.*

Gaby *picks up the phone.*

Gaby   Is that the community centre. The U3A please? The art class . . . Oils. I need to speak to Marjorie. Can't remember her surname. They're all busy painting? I don't care, it's urgent. Call me back. It's Gaby at the Jobcentre.

She puts the phone down.

Kay!

Kay *comes over.*

Gaby I want to dictate a letter.

Gaby *paces, dictating*

Gaby   Dear Matt/Jed/Debra. . . . A copy to each.

Kay   Couldn't I just put Dear Sir or Madam, or to whom it may concern?

Gaby   No. (*Dictating.*) Due to unforeseen circumstances, I am afraid I am having to terminate our working relations. I wish you all the very best with your future artist endeavours. Yours sincerely, etc.

Kay   They can't sue?

Gaby   Of course not, I know how to draw up a contract. Years of working here have served me well.

The phone rings.

(*On phone.*) You have? What do you mean there are six Marjories in 'Intermediary oils?' Look, she has grey curly hair . . . they all do . . . right . . . a cardi, plaid skirt . . . that narrows it down to five. (*To* **Kay**.) Did you see an old lady came in here a couple of weeks back?

Kay   We don't get many senior citizens on this floor since they relocated pensions . . .

Gaby   Did you see her! Yes or no!

Kay   No. Why the rush to find one old lady?

Gaby   Because if we don't find her, and get her and all her friends to sign up with us, some other art dealer is going to steal them away and exploit them.

Kay   You're trying to save her from being exploited?

Gaby   Hello? No, I'm trying to exploit her before someone else does.

Enter **Marjorie***, carrying a small watercolour painting.*

Gaby   Oh my God! Marjorie!

Gaby *rushes up to her.*

Gaby   Do have a seat. Tea? Coffee? Doughnut?

Marjorie *hands the picture to* **Kay**.

Marjorie   Here's the painting you bought.

Kay   Oh, right . . . you know it had completed slipped my mind.

Marjorie   Then you'd have had nothing for your seven pounds.

Gaby   Seven pounds? Do you know how much a watercolour like this is worth, Marjorie?

Marjorie   I usually sell them at nine fifty but I gave your colleague a discount because she loved this painting, and it's important to have what you love, isn't it, dear?

Gaby   How much do you want for it?

Kay   Eh?

Gaby   I want that painting, Kay. Ten pounds, how about –

Kay   Seven hundred. And double the redundancy package Roger offered. Now you're such a star at head office I'm sure you can get it for me . . .

Gaby   Okay, okay, I'm thinking about it. Just get out of my sight, go on.

Exit **Kay** *with the painting.*

Gaby   I don't suppose you could paint me another one just like that?

Marjorie   Oh no.

Gaby   If I told you I could sell it for thousands?

Marjorie   No, because the poppies aren't out this time of year. If I painted the hill now, it would be with daffodils poking through the frosted grass . . .

Gaby   Do it. Go up there and do it.

Marjorie   Oh I'm all done with daffodils, dear. Must've painted them at least thirty times over the years . . .

Gaby   And where are the paintings?

Marjorie   In the loft mainly. Along with my ones of the primroses and bluebells, in the Lake District and Cornwall.

Gaby   Can you bring them all down here? I could sell them for you.

Marjorie   That would be very nice of you, my dear.

Gaby   I get commission of course.

Marjorie   Of course.

Gaby   And you like *The One Show*? I could get you on there.

Marjorie   I suppose Val Doonican doesn't have a programme anymore?

Gaby   It's a national tragedy. (*Beat.*) And will you start painting watercolours again? You see oils don't sell so well.

Marjorie   Oh I don't paint in oils.

Gaby   But you joined that class. U3A.

Marjorie   I went to the taster session. But it wasn't to my taste. Garish. Give me a nice subtle watercolour any day. Trouble is I've run out of views to paint. After a while it gets boring – same old hills, they don't inspire me these days. If I could afford a holiday, somewhere picturesque . . .

Gaby   Third week in April. What're you doing?

Marjorie   Probably the WI, my bridge club . . .

Gaby   Come to Venice with me!

Marjorie   Venice!

Gaby   An all-expenses paid trip, I won it in a competition and I've no one to take.

Marjorie   I've always wanted to paint the canals . . .

Gaby   And so you shall.

Marjorie   You never know one or other of us might even meet some nice man . . .

Gaby   It's a thought.

Marjorie   But weren't you already working with some artists? Wouldn't they like to go to Venice?

Gaby   Probably, but then they wouldn't be available to sign on, would they?

Marjorie   Very well then – Venice in April sounds lovely.

She gets up.

See you later, dear.

Gaby   Bye, Marjorie. Keep painting, eh?

Exit **Marjorie**.

Gaby *puts her sign back up on her desk*: *'Employment Adviser'.*

Gaby   Next!

The End.

Lockdown Tales

Scripts

Judy Upton

Signed, Sealed, Delivered

Produced as a short film by National e Theatr, April 2020, available on YouTube:
https://www.youtube.com/watch?v=zwie5MxGjd4&feature=youtu.be

Actor: Alice Merivale
Director: Jessica Mensah
Producer: Barry McStay

The White Hart

Produced as a short film by Lights Down Productions. June 2020, available on YouTube and Scenesaver:
https://www.youtube.com/watch?v=IUJiAvf1piA
Scenesaver: http://www.scenesaver.co.uk/production/the-white-hart/

Actor: Jodyanne Fletcher Richardson
Director: Leah Townley
Producer: Caley Powell

Winner of OnComm, the Offies Commendation for online shows, 10 July 2020, for best work broadcast or screened during the COVID-19 crisis.
http://offies.london/oncomm/

Rehearsed reading on Radio Reverb's 'Sapphic Voices' show, 9 p.m., Sunday 21 June 2020.
Actor: Aileen Archer
www.radioreverb.com

A Cat Problem

Produced as a short film by Write Now Berlin, premiered at 7 p.m. on Friday 31 July 2020 and available on YouTube:
https://www.writenow.berlin/plays/a-cat-problem/
https://www.youtube.com/channel/UCPv-viOPO2bKOesNXsrt2IQ

Actors:
Dylan Baldwin, George Bloomfield
Director: Emma Jude Harris
Producer: Secil Honeywill

Urban Foxes

Produced as a short film by Chalkroots Theatre, May 2020, available on YouTube:
https://youtu.be/cubuHO8UIC0
https://www.youtube.com/watch?v=cubuHO8UIC0

Actor: Jess Kinsey
Director: Saulius Kovalskas
Producer: Chalkroots Theatre

Bees

Premiere on 17 September 2020, as part of the New Moon Monologues
by Queens of Cups Productions, available on YouTube:
https://youtu.be/qC6PIcfj5lY

Actor: Ruchika Jain
Directors: Grace O'Keefe and Erin Holland
Producer: Queens of Cups Productions

Signed, Sealed, Delivered

A monologue

Scene One

Flo is in her first term at university in London.

Flo   It's surprisingly easy to obtain cardboard. You can find loads outside shops on the night before their bin collections. You can quickly build up quite a haul. You do need to be picky though – be careful with the type and quality. You want the strong, thick stuff – and ideally a box that has been used to deliver a large item like a freezer or a chest of drawers. You don't want any that have contained anything smelly either. You can make a large enough box out of several smaller ones of course, but if you do that, then you'll need to make sure you allow a very generous overlap at all the joins. The joins are always going to be the weakest part.

I'm the first in my family to go to university. When I checked it all out online I couldn't believe how exciting it was going to be! All those multi-levelled libraries, state-of-the-art lecture theatres, leisure and study spaces with their own coffee shops . . . In the photos and videos everyone seemed to be strolling around, laughing and smiling – without a care in the world.

My school was nothing like that. It was the kind of place where if you laughed, or even dared force a timid smile, someone would ask you what your problem was. Or more likely still, kick you in the teeth. I'm not saying I was singled out or anything. Others had it far worse with bullying and that than me. I quickly learned to keep my head down, not to make eye contact – to be invisible basically. Don't stick your hand up, if you know the right answer. If you do, even the teacher will mock you over it. Just say nothing, just get through the day.

University was definitely not going to be like that. Here people would actually want to meet me, be my friend and hear what I had to say. Or so I thought . . .

In freshers' week people gave me flyers for every kind of hobby or activity. I was invited to join sports teams, political groups, choirs and drama clubs. I went along to just about everything – sitting there while people who were far more confident and interesting than me spoke and were listened to. I didn't mind though. I was dazzled to be among all these ideas and opinions.

It was a couple of weeks into the term before I really noticed it. The fact no one had noticed me. By then the invitations had started to dry up. I saw and heard people heading off out to this and that, and occasionally I'd still go to a bar or a coffee shop. But when I did, I'd always somehow find myself on the very edge of the crowd, forcing a smile and trying not to look too lonely and desperate.

What's wrong with me? Why am I not an interesting person? How do you become someone other people want to talk to?

They make parcel tape in several different strengths, widths and lengths. It's actually rather overwhelming, having to make your choice. Also, for me at any rate it was hard to estimate how much I actually needed. I'd never done anything like this before. I ended up buying three rolls, just to be on the safe side. Previously, I'd imagined parcel tape just came in that shiny brown colour, but you can buy a clear one too, and – my choice – a white one with the word 'Fragile' written on it in red. Not just because of how I was feeling obviously . . .

Larger parcels are often stapled with huge metal staples, which are nothing like the ones you use to hold the pages of an essay together. Of course you can't very well staple a box together from the inside though, and the backs of staples can be quite sharp, so I didn't bother with any of those.

My family just don't understand how I feel. They're all so proud of me. Both my sisters told me I was so lucky to be going to uni and not into low-paid jobs like them. Getting a degree in environmental science was a great way to escape my hometown, with its zero-hour shift work with zero prospects. But I had friends back there. Neighbours I'd grown up with. People who talked like me and thought like me. I belonged. I was happy. This term has been even harder than last. If anything, I've felt even more homesick. I almost didn't return after going home for Christmas. But I knew they'd be disappointed, Mum and Dad.

Then this whole crisis happened and suddenly the university said they were planning to close for the duration. We were all told to go home.

Unlike most people I was relieved. Fine, I thought. I'll just go back to my parents' and watch the live-streamed lectures and upload my essays. For me that might work better than actually being here. At the very least it might give me some time to get my head together.

If Dad hadn't had to give up driving, I knew he'd have driven straight down here to get me. Mum has a car, but she's currently busy making grocery deliveries to those who can't get out.

The first thing I did, after checking that trains were still running, was to look up the price of the fare home. I knew it would be expensive, as I wouldn't be buying the ticket in advance, but I was still completely shocked at how much it cost. It's a figure that's larger than my current bank balance.

I heard my fellow students leaving and watched them packing their wheeled cases and boxes into waiting cars. And I didn't know what to do.

That night I sat at my window in the now eerily quiet accommodation block, watching the traffic racing by below. I wished I could persuade one of those drivers to give me a lift, at least part of the way. I looked online at car-sharing sites but there was nothing that would take me where I needed to go. Also I didn't know how safe it would be getting into a car with a complete stranger. Not very safe at all, I imagined.

But then as I sat there watching the vehicles streaming past, I noticed something. There were still loads of white vans from courier companies collecting and delivering parcels. A while back I'd overheard a guy on my course explaining how he sells his old textbooks, CDs, DVDs and even clothes online, parcelling them up in boxes for a courier to collect, postage free. The address of one of these wholesalers who will buy your old stuff, is on an industrial estate a few streets from my family's house.

That's when I came up with the idea.

Is it possible to post yourself?

When I was a kid, my parents brought the groceries in cardboard cartons from the shops. I used to draw on those boxes with my felt-tip pens, making houses, stables, and even a spaceship – then sit inside playing for hours It was quite comforting to be inside a box. Not claustrophobic at all.

But is posting yourself really possible? – I looked online.

In the early twentieth century, a man called W. Reginald Bray posted himself. He became famous for it. The reason he did it apparently was just to test the Royal Mail. He took himself to his local post office, in Forest Hill, south London, along with the correct postage and an address label. I haven't been able to find out whether he actually put himself in a box though. And also he did live only a street away from the post office.

I doubt I could've afforded the stamps to travel by Royal Mail. With my plan of using a courier, all I needed to do, I hoped, was make my reinforced box and cut into it lots of large air holes. Then I could call the company, climb in through the little door I'd left, before sealing myself inside. If the courier did find me, and decide to charge me for the journey, I'd be home by then anyway. I could borrow the money off my parents. With a bit of luck.

So now my box is built and I'm ready. The most worrying thing now is trying to estimate how long I'm going to have to stay inside it. I think I might need to sit here for up to three hours, so that's what I've been practising for. I've room to make a few small stretches, just so I don't get cramp. I have to sit hugging my knees though for most of the time. I've a cushion, three bottles of water, a pack of sandwiches, a torch and a pair of scissors. The scissors will be needed to get out when I arrive of course. And give me the option of making extra air holes, should I feel I need them.

So now it all systems go basically. Wish me luck!

Scene Two

A little time has passed.

Flo   Okay . . . Well as you can see I'm still here.

So this is what happened, right? I carried the box down into the hallway of my block, climbed inside and waited. I'd already booked the slot for the parcel pick-up, so that's all there was left to do. Unfortunately I hadn't realised that a pick-up slot just vaguely meant any time on a particular morning or afternoon. I sat in my box for over an hour. I checked the time on my phone occasionally, but I didn't use it apart from that. I needed to keep as much battery as possible, in case of emergencies.

I was just debating whether I could risk getting out for a quick loo break, when I heard someone coming down the stairs. I thought everyone else had already gone. I didn't think anyone but me was still in this accommodation block. Clearly I'd been mistaken. I peered out the nearest air hole. A young woman with curly blue hair was descending, a bulging bag-for-life on each arm and her hands clasped around a hamster cage. She sat down near the bottom of the steps and started checking her phone. I recognised her then as someone I've previously passed in the hallway or foyer. I hoped that whoever she was waiting for, with all her packed-up belongings, would hurry up and collect her. Staying completely motionless and silent was an extra stress I certainly didn't need.

That's when it happened. I tried and failed to stifle a sneeze. It burst out and it was loud – incredibly so – or maybe that was just the surrounding cardboard making a kind of echo chamber? So I sneezed, and my block-mate screamed. Looking through an air hole I could see her fearful eyes staring at my box. She stood up then and warily moved towards me. I didn't know what to do. I just froze. Stupid really.

'I know someone's in there,' she said, voice a little unsteady. 'Um, are you okay?' She walked around the box, still staying nervously at a slight distance. 'Are you okay?' she repeated. 'Can you understand me? Do you speak English?' It occurred to me then that possibly she thought I was somehow a captive in the box, or an illegal migrant, being trafficked. She took out her phone again and looking very serious and concerned started to dial a number. Who was she calling? The police?

'It's alright,' I said. 'I'll come out.'

Karly recognised me as a neighbour as soon as I emerged and started laughing. At that point she thought it was some kind of prank. And she simply couldn't believe it, when I admitted what I'd been trying to do.

Karly made the point that even if my box was collected, I might very well end up in a locked-down van or depot, rather than getting home. At that point of course we'd no idea how strict or not restrictions on working and travelling might get.

Then she told me her brother was driving down from Dundee to collect her and take her back there. When I said where I was trying to reach, she said that dropping me off in my hometown wouldn't be a big detour for them. They'd be happy to do it. Plus it would be nice to have someone to chat to on the way, as her brother tended to be a bit on the quiet side. 'Go and collect some things together. Jake'll be here in a minute.' Karly grinned and gestured to my box. 'And you might just want to drop that off at the recycling bin before we go.' I smiled too then.

While we were chatting, I heard Karly's hamster rustling about in his bedding. She said his name was Gus. She'd bought him as company for herself, as she'd found being away from home for the first time a little bit scary. 'I just feel sometimes that I'm too weird . . . too out there for other people to relate to,' she said.

'Weird? You're not the one who was trying to post herself,' I reminded her. She laughed at that. 'Yeah, fair point, Flo, but I think it's great to do things differently . . .'

'To think outside the box?' I teased. We were both laughing now. Then she spotted a car passing by slowly and jumped up. 'That's Jake – looking for somewhere to park, probably. Can you wait here a sec with Gus?'

Now Karly's coming back in, and she's with a guy who looks like a shorter version of herself, though he has fair rather than blue hair. 'Jake, this is Flo. – Come on, grab your bags, girl, we're going home!'

Flo *picks up her bags, and calls to the unseen* **Karly***.*

Flo Coming!

She leaves.

The End.

The White Hart

A monologue

Jen *is a lorry driver in her forties/fifties.*

Jen   I swore as I checked the mirror and braked hard. Just before 2 a.m. it was. When I got home, I went straight to bed as soon as I'd eaten, but its red eyes were still there, burning beneath my lids. I couldn't sleep and the sunlight pouring through the curtains made it worse. That material's far too thin and flimsy. If I worked regular nightshifts I'd get blackout blinds, but I've no time to do anything about it now. I suppose I could stick old newspapers over the windows. I don't get one delivered myself, but there're usually a few kicking about in the waiting area.

All us drivers are confined to one corner of the warehouse now, while our trucks are loaded. There are five plastic chairs, all spaced apart, and that's where we have to stay. After we protested to management yesterday, we now also have a single port-a-loo for our use. Lucky us, eh? Drivers had previously used the general staff toilets, until we were banned last week. So while it's still fine for the wholesaler's own staff to use their facilities the drivers, for reasons unknown, are treated like lepers. We sit on our designated chairs, fenced off by a line of hazard tape, eating our homemade sandwiches and drinking lukewarm coffee from our thermos flasks. There's a coffee machine, but it's now on the other side of the tape border and reserved for packers and forklift drivers.

I miss hearing all the news and gossip from my friends among the warehouse workers. I won't be able to have a chat with any of the supermarket shelf-stackers on arrival either, and supper will be in my cab, as the café at services is closed. As a trucker I'm used to being on my own for long periods of time, but now, like so many people, I don't see anyone outside of work either. I live alone in a one-room box, and most of my friends aren't yet into virtual conversations. We do Skype, but we're all a bit awkward and quickly run out of things to say. It's not the same as when we'd go for a meal or to the pub in a big group. Mum rang just now, even though I'd told her not to call during my downtime. She can't adjust to me working nights. I'd said I'd drop in any shopping she needs on my way home, but all she wanted was her bleeding lottery tickets. 'Can you get me three and a couple of scratch cards, Jen? They won't put any of those in my food parcel will they?' I don't think that was a serious question, but you never can tell with Mum. I told her the supermarket wouldn't be open when I arrived, and that I wasn't going out again later just so she could waste her money. Why do people in their eighties want to win the lottery anyway? Mum always says she has no idea what she would do with a million if she won it. Why then ask your daughter to risk her health for something pointless?

When that stag stepped out in front of my truck last night, I was certain I was going to hit it. I'm seated too high in the cab for that kind of impact to do me damage, unless it was thrown into the air, of course. Knowing my stopping distance, even at only a little over 30 mph, I didn't think the deer stood much of a chance. It disappeared and I feared it had gone underneath, despite not feeling so much as a judder. When I got out to take a look though, there was nothing there. Not a mark on the truck, no movement in the trees, and no sound of any living thing on that deserted stretch of road. The stag had melted away, as if I'd driven through a ghost. At least that meant it didn't have to go in the incident log.

It's only since this crisis began that we've been asked to drive at night. Previously we were used to setting out before the sun was up, but doing whole trips in darkness is a new experience. No one likes to hear heavy lorries thundering past their home in the early hours, or at least they didn't before empty shelves became a problem. At night the motorway lights can become hypnotic and with few vehicles apart from other trucks out there, there's less than usual to occupy your mind. You leave the radio on for the traffic reports and notice how the DJs struggle to play appropriate songs after each news bulletin. Follow it up with something cheerful and it appears insensitive, choose a downbeat track and it'll make us feel worse. In the end they usually just play the bland stuff. It's middle of the road music for the middle of the motorway in the middle of the night.

I'd already left the motorway by the time I saw the white stag. I was delivering to a store in a village where there's a winding lane with a tree canopy for several miles before you reach the high street. That's where it happened. He stepped boldly out from the shadows of the trees. His head was held high and his huge antlers branched wider than a Christmas reindeer. In those few seconds, as he turned his head to confront my 7.5 tonne lorry, he appeared utterly fearless.

Taking out my phone I search 'white stag' and discover that they're actually quite rare. There are several species of deer in this country but by his size I think he must be a red deer. They shed those massive antlers around this time, in March or early April, and grow a complete new set by autumn. A large white stag is also known as a 'White Hart' – like in the name of a pub or in White Hart Lane. It says they're surrounded by superstition and folklore. Mum's superstitious, but I'm not. Not usually. Though I do suddenly feel the urge to discover whether, like a black cat crossing my path, a white hart is associated with good luck, or with bad. It's mainly because of the way it looked directly at me – those burning ruby eyes meeting mine as if it was trying to tell me something.

If I tell any of the other drivers about it later, they won't let me take this mysterious white hart stuff seriously. 'You nearly hit a stag – oh deer!' That's how it'll be. Then Markos would be telling, for the umpteenth time, the story of the squirrel that got trapped in his cab, whilst proudly showing the teeth-marks left in his thumb. Richard though might be more interested. He has a dream-catcher hanging above his windscreen and likes folk music. Catch him in the right mood and he'll talk about things like water divining and ley lines.

Richard might know if it's lucky or unlucky to see a white hart. I'll text him later and send him links to some of the stuff I've found about them. A couple of websites mention white harts as part of the legend of Herne the Hunter. He's an antler-wearing lord of the forest who watches over the natural world. Celtic people once saw white harts as messengers from a place called 'the otherworld' – a land of spirits. My gran was from County Wexford and she was superstitious. Perhaps that's where Mum gets her love of the ruddy lottery. Now I've just found a site about English folklore and it says a white hart appears at times of great turmoil and it signifies change. That's certainly interesting if, at present, a little unnerving.

These days, when your truck is loaded, a man wearing a mask from a DIY shop appears, and beckons you, from a social distance with his blue-gloved hand. I think yesterday it was Steve but it could've been Dave as they're both bald and around the same height. Either would've been a friendly face, in normal times. You quickly start to miss smiles when they're not visible.

Well, it's time to go to work. A white hart can lead you down new roads, the folklore website says, which to me sounds suspiciously like a detour ahead. 'It can also symbolise new beginnings, new knowledge and a greater understanding of the world.'

The white hart might not be the lucky black cat I was hoping for, but at least it's no prophet of doom. I'm toying with printing a photo of one later. I could stick it up in my cab, like the way people are putting rainbows in their windows. I will pop out later and buy Mum her lottery tickets too, I've decided. I'll take them round and put them through her letterbox. It's not because seeing a white hart has made me feel particularly fortunate. It's just that at the moment, we all need to believe in something, whether that's family, friends, luck, or something more spiritual. In this time of uncertainty, there's one thing I now feel certain of. At some point I'm going to see the white hart again. Maybe sooner, maybe later, somewhere down the road.

The End.

A Cat Problem

A short play for two (self-distancing) actors

Larry *is in his forties/fifties. He is making a video call from a small reasonably office-like space (actually, we discover, in a prison). He is video calling his son, **Joel** (twenties/thirties), who has his own flat (for now at least). It's during the first 2020 lockdown.*

Larry   Alright, Joel.

Joel   Hello, Dad. You've got ten minutes, Lacey was saying?

Larry   Ten minutes a week, yeah. So I called your sister last week, and it's your turn this time. Nothing personal, just I thought it oughta be ladies first, or is that sexist and all nowadays?

Joel   So where exactly are you?

Larry *is amused.*

Larry   The International Space Station. That Tim Peake dropped in for a cuppa this morning. And Major Tom – David Bowie's mate, not the one walking round his garden.

Joel   Yeah, alright, I meant is this a special room or something they're letting you call from?

Larry   It's an office of some sort I think. Never bin in here before. Just somewhere the screws or guv'nor use maybe.

Joel   And how're you keeping?

Larry   Mustn't grumble. So far. Couple of screws off sick and it's all over D Wing like the bubonic, but so far no cases on this landing as far as I know. Seen more masks and gloves than the Great Train Robbery, but it's only the usual smokers, tokers and jokers who are coughing up here. How's things your end?

Joel   Could be better. I mean it's been very quiet, with no services or MOTs to do, and fewer people knackering their suspension on the potholes. That's been a bit of a problem actually. Course the landlord still wants his rent and I was already late with it. If I can't come up with it, he's talking about having me out next week.

Larry   Can he do that?

Joel   Well, yeah.

Larry   I mean don't you have any rights?

Joel   Not when he's me ex's brother-in-law and it's all a bit unofficial like.

Larry   Ah. You'll have to move in with Lacey, Jack and the kids.

Joel   Can't do that. With Crystal's asthma, they're shielding. Won't let anyone in or out. Fort Bloody Knox, but understandable really.

Larry   Can you get a loan?

Joel   Another one? Can't see that happening.

Larry   I wish I'd been able to hang on to my place . . .

Joel   It's okay, Dad.

Larry   I thought there was a chance of them letting me out and all. My lawyer thinks they still might. But when I told 'em I'd somewhere to go, I meant I was gonna stay with you. There's no room in any of the hostels apparently. That might be why things are stalling. I hadn't got my hopes up too high anyway, but now you say you won't have anywhere to live neither, I don't know what I'll do, if I do get out. Still it's gotta be better than being banged up 24/7 . . . even if I do end up self-isolating in a shop doorway.

Joel   Dad . . . it's not gonna come to that. I've got a plan. I'll make good me rent, don't you worry. Then you can stay with me. Anyway, I'm really glad you called. Cos I could do with a bit of advice, like.

Larry *is slightly suspicious.*

Larry   Oh yeah?

Joel   What do you mean 'oh yeah'?

Larry   I thought you seemed happier than usual to hear from your 'waste-of-space' old man. Thought perhaps it was the video call – seeing me for once, making you all matey. Was a bit surprised you even remember what I look like really, seeing as how little you visit.

Joel   Honestly, Dad, it's like I've told you. I've been working all hours. Before the lockdown I mean. That's all it was. I'd have come more often if I could. And it's a long old round trip . . .

Larry   Yeah, yeah.

Joel   . . . And, er, look, now I've time on my hands and I can get to you without getting caught in an hour long tailback like what happened last time, well, there's no visiting.

Larry   Same as the zoo, so I've heard. Yeah, look, alright son . . . tell me, what is it you want to know?

Joel   Cats. I need some advice about cats. Do you know anything about 'em?

Larry   Cats? Like old Moggie when you were a little 'un? You thinking of getting one? Be another mouth to feed and if you might be getting evicted any rate –

Joel   Cats – catalytic converters.

Larry   Oh, you mean like on a car?

Joel   Do you know anyone who deals . . . I mean did you ever . . . when you were fencing . . .

Larry *looks around, checks he is alone in the room.*

Larry   I wasn't fencing. I was just buying and selling.

Joel   Receiving stolen goods.

Larry   No. Well . . . Just got a bit unlucky.

Joel   Yeah, more than once. Look, what I need to know is – do you know anyone who'll fen . . . I mean want a number of catalytic converters?

Larry   Can't think of anyone off-hand-like. Why?

Joel   Only I was having a bit of a clear-out at the lock-up where I do me private jobs and, well, it seems I've got quite a few I could be flogging off . . .

Larry   Stick 'em online.

Joel   Well, that's the thing . . . Er, is anyone there with you? Screws listening in?

Larry   Not that I'm aware. I'm in this room on me own cos I'm trusted . . . but who knows if they're eavesdropping somehow – I don't know much about this technology . . .

Joel   Right . . .

Larry   Ah. You mean they're not completely legit? Trust me, Joel, you don't wanna to go down that route. You stick to the straight and narrow. For a few hundred quid's worth of old car parts, it's not worth it . . .

Joel   Listen . . . It's a lot more than that, Dad. These are catalytic converters from hybrids – cost at least a grand to replace. Each. That's because of the rare metals they contain see? They're used to reduce the pollutants from the engine yeah? Anyway these rare minerals – there's palladium . . .

Larry   Palladium? Seriously? Like 'Live at the London Palladium'? You're winding me up.

Joel   Palladium and rhodium. They're in short supply apparently and rhodium is currently, per ounce, worth six times the price of gold.

Larry   Yeah? . . . So worth its weight . . . and then some . . .

Joel   I've heard scrap metal dealers will pay between 300 and 500 per cat. But when I rang the one near me, the rip-off merchant was trying to offer me 50 quid each. I mean at that price it's not worth the effort. What I need is to bypass the scrappers and deal with the guys shipping the stuff abroad. That's where it all goes – back out the country.

Larry   Where you getting them – the cats?

Joel   You don't want to know, Dad.

Larry   You're on the bloody rob.

Joel *indicates to* **Larry** *to keep it down.*

Larry   My son's on the bloody rob. Typical. That's all I bloody need. You were the one person in this family who was gonna do well, make it big. And by honest toil.

Joel   Yeah. I was. I was doing alright till this stinking virus came along.

Larry   So let me get this straight . . . Are you . . . acquiring them yourself?

Joel   It doesn't take long. If you know what you're doing. Couple of minutes max each one.

Larry   You're not one of those scumbags – the hospital car parks . . .

Joel   No! God no. Nothing like that. I swear on Mum's life.

Larry   And how many?

Joel   Nearly two hundred.

Larry   What? Someone's been busy.

Joel   I gotta friend grafting with me. He'd need to get his cut and all.

Larry   Oh God. Right . . . well, normally as things stand, I do happen to know a bloke who might be interested . . . though getting word to him now there's no association won't be so easy. Leave it with me, right. Give me a couple of days. And someone'll contact you. But Joel, this is a one-off, right . . . you hear me?

Joel *has got up and gone to his window.*

Joel   Sorry, Dad, just looking out the window. Flashing blue.

Larry *laughs.*

Larry   Getting jumpy, lad? Welcome to my world.

Joel   It's an ambulance.

Larry   Word to the wise – they won't come with the old blues and twos going. First thing you'll know is when you wake up to the door going in.

Joel   Oh . . . oh right. Looks like it's old Mrs Cambridge downstairs. Two paramedics going in. Been doing a bit of shopping for her, collecting prescriptions.

Larry (*sarcastic*)   Do ambulances have cats? You might just about have time to jack it while they're busy in there.

Joel   Dad! I don't actually feel that great about what I've been doing, to tell you the truth. I'm only doing what I gotta do.

Larry   Alright, son. Same here. I'm only helping cos I have to. I've been a crap dad, but I'm making it up to you okay? I'll do you this favour and then we're even.

Joel   You weren't really that crap . . . I know I've said that in the past, and you were away a lot . . . but when you was there, we had a laugh . . .

Larry   Yeah . . . I know. Listen, screw's just put his head round the door telling me to wrap it up. I gotta go. I'll see what I can do about your cat problem. Someone will be in touch later this week with a bit of luck.

Joel   Thanks, Dad, bye now. Stay safe.

Larry   Bye, son. Er, stay lucky!

He turns off his screen.

The End.

Urban Foxes

A monologue

Hannah *is in her early twenties.*

Hannah   Life's hard on the streets of Brighton. The constant uncertainty of getting enough to eat, and finding somewhere to sleep that's both safe and reasonably dry and warm. I can't help worrying about Esme – she's alone, she's pregnant . . . and she's a fox.

When I first met Esme it was early last autumn, the start of my ecology degree. I went on a freshers' pub crawl, wearing the same beer-company sponsored t-shirt as everyone else. I drank too much and ended up in a big crowd, skinny-dipping at 4 a.m. Esme though has never felt the need to conform. She does exactly as she pleases. She doesn't skulk or keep close to the walls and hedges. She's bold and swaggering, sass personified. Her fur shines like burnished copper, her brush is full and ermine tipped. She's the vixen queen and she knows it.

I tried to make friends with the two other girls I was flat sharing with – probably tried too hard. I had thought I was lucky to get that room. The third girl in their group had decided to take a year out from her course, so her room was empty. Only then she changed her mind and returned, wanting her room back. She and the other two suddenly wanted me gone and stupidly I hadn't insisted on some kind of contract. It meant I had to find somewhere else to live in the middle of the term when there weren't any vacancies. I did find somewhere. I do have a roof over my head, even if the situation isn't ideal.

I often spend hours crouched in the street, or in a shop doorway watching Esme or other foxes. Some nights I stay out until dawn. It's awkward now there's the lockdown, but I'm stealthy and wary as a fox. I stay in the shadows. The police cars go by without spotting me. If I stay out all night, I don't see Tim, who owns the flat I'm staying in. He works at a DIY store and they're open again now, thankfully.

When I first met Esme she would stand or sit with her head pointing at the sky, and screech. At first I thought something was wrong, she might be in pain but it's actually a mating call. Fox sex is brutal – the male bites the back of the female's neck and his penis is barbed and becomes temporarily stuck inside her. She screams at every painful thrust. I've seen foxes mating, though not Esme, I don't think I could stomach it. Not with the way things are in my life.

Male or dog foxes do tend to stay with their partner while the cubs are young though, bringing them food. It's a relationship built on raising young together. I've called Esme's mate George. Sometimes she can be short tempered and nippy with him, but often after a night's hunting they greet each other excitably like dogs.

My parents live in Australia and I couldn't afford to go there at the start of lockdown. I didn't like to ask them to send me the airfare, as I know their business isn't doing well at the moment. Now of course it's too late until normal flights resume. I'm stuck in this situation, even if it is of my own making. I can't tell anyone but Esme about it either. I just know they'd judge me.

When I answered Tim's ad. I knew what I was doing, and it seemed like no big deal. The room was rent-free and he wasn't repulsive or anything. In fact he seemed quite normal. He said he'd only want sex a couple of times a week, and I thought fair enough I could handle that. I'd had a few loveless encounters before, who hasn't? I didn't fancy him, but as I say he didn't really turn me off. But I hadn't thought about how it would make me feel. I hadn't thought about that at all . . .

Tim isn't rough, but it's meaningless, it's mechanical. I'm just an object to satisfy him. He has a girlfriend who is teaching in India at the moment, and our sex for rent arrangement is, he says, just a convenient way of getting what he needs in the meantime. But living like that was killing me; it crept into my soul and ate it away, day by day, week by week.

But I'm turning into a shadow. I've managed to avoid even seeing Tim at all for two weeks by staying out with my fox. Perhaps I'm gaining some of Esme's spirit. I'm becoming a wild creature. I have become one. I trust no one now. I show no one my vulnerabilities. If any human comes near me I shrink back, muscles tightening, ready to fight or flee. It's as if like Esme, when under threat, my hackles are rising, I'm baring my teeth.

****

Esme has had her cubs! There are four of them. Her den is under some decking in the garden of an empty house. I saw them for the first time today. I think it must've been their first time popping up above ground. They've big blue eyes at this age and they're into everything – one chasing a grasshopper, another trying and failing to eat a worm – living spaghetti. As I reluctantly headed home in the early hours, Esme was alert, agitated, running to the hedge, and then returning to the den. Two streets away I discovered why. The body of George, her mate was lying in the road. There's more traffic at night now as it's when the supermarkets get their deliveries. Whatever had hit George looked like it had killed him outright.

This morning Tim told me he's having an illegal party tonight at the flat. He's invited a few friends around despite the risk of Covid-19. He wants to introduce me to some of them. Actually what he really wants to do is share me with them. He's even offered me money. I said 'Yeah, alright', in a little meek voice, like the ghost that I've become. I took his stinking money. I nodded and forced a smile when he told me to 'dress up for once, not those grungy old jeans'. The fridge is full of food ready for later – pizzas, burgers, sausages. He ordered it all in earlier. Now he's in his bedroom getting ready. Stealthy as a fox, I emptied it all into two shopping bags. My belongings are already stashed in my suitcase in the front garden. All I need do is slip out the door.

Foxes cache their food to make it last. Esme will now have enough to feed her cubs through their most vulnerable weeks. Me, I reckon I've enough to live on for a while too. Before leaving I'll steal a chisel, to loosen the basement window of the empty house. My new home's far enough away from Esme to respect her little family's privacy, but near enough for us to keep each other company. She knows me and knows I mean her no harm. Together, living on our wits, and what we can scrounge, I know we'll be okay.

The End.

Bees

A monologue

Suhana *is a machinist in her forties.*

There's a bee buzzing against the window. My eyes keep drifting up to it as it pushes itself angrily at the grimy glass. I think it wonders why it can see the light but never reach it. If I could, I'd get up and let it out, but leaving my work station really isn't worth the hassle that would cause me. They fine you for everything here. A minute late in the morning, too long in the toilet or getting a cup of water – whatever. Dust sparkles in the air, and the machines whirr in your ears night and day. Anala who sits in front of me is coughing. If she's sick she still won't go home. There's no pay if you're ill at home, but there's rent and bills and mouths to feed no matter what.

I'm inserting a mesh panel into the front of a sparkly top. It's the kind of thing a young girl might wear in a nightclub, but there aren't any clubs open now, so why are we even making it? I know there are illegal parties, but haven't people enough things in their wardrobe? Why don't they get us making protective clothes for doctors and nurses instead? If I was doing something like that, it wouldn't be so bad. The bee's in the same situation. It should be outside collecting honey for its family. Instead it's stuck in here going up and down a small pane of glass as I guide my needle up and down this piece of cloth. If someone swatted the bee, would anyone back at the hive or wherever it lives miss it? My family would miss me if I died here, but no one else would really notice. A woman was taken ill, late last year. Fainted on the floor. It was just after midday and by three o'clock someone else was sitting at her sewing machine completing the skirt she was making. Busy like a bee, then swatted, and gone.

If this place and the other factories closed though, where would we go? How would we live? On my way home I often look in the windows of shops and cafes and I used to think 'I'd like to work there'. Because you see people walking by. And you don't get fined for chatting, as far as I know. Now though those places are only just starting to open again, and some of them still have their shutters down. Maybe some of them won't come back.

I've heard there are long queues at the Jobcentre now. I went there once, but they said 'you've got a job already'. I said it doesn't even pay the minimum wage. 'Well, it should do,' the man said. 'That's the law.'

'And how am I supposed to make them obey that law?' I asked him.

'Join a union. Go on strike.' I tried to explain. In my job you can't join a union, there are no strikes, you're either working or you aren't.

'You do have right to work here legally?' the Jobcentre man said. He was looking at my National Insurance number. It was right there in front of him. I had to fill it in on a form before I even got to see him. He was wearing a rugby shirt under his suit jacket. It had stripes on it. Orange and black like a bee. I think our company might have made it. We did a lot of rugby shirts last year. I remember seeing one in a sports store when I went to buy our two their football kit for school. I couldn't believe the price.

If I went to the market, bought the material and made the shirts myself, I'd make a profit for myself. I could do it from home on a second-hand sewing machine. I even asked in one of the smaller shops if they'd want to stock some shirts and tops if I made them. The woman said 'no'. They already had their suppliers. I asked her how much she paid her supplier for each shirt. She wouldn't tell me. 'Trade secrets'. Her shop is shuttered now. I don't know if she's going to re-open. I think everyone buys their clothes online anyway. Would it be any use trying to sell things through a website? Would anyone see my little webpage with a few items on it? I just don't know.

It would be a big risk to set up my own business if I had to give up this job to do it. How do you start something up when you've nothing to spend? When I come in from work I can't face more sewing. I have to soak my fingers in salt water to soften the hard skin and soothe the cracks and blisters. How do I find time to make items to sell?

The bee has stopped buzzing. It's sitting quietly on the windowsill now. It's learnt that escape is hopeless. It has accepted its fate. It will spend its last minutes or hours in this hot, airless place. For the bee, the memories of flowers – their beauty, their colours, their perfumes – are fading. Anala is coughing again. 'It's so hot!' she says.

My supervisor is at the other end of the room, by the fire-escape door, trying to get a phone signal. I dart across to the window. I open it a little. I know there are no flowers outside, just concrete, brick and rubbish down below. But as I return to my machine the bee has crawled towards the crack. I can feel the breeze and as soon as my supervisor realises the window is open he will close it again. He always does for some reason. The bee has only a short time to gain enough strength to crawl outside. I find myself whispering, 'Go on, bee. Go.'

The bee is outside the window now! I don't know if it's just resting there or if it has gone on its way. I really hope it's taken to the air and it's flying back to the flowers, and back to the other bees. I hope now it's free and living again – properly living in the cool, fresh air.

The End.

www.ingramcontent.com/pod-product-compliance
Ingram Content Group UK Ltd.
Pitfield, Milton Keynes, MK11 3LW, UK
UKHW020658280225
455688UK00004B/167